Faith and Fiction

Faith and Fiction

Christian Literature in America Today

Anita Gandolfo

Westport, Connecticut
London

Library of Congress Cataloging-in-Publication Data

Gandolfo, Anita.
  Faith and fiction: Christian literature in America today / Anita Gandolfo.
    p. cm.
  Includes bibliographical references and index.
  ISBN 978–0–275–99196–8 (alk. paper)
  1. Christian fiction, American—History and criticism. 2. Christianity and literature—United
States—History—20th century. 3. Christianity in literature. I. Title.
PS374.C48G36 2007
810.9'3823—dc22   2007016222

British Library Cataloguing in Publication Data is available.

Library of Congress Catalog Card Number: 2007016222
ISBN-13: 978–0–275–99196–8

First published in 2007

Praeger Publishers, 88 Post Road West, Westport, CT 06881
An imprint of Greenwood Publishing Group, Inc.
www.praeger.com

Printed in the United States of America

The paper used in this book complies with the
Permanent Paper Standard issued by the National
Information Standards Organization (Z39.48–1984).

10 9 8 7 6 5 4 3 2 1

For Emily Rose, already a talented writer,
with confidence that she will fulfill her potential

Contents

Preface

…in America, religion is the road to knowledge….

—Alexis De Tocqueville, *Democracy in America*

On Good Friday in 1966, *Time* magazine's cover story posed the question "Is God Dead"?, a question that reflected the turbulent times known as The Sixties, and the secularization of American society that seemed to be the major development of those times. However, a generation later in 2005, *Newsweek* featured a cover story on the proliferation of "Spirituality in America," indicating that in the United States, the response to *Time*'s question has been a resounding no. Polls show Americans to be among the most believing citizens in the world, and the field of publishing confirms this obsession with religious themes. Christian publishing has burgeoned in recent years, featuring not only nonfiction best sellers designed to inspire the faithful but almost all types of fiction from romance through mystery and suspense.

Ironically, however, religion appears to be more divisive than unifying in contemporary American culture, as political reporters repeatedly speak to the tensions evoked by religion in American society. Even religious denominations are experiencing conflicts among their own members over church discipline and provocative social issues. While it is difficult to sort out all the elements involved in contemporary American religion, the purpose of this study is to analyze contemporary literature to provide some insight into the nature of the religious tensions among the people of the United States.

Every popular art form is a reflection of the society that produces it, and the literature of a culture is inextricably tied to its faith experience. Ever since the Anglo-Saxons converted to Christianity in the seventh century, sublimating their pagan past to the Christian present in their writing, the literature of the English-speaking world has been infused with religion. This book is not a history of that association, but an analysis of the current moment in contemporary American fiction as it reflects the religious tensions in American society. My goal is to show how that fiction can provide insight into the contours in the landscape of American religion.

It is important to note that in this study, I am using the word "literature" without regard to the traditional criterion of artistic merit but according to the basic dictionary definition of "the body of written works of a language, period, or culture." My purpose is to highlight the current cultural moment by examining imaginative texts that are significant documents of that moment. Some other key terms require clarification.

The concepts of faith, belief, and religion are often used interchangeably in casual conversation, but there are important distinctions to be made. Faith is a quality of the person. One can have faith in God—or in the stock market—but when used in religious terms, faith refers to the individual's relationship to Transcendence. It is a quality of the person and involves the totality of the individual, affecting the way that person views the world and its other inhabitants. Faith is often engendered by religious tradition, but religion is related to the institution; one *is* a person of faith; one *belongs to* a religion. In terms of religion, belief is the attempt to translate the relationship with Transcendence into concepts or propositions. An individual can have belief, but when belief is associated with a religion, it is commonly referred to as doctrine or dogma. Ideally, individuals associate themselves with a religion whose doctrines most closely adhere to their own beliefs. But the reverse is also true; people's adherence to a specific religion may cause them to reexamine and perhaps revise their personal beliefs.

The experiential situation is more complicated, since American individualism is one of the salient features of the religious landscape in the United States. As we will see in this study, the lived experience of Americans in relation to religion defies easy categories, which is why analyzing religious fiction can be especially productive. Novels do not sell phenomenally well primarily because of their artistic merits but because they tap into the *Zeitgeist,* the intellectual and cultural climate of the times and thereby appeal to vast numbers of people. Thus, in looking at some very successful fiction, we can gain insight into various segments of readership that reflect aspects of the contemporary American religious landscape.

In this study, I refer frequently to evangelical Christians, and it is important to note that this is less a particular denomination than a religious attitude common to Christians who may belong to various denominations, although there are also predominantly evangelical congregations as well. As the name "evangelical" implies, the core attitude among this group of Christians is the mission to share the good news that Jesus Christ is the one, true Savior. Spreading this word is critical because evangelicals believe that accepting Jesus as one's Savior is necessary for salvation, and thus by helping others accept Jesus and be saved, they are doing God's work. Evangelicals also believe in the inerrancy of the Bible as God's authoritative word on earth. This triumvirate of beliefs—Jesus as

Savior, the importance of sharing that good news, and the Bible as inerrant word of God—form the basis of the evangelical religious consciousness.

In addition, I will frequently refer to "conservative Christians." This group includes evangelicals but also many other Christians who have a similar social outlook, principally a view that the dominant culture in American society today tends toward degeneracy in its acceptance of sexual promiscuity, abortion, homosexuality, and tolerance of vulgarity and profanity. Although conservative Christians may not share all of the beliefs that mark the evangelical, they are commonly allied on social issues. Like evangelicals, conservative Christians can be found in many denominations. In fact, as will be discussed later in this study, individual denominations are often divided between conservative and liberal members, frequently resulting in difficulties within the church when provocative issues surface, as in questions of homosexual marriage or ordination.

The impetus for this book is a very well-known phenomenon in the publishing industry, the vast sales of "Christian fiction," a term I put in quotation marks because it refers to a very specific subgroup of fiction produced mainly by evangelical publishers, but now often published by special labels of mainstream publishers as well. This phenomenon, however, does not exist in isolation but in the context of contemporary American literature in general, more specifically, literature that is informed by religious concerns. The purpose of this study is to place the distinct publishing phenomenon of "Christian fiction" in a context that explains both its incredible sales and its significance in reflecting contemporary American culture.

In my first chapter, I try to provide the necessary introduction with a historical account of this relationship of religion and literature in American society. My second chapter, devoted to an ancillary publishing phenomenon, *The DaVinci Code,* uses the sales and responses to that novel to gloss the current cultural moment, identifying the key factions involved when the subject is religion. Chapter 3 explores those factions in more detail, focusing on the social and political concerns that inform the Christian fiction market. In Chapter 4, I discuss some of the most popular contemporary Christian fiction in an effort to explain its widespread appeal, reserving the next chapter for the most salient of this subgenre, the Left Behind series, a publishing phenomenon in its own right and a group of books very different from the Christian fiction described in the preceding chapter. Chapter 6 explores some of the concerns related to contemporary Christian fiction, especially its relationship to mainstream fiction. In Chapter 7, other fiction that is informed by religious concerns but does not fit the evangelical pattern is explored, and in Chapter 8, I attempt to bring this study to conclusion.

In choosing the fiction to discuss, of necessity I have had to be selective rather than exhaustive. In every case, I have tried to present representative fiction for the topic under discussion, but it is literally impossible to discuss the vast number of novels that could be included. Thus, the informed reader may find his or her favorite works or favorite authors missing from these pages. I believe, however, that the reader will be able to place those novels or authors within the parameters of the discussion in these chapters and will see how they fit into the pattern that is presented. Moreover, my analysis of this fiction cannot be comprehensive. I am looking at the individual works from a specific vantage point, as explained in the separate chapters, and my discussion is therefore focused, conditioned by the scope and substance of this study.

There are many variables involved in the appreciation of literature, and one of them is always the situation of the individual reader. Thus, for examples, there are those who loved *The DaVinci Code* and those who hated it, those who thought it was dangerous to religious faith, and those who believed that it inspired more mature faith. In every discussion of a literary work, I have tried to simply account for the varied reactions while remaining personally neutral. The goal of this study is not to make value judgments but to explore how sales of particular fiction may reflect the contemporary American religious landscape.

This study originated with a suggestion by Suzanne Staszak-Silva, my editor at Praeger Publishers, whose advice in the early stages of planning was invaluable, and I am indebted to her for her wise counsel. There are critics that I cite in this study who are critical of technology, especially the Internet, fearing its negative effect on the printed word. I can attest to its positive effect. The Internet was an invaluable asset to me throughout the process of developing this study, as perusal of my endnotes will indicate. The information available online for the serious researcher is incalculable, and only a scholar who learned the trade in the dusty stacks of uncomputerized libraries can fully appreciate its true value. Finally, I am indebted to all those from whom I learned to appreciate literature over the years, my teachers and my students.

1

"Still Got Religion"

America is the only country in which it has been possible to witness the natural and tranquil growth of society, and where the influence exercised on the future condition of states by their origin is clearly distinguishable....

—Alexis De Tocqueville, *Democracy in America*

In the course of a murder investigation in a contemporary mystery novel, Detective Terry Flynn encounters a priest who, although key to the investigation, is abrasively uncooperative. Flynn tells the clergyman that it's fortunate he's a priest because otherwise Flynn would begin to use his fists to elicit compliance, to which the priest snidely replies, "I thought you weren't a Catholic, Detective Flynn"? Staring contemptuously at the priest, Flynn responds, "I still got religion."[1]

That interaction speaks to the situation of religion in American culture today. Despite the appearance of rampant secularism in many aspects of society, Americans are among the most religiously observant people of any developed nation. A 2003 Gallup Poll reported that six out of ten Americans said that religion was "very important" in their lives. In contrast, in Canada and the United Kingdom, only 28% and 15% respectively described religion as similarly important to them.[2] In addition, a 2001 survey done by the City University of New York Graduate Center concluded that by most standards, the United States was a more professingly religious country than any European nation except Ireland and Poland, with 85% of Americans identifying with some religious faith.[3] Overall, despite the evidence of secularization in our society, like Terry Flynn, we've "still got religion."

However, sociologists also frequently observe that American religion has endured as a salient feature in society because of its responsiveness to cultural changes over the years.[4] Terry Flynn's vestigial Catholicism is a very different religious experience than that of his parents or grandparents, just as the American society he lives in is different in many ways from that of his ancestors.[5] Thus, before we proceed to analyze the current situation of faith and fiction in American literature, it is essential to understand how the variously intertwined threads have been woven into the contemporary cultural tapestry of American religion. And since this is a study of religion and literature, it is also important to note why those two threads are so closely intertwined.

Literature and Religion

Both literature and religion belong to the same domain of experience, the attempt of the human heart to delineate the ineffable. The theologian John Shea explains the relationship of life experience to faith in this way, "We participate in a larger Mystery which is the permeating context of all we are and in relationship to which our destiny is worked out."[6] Faith is an aspect of the person independent of any formal belief system. Most often faith is mediated through religion, but the latter is not essential to the former. A person can be converted to religious faith from agnosticism or atheism, but more often religious conversion involves a turning, or *metanoia,* in which the individual develops a renewed faith life from a singular experience. The classic conversion tale is Paul on the road to Damascus. He was a devout Jew dedicated to extinguishing the new sect formed by disciples of the recently executed Jesus of Nazareth when, as the Scripture explains, on a journey to Damascus, he has an experience of the Risen Lord. Thus, the mission for Christ that he then subsequently embraces did not develop without any religious background. It was, instead, a true *metanoia,* a turning toward God that gave new meaning to his faith life.[7] Life experience informs religious faith.

As in any relationship, reality is manifest through events that communicate meaning. The human inclination is to reflect on those events through storytelling. Lovers have stories of how they met, and children want to know the stories of when they were born, for we tend to put our significant life experiences into story form. The Bible is an archetypal example of this impulse. It is commonplace to note that the Judeo-Christian religion is a Biblical religion. Less commonly observed is the fact that the Bible is a form of literature, composed of narratives of human experience of the Divine. Whether it be the stories of the Israelites in Genesis and Exodus, the poetic Psalms of relationship to Yahweh, the events in the life of Jesus in the four Gospels, or the conversion narrative of Paul on the road to Damascus, the Bible represents the human effort to encapsulate and express the faith experience of human beings. So it is hardly surprising that beyond the canonical texts of Scripture, aspects of people's faith experience permeate our literature, since American society has been steeped in religion since its founding.

Although the relationship between religion and literature in Western society is extremely complex, the cultural critic Giles Gunn provides a useful classification that considers the literary work as complementary, oppositional, or alternative in its response to religion.[8] While contemporary literature may contain any or all of these approaches, Gunn's categories are inherently historical, and the earliest literature in the United States reflected the initial complementary relationship of literature to religion. This complementary mode in which religion is considered integral to life and supported by social structures mirrored the attitude toward religion in Western society at the time and correlated with the historical circumstances of the nation's origins.

The Early Years

The circumstances of the founding of this nation instilled religion as a central aspect of our culture, the founding *mythos,* as it were. As one sociologist of religion explains, "The myths with which a society is legitimated must be powerful and authoritative, must ground the public's devotion, and must give the society an awareness of its origin and destiny."[9] Of course, these colonists were not seeking religious freedom as we would understand it today; theirs was an attempt to escape an established religion that was not their own, and the initial tendency in the early colonies was to establish the founders' religion and merely tolerate others.[10] However, it is important to note that the settlement in this new world was conceived as a religious mission, an "errand into the wilderness" to found a "city upon a hill."[11] The theme of the "American Israel" was a founding metaphor. Europe was Egypt; America was the Promised Land. And the journey was inspired and guided by God, who called his people to establish a special nation.[12] Thus, at its founding, this was a faith-based society, and religion was inextricably part of the political realm. As with the Israelites, the colonists held the belief that fidelity to God's laws was necessary in order for this new country to prosper.

Understandably, in such a generally cohesive society, religious expression was a natural part of ordinary discourse. And the country's earliest literature was complementary, tending to assume the presence of an inherited religious tradition and promote its values. The seventeenth-century poet Anne Bradstreet, for example, one of the earliest writers in the colonies, published poetry with homely subjects related to her husband and children, and she unselfconsciously reflects the Judeo-Christian perspective that underlies her worldview and that of her readers at the time. For example, in her much-anthologized poem "Verses upon the Burning of our House," she records her first thought when she learns that the house is ablaze, a thought of the Divine source of life:

> I started up, the light did spy,
> And to my God my heart did cry
> To straighten me in my distress
> And not to leave me succourless.

And when the flames have consumed her home, she responds in language with clear Biblical echoes, "I blest his grace that gave and took,/That laid my goods now in the dust."[13] This assumption of a shared belief in God that infuses human experience reflects the complementary relationship between literature and religion.

Later, when Cotton Mather writes his history of the colonies in 1702, his title reflects the strong Christian ethos of those settlements, *Magnalia Christi Americana (A History of the Wonderful Works of Christ in America)*. Mather sees himself both as a chronicler of the past and as a defender of the values of those original settlements that he believes are already "under attack from new forces of secularism."[14] His approach reflects a central aspect of literature in a cohesive society; it functions to promote the *mythos,* the story that the society regards as its truth.

Those new forces of secularism in the seventeenth century were somewhat contained by two movements in the eighteenth century that radically affected the development of religion in the New World. Toward mid-century, an evangelical revival, The Great Awakening, both invigorated and divided churches throughout English-speaking countries. Those denominations that welcomed the evangelical emphasis on rebirth inspired by preaching of the Word flourished, and by the nineteenth century, Presbyterians, Baptists, and Methodists were the largest American Protestant denominations. Jonathan Edwards' much-anthologized sermon *Sinners in the Hands of an Angry God* is a product of the evangelical movement.

However, another movement, Deism, affected far fewer people but was probably more influential in the development of our country. A product of the rationalist emphasis of the Enlightenment, Deists encounter God through reason rather than Scripture and thus would be antithetical to orthodox Christianity. Although far fewer Americans were drawn to Deism, its adherents were typically of the upper class, men like Thomas Jefferson and John Adams. The unique American form of Deism, heavily influenced by the strong religious heritage of the colonies, holds to specific universal truths that should guide all people. And that philosophy informs our documents of independence—"certain truths are self-evident, that all men are created equal, that they are endowed by their Creator with certain unalienable Rights, that among these are Life, Liberty and the pursuit of Happiness."

It is this "American Deism" that provides the inspiration for what will be our nation's civil religion. As the sociologist Robert Bellah has explained,

> The words and acts of the founding fathers, especially the first few presidents, shaped the form and tone of the civil religion as it has been maintained every since. Though much is selectively derived from Christianity, this religion is clearly not itself Christianity....The God of the civil religion is not only rather "unitarian," he is also on the austere side, much more related to order, law, and right than to salvation and love.[15]

This civil religion is reflected in the motto of "In God We Trust" on our coins, and the recently controversial words "under God" added to the Pledge of

Allegiance in 1952, as well in countless benedictions in public ceremonies. While the United States has not established any religion, its *mythos* is based in a civil religion that reflects the colonists' belief in their mission from God. And the persistence of that belief as part of our civil religion is underscored in our public discourse. For example, President Johnson in his speech to Congress in 1965 asking for a strong voting-rights bill said, "Above the pyramid on the great seal of the United States it says in Latin, 'God has favored our undertaking.'" And he continued in the same vein, "God will not favor everything that we do. It is rather our duty to divine His will. I cannot help but believe that He truly understands and that He really favors the undertaking that we begin here tonight."[16] This tendency to invoke the Deity on ceremonial occasions is evident in American life from Presidential inaugurations through college commencements and is evidence of this civil religion which has nothing to do with specific denominations or actual worship.

It is important to note the function of popular literature in perpetuating the civic *mythos*. As one historian has noted, several men too young to have participated in the Revolution published works that taught Americans to venerate it.[17] One example is Mason Locke Weems, a writer and clergyman. Hearing of George Washington's death, Weems, a fervent admirer of the first President, wrote a popular, "largely fictionalized" biography that "turned him into a down-home, evangelical hero for a rural and increasingly religious nation."[18] From Weems we get the Washington of cherry tree fame who cannot lie. The function of these popular works that magnify the virtues of the founders is to promote nationalism in support of the new nation. As we will see, popular fiction will later be a similar force in creating devotion and strengthening the ties of believers to their religious heritage.

A Literature of Our Own

As literature mirrors the society that produces it, our early literature is the unique mixture of a strong Christian foundation, the Deist emphasis on reason and understanding, and the idealism of our founding documents. The first generation of major American writers in the nineteenth century, Emerson, Hawthorne, Thoreau, Whitman, and Dickinson, often referred to as "Transcendentalists," had a dual mission. They were consciously trying to create a uniquely American literature not tied to the traditions of England or Europe. And they were also exploring the nature of faith and religion in light of the changes in knowledge and culture— the Enlightenment with its emphasis on logic and reason; the Romantic Age with its emphasis on more intuitive thinking and appreciation for sensory experience; and the new Biblical criticism that looked at the Scriptures from the perspective of literary analysis. They reflect the transition to literature's oppositional relationship to religion, an opposition that was not directed at belief in God. Rather, it was a challenge to orthodox forms of religious expression and is most evident in questioning institutional religion.

Ralph Waldo Emerson provides an example of the oppositional approach in both his life and his writing. He was a preacher who had renounced the pulpit, yet he did not reject religious values. Emerson and his literary colleagues of the period spent time analyzing social conditions and exhorting their fellow citizens to live more wisely.[19] In particular, he and Henry David Thoreau castigated the materialism of the emerging consumer economy. This apparently secular voice of literature was not agnostic, but oppositional. It was deeply spiritual but opposed to the controlling force of institutional religion. Note, for example, how Emerson's comment in his essay "Self-Reliance" includes both presence in church yet cynicism about the service itself: "I like the silent church before the service begins, better than any preaching."[20]

And Thoreau encapsulates the Deist emphasis on rational thought and learning from the Book of Nature in his famous lines in "Walden":

I went to the woods because I wished to live deliberately, to front only the essential facts of life, and see if I could not learn what it had to teach, and not, when I came to die, discover that I had not lived.[21]

In that same essay, he expresses dismay that "most men" have "*somewhat hastily* concluded that it is the chief end of man here to 'glorify God and enjoy him forever'."[22] For both Emerson and Thoreau, the individual should not simply embrace the traditional doctrine of institutional religion but seek God through His works and action in the world rather than via "any preaching."

However, what Emerson and Thoreau and their fellow Transcendentalists express most clearly is the strong individualism that will be the major thread in the tapestry of American religion. That individualism will continue to foster a consistent criticism of institutional religion. For the literary giants of the nineteenth century, there is a strong emphasis on the God within, the primacy of personal spiritual experience, epitomized in the title of Walt Whitman's "Song of Myself" and expressed succinctly in a letter from Herman Melville to Nathaniel Hawthorne, "I feel that the Godhead is broken up like the bread at the Supper, and that we are the pieces. Hence this infinite fraternity of feeling."[23]

Nathaniel Hawthorne's *The Scarlet Letter* is, of course, the novel that is the most famous comment on religion in American literature of this era. Although the setting of the novel is Puritan New England, the time of a complementary relationship of literature with religion, it reflects the oppositional sensibility toward religion of literature in the 1840s. In the novel, personal spirituality is determined by responses to moral choices rather than attendance at religious services. The scarlet letter is at once both the religious institution's simplistic solution to Hester's adultery and her own "red badge of courage," as she refuses to let it define her. Hawthorne's fiction makes it clear that sin and redemption are far more complex than reductive church tenets suggest. The community's decision to ostracize Hester assumes that sin can be simply cast out of a society by exiling the sinner, failing to recognize that sin is an aspect of the human condition that can't be so easily excised, as Hawthorne shows in the complex characters of Dimmesdale and Chillingworth.

The writers of this era reflect a cleavage in society that remains a major chasm in American religion today. Alienated by the "fire and brimstone" rhetoric of the evangelicals, the faith experience of these artists becomes more eclectic in expression. For example, there is no absence of belief itself, as in the opening lines of Emily Dickinson's poem #501:[24]

> This World is not Conclusion.
> A Species stands beyond—
> Invisible, as Music—
> But positive, as Sound—

And as she notes in poem #1551:

> The abdication of Belief
> Makes the Behavior small—
> Better an ignis fatuus
> Than no illume at all—

Here Dickinson insightfully comments that even the presence of a "false light" (ignis fatuus), that is, institutional religion, is preferable to its absence, since religion seems to have the effect of restraining pure self interest (Behavior small). Skepticism about institutional religion is not necessarily antagonistic but, as in this poem, can be tolerant of the value of religious institutions for the good of society. What is clear, however, is that the voice of moral authority is no longer ceded automatically to pastor or bishop. However, during Dickinson's rather cloistered lifetime, the country is experiencing a major cataclysm that will lead to more dramatic changes in the society and its religious expression.

The Civil War and Its Aftermath

The Civil War will mark the beginning of a radical change in American culture, as the nation moves from an agrarian to an industrial society in the years following this conflict. But the war is also a major moment in the country's civil religion. In light of the national self-understanding of America's "mission" to be a democratic republic guided by God, we can better appreciate Lincoln's expression of the challenge of the war, a conflict that he saw as not principally about slavery but one that would determine "whether that nation, or any nation so conceived, and so dedicated, can long endure."[25] If the founding was our Exodus, the Civil War became our Easter. The vision of the Civil War as our nation's death and rebirth is reflected in the contemporary association of the assassinated President Lincoln with Jesus Christ to convey an understanding of his role as the national savior. The historian Richard Wightman Fox reports that only five hours after

Lincoln's death, James Garfield, then a Congressman but later our second assassinated president, addressed a mass audience in Manhattan, "It may be almost
impious to say it, but it does seem that Lincoln's death parallels that of the Son
of God." Fox also quotes a minister explaining that "Jesus Christ died for the
world." And "Abraham Lincoln died for his country."[26]

That the American people could see this event in such strong religious terms is
testimony to the strength of the religious thread throughout the country's rich
tapestry. That thread maintains its strength despite social changes because of its
flexibility. As the nation develops through the vast changes that mark the time
between the end of the Civil War and World War I, the critical question is asked
by Melville in his 1876 poem "Clarel,"

> But now our age,
> So infidel in equipage,
> While carrying still the Christian name—
> For all its self-asserted claim,
> How fares it, tell?[27]

In the more secular, pluralistic country that develops, it is more common to see
religious values expressed in fiction through human relationships than in specific
references to God, Christ, or church. A clear example of this is in Mark Twain's
masterpiece, *Adventures of Huckleberry Finn*. Although published in 1885, the
novel is set in the years before the Civil War, both to establish the moral conflict
for Huck and give the reader a perspective on that conflict. Encountering the runaway slave, Jim, Huck is initially impelled to report him to the authorities, as his
society dictates he should. But marooned on the raft with Jim, Huck gets to know
the man and in the moral climax of the novel, decides not to turn him in with the
words, "All right, then, I'll *go* to hell."[28] Believing that he will be condemned
for this sin of defying the civil law, Huck nevertheless chooses Jim's welfare over
his own, thus vividly portraying the Christian principle, "Greater love hath no
man than that he lay down his life for his friend" (John 15:13).

Most modern literature of any complexity can exhibit some or all of the characteristics of Gunn's categories simultaneously in their expression of religion.[29] In
Twain's *Adventures of Huckleberry Finn,* the stance of literature in opposition
to religion is apparent in the reader's awareness that Huck is making a decision
that is contrary to the laws of the society of his time, but one that readers of this
novel, published well after the Civil War and the demise of slavery, understand
to be a correct, moral decision. In other words, the character in a novel, the untu-
tored Huck Finn, speaks with a stronger moral voice than was available in his
culture at the time. Similarly, from a religious perspective, Huck believes he is
condemning himself for saving Jim, whereas the reader can see this as an expression of Christian virtue. In this adolescent's ability to act with the highest degree
of religious sensibility by relying on his native intelligence and feelings, Twain
creates a fiction that approaches Gunn's third category, literature as an alternative

or substitute for religion. Huck can act with Christian virtue despite no actual reference to religion as a source of guidance.

More than sixty years later, another American teenager is adrift in a novel with striking parallels to *Adventures of Huckleberry Finn,* but this time he's not on a river. Holden Caulfied in J.D. Salinger's *The Catcher in the Rye* wanders the streets of New York City, as alienated from his society as Huck is from "siviliza-tion." The difference between the protagonists is that Huck learns to trust his intuition and makes a positive moral choice, whereas Holden is frustrated in trying to achieve in the real world the role he fantasizes. To be a "catcher in the rye," to protect innocent children, is to be, in essence, a savior. His desire to help and protect is shown when he cleans the "F-word" from a building because he doesn't want children to see it. Holden has inherently good instincts but cannot find a way to express them in his social world of the 1950s.

In terms of the relationship of fiction to religion, Salinger's novel, as a par-allel to Twain's, reflects the weakness of the opposition to religion without a strong, faith-based culture from which an individual can derive meaning. Huck is able to make a Christian choice to save Jim because he has been raised in a culture imbued with Christian values even though those values were not always enacted in the social realm, witness the institution of slavery. Holden, on the other hand, cannot find any support for his idealism in his society. Salinger's novel is prescient in its depiction of the secular, "God is Dead" culture that will emerge in American society within a few years. Ironically, both of these novels are among the most banned books today, and it's the development of American society in the years between Twain's novel and Salinger's that accounts for this myopic view of literature in which readers respond at only the most literal level.

To World War I and Beyond

From the end of the Civil War, as the United States experienced the trans-formation from a rural, agrarian society to a more urban, industrialized land, religion moved from the public sphere to the private. As daily life in the new urban world became increasingly impersonal and uncongenial, religion became "feminized," a haven of love and acceptance in the harsh, cruel world.[30] And as American society progressed through World War I, Prohibition, and the Depression, there was increasing social unrest and conflicts in values. Marxism and Freudianism challenged traditional social thinking and contributed further to confusion and conflict. Religion increasingly became a safe haven, not for theological answers to modern issues, but as a stable presence in a chaotic world. The church community or parish was the center of religious life, and in the religious community, adherents sought acceptance and love. Theological precepts or doctrines were less relevant in themselves than as they influenced pious practices, the level at which most churchgoers experience religion.[31]

During the period between the world wars, there was a major shift in literary expression that has been labeled "Modernism." Begun in painting with the Impressionists, it gradually influenced all of the arts. The Impressionists turned from objective reality to subjective impressions. Applied to literature, this emphasis on the subjective often meant depicting the "actual" mind of the protagonist as the core narrative. Thus, the emphasis was not on story but on fragments of information, the "stream of consciousness," from which the reader must infer the story. One way to understand the difference is that in traditional narrative, the reader is a consumer of meaning, absorbing the coherent story provided by the author; whereas in a modernist novel, the reader must be a producer of meaning, must infer meaning from the various fragments of expression presented by the author rather than from a coherent narrative, the traditional form of storytelling. The best-known modernist novelists in Europe were James Joyce and Virginia Woolf, and in America, it was William Faulkner. American modernist poets include T. S. Eliot, Ezra Pound, Wallace Stevens, Hart Crane, and William Carlos Williams.

The techniques of modernism derived from a philosophic basis that was a response to a sense of loss of old certitudes. Not only had the country experienced the horrors of World War I and the decimation of the civilian population in the influenza epidemic of 1918, but at the same time, a theological liberalism was calling some traditional beliefs into question. Americans encountered both Marxism, with its emphasis on being controlled by forces outside the self, and Freudianism, with its emphasis on being controlled by unconscious forces within the self.[32] The traditional American reliance on self-determination was shattered, best expressed by the line from T. S. Eliot's *The Waste Land* that encapsulates the sense that the artist's form of expression mirrors an interior sense of dissolution, "these fragments I have shored against my ruins."[33]

The American novelist Willa Cather noted that "the world broke in two in 1922 or thereabouts."[34] Not coincidentally 1922 is the *annus mirabilis* of modernism, marking the publication of both Joyce's *Ulysses* and Eliot's *The Waste Land,* the quintessential modernist novel and poem. Cather's comment reflects the fact that the result of this strikingly esoteric and arcane literature was a stronger cleavage between the "serious" and the "popular." As "serious" literature became increasingly arcane and obscure, its readership was significantly narrowed to the highly educated elite, with a concomitant increase in all forms of popular literature for the masses. And while popular fiction may be denigrated and ignored by the literary establishment, the books that large numbers of people are reading are highly significant, as we will see in the chapters that follow.

Literary modernism should not be confused with another movement known as "modernism" that is specifically related to religion. Beginning with critical study of the Bible in the late nineteenth century, religious liberals, also known as modernists, called many traditional beliefs into question. Since they no longer viewed the Bible as an infallible record of divine revelation, modernists also rejected any religious belief based on authority alone and called for a rethinking of Christian doctrine to accommodate this new knowledge. Like literary modernism, this movement was intensified by the cataclysm of World War I, further calling into question traditional values and morals. Liberals stressed the immanence rather than the transcendence of God, which led to a focus on the social gospel, the mandate to challenge the corruption in the world that was, in turn, corrupting man. Clearly, this movement would be anathema to conservative and especially hierarchical religions, so it is hardly surprising that the Catholic form of modernism was condemned by Pope Pius X in a 1907 encyclical.[35]

While the Bishop of Rome may have worried about the inroads of modernism, the Bishops of the United States in the mid–nineteenth century had far more pragmatic concerns. The vast tides of immigration brought large numbers of Catholics to America from diverse cultures, and this posed a special challenge to the Church. These immigrants would have to adjust to life in the United States, and the Church also sought to insure their continued fidelity to Catholicism. From the diversity of languages and cultural heritage, the Church's challenge was to create a religious unity.[36] The story of that accomplishment is far too complex for these pages, but one aspect of that unifying and proselytizing mission was the development of a uniquely Catholic popular literature that developed in the late nineteenth century and blossomed well into the twentieth. In fact, one of the editors known for promoting American nationalism through his popular literature, the Irish Catholic Mathew Carey, was equally instrumental in creating popular fiction to unify and edify Catholics.[37]

As noted by sociologists, for the typical worshipper, religion is less a matter of theology or dogma than it is about personal experience.[38] Fiction, whether in popular novels or magazine stories, enabled the Catholic writer to promote the Church's values and the tenets of the faith through simple stories of "real life" people. The Catholic fiction of this period consists mainly of narratives constructed "to give metaphoric reinforcement to ideology."[39] They are primarily cultural artifacts without artistic merit. Interestingly, they parallel the eighteenth-century American fiction designed to promote nationalism, and we will see this phenomenon recurring in contemporary religious fiction as well. Whether promoting nationalism or religion, this use of fiction to promote ideology is a consistent phenomenon throughout history. Obviously, this proselytizing fiction works best with unsophisticated readers, and the typical American Catholic during this period, less educated than industrious, was well suited to be a consumer of this ideological fiction. Flannery O'Connor, who is the most acclaimed Catholic writer of the post—World War II era, pronounced judgment on this type of religious fiction with the comment, "When the Catholic novelist closes his own eyes and tries to see with the eyes of the Church, the result is another addition to that large body of pious trash for which we have so long been famous."[40]

Although O'Connor writes in the second half of the century, she not only presents an appropriate contrast for the "pious trash" school of Catholic fiction during the earlier part of the century but also represents another issue for the writer with an underlying religious philosophy. As an accomplished writer with a unique style, highly influenced by the Southern Gothic tradition and its fascination with the grotesque, O'Conner's fiction is dense and difficult, and frequently violent. Her work was much lauded by critics, and rightly so, but critical reception is conditioned by expectations. The lesson of the modernists was that "serious" literature was difficult to interpret and required extensive close reading. O'Connor, with her rich use of symbols and often mystifying dramatic action, fits the modernist model of serious literature. However, her fiction, much like Joyce's novels or Eliot's poetry, is also rather inaccessible for the average reader without extensive exegesis, which is why her stories are so frequently anthologized in college literature texts. Her fiction is also not the inspiring or edifying type that the average reader expects from a religious writer.

Thus, the reader who is looking for a closer association with his or her religious tradition through literature might be more fulfilled by the "pious trash" of popular fiction than from reading the very accomplished prose of Flannery O'Conner. This is important to note. And it is equally important to note this wide divergence in something as apparently monolithic as the "Catholic novel." We will encounter this issue in contemporary religious fiction in subsequent chapters. What literary critics regard as "good" literature is often not as widely read as literature that fulfills the needs and expectations of its readers.

World War II and Its Aftermath

Sociologically, World War II was a watershed in American history. Principally as a result of the G.I. Bill, the level of education among Americans increased dramatically in the years immediately following World War II. The effect on religion was equally dramatic, since education began to create a cleavage within denominations.[41] Those with more education were more likely to be liberal, and those with less education were just as likely to be conservative. Those with advanced education were also likely to be unaffiliated with any religion, since higher education also operated "as a missionary outpost of secular culture weaning the young generations of the mainline churches away from their tradition."[42] The liberalism of the academy, however, was countered by the growth of evangelicals during this period, whose numbers increased, drawing from mainline denominations via youth movements and crusades from powerful evangelists like Billy Graham, Oral Roberts, and Rex Humbard.[43]

The literature of this period illuminates this social change. As a consequence of the accessibility of education, the period of 1945–1960 marks the democratization of American literature. It is not only the regional and ethnic voices that are new, but the focus on their own experience with a return to traditional narrative in presenting those experiences to the reader. This is the era of Ralph Ellison's *Invisible Man* (1952), and James Baldwin's *Go Tell It on a Mountain* (1953), giving white America an insight into the African-American experience. And this is the era of Saul Bellow, Bernard Malamud, and Philip Roth, writing from the perspective of second-generation Americans and exploring their ethnic identity.

As Will Herberg pointed out in his landmark study of American religion, "Religious association...became the primary context for self-identification and social location for the third generation, as well as for the second generation, of America's immigrants."[44] Thus, as we see in the literature of the period, even those not formally practicing their religion identify with a religious heritage that they struggle to understand.

A much-neglected story by Philip Roth from his first short story collection, *Goodbye-Columbus,* is emblematic of this ethnic fiction.[45] In "Defender of the Faith," a young Jewish-American Army sergeant, Nathan Marx, has returned from combat in Europe, and while awaiting his discharge is also trying to understand his place in society in terms of both class and religion. In the story's narrative conflict, Marx encounters a recruit, Sheldon Grossbart, who tries to elicit favors by exploiting their common religious heritage. In trying to deal with Grossbart, Marx experiences tension in his identity as a Jew in American society. Irritated by the conniving recruit, Marx wants to assert military discipline, but he also struggles with the casual anti-Semitic remarks of his commanding officer, causing him to feel a bond with Grossbart despite the latter's unacceptable behavior.

Marx's struggles with Grossbart are an externalization of his own interior conflict to resolve his postwar identity as an American citizen—a Jewish-American citizen. The challenge of coming to terms with one's heritage in the postwar world informs much of the literature of this period. In terms of Gunn's categories, the story, like Marx himself, oscillates between the complementary view of religion as an inherent part of experience, which is the basis for Grossbart's claims for special consideration, and the oppositional phase of literature that questions the priority of institutional religion, a position that is forced on Marx by Grossbart's manipulative behavior. Marx understands that he cannot inhabit the religious world of his grandparents, but in rejecting Grossbart's model of a contemporary Jew, he is uncertain how to incorporate his religious heritage into his life. His attempts to decide on a future career after his discharge from the Army suggest the potential to substitute vocation for religion. A career in law or academia can be an alternative mode, one that will provide meaning and values for the individual as a replacement for an abandoned religious heritage. In the story's climax, the reader understands that religion is complex and involves the whole of the individual beyond pious practices, and this complexity is intensified in the postwar years in America, as increased secularization challenges the inherited traditions of religious observance.

Politically, the democratization of American society reflected in literature during the postwar period provided support for the Civil Rights Movement, which would have a profound effect on the role of religion in American society.[46] Having retreated from the public arena to home and hearth, religion was suddenly back in the public realm, a major factor in the Civil Rights Movement, evidenced not only by the fact that its major voice, Martin Luther King, was a minister whose oratory was grounded in Biblical language but also by the fact that

religious leaders were among the major, and most visible, supporters of the movement. On the whole, Americans could appreciate the value of moral leadership
from the churches on this issue.

However, as The Sixties progressed, religious leaders continued involvement
in more divisive issues: the Vietnam War, pornography, abortion, and homosexuality, often dividing their congregations.[47] Having entered the public sphere
in championing civil rights, religion could no longer be relegated to home and
hearth, whether or not the American people appreciated its voice in the political
arena. A consequence of the pull to the left in American society in the late 1960s
would be to strengthen the cleavage between liberal and conservative within
religious groups. Ultimately those labels, rather than denomination, will be the
central difference in the religious perspective among Americans.[48] Thus, today
we find conflict within denominations over church discipline and practice, as in
the current controversy in the Episcopal Church over the ordination of gay
bishops that may result in a major schism.[49]

The liberal/conservative divide in contemporary American culture is reflected
in contemporary efforts at book censorship, particularly fiction for young people.
Sociologists' correlation of conservatism with a lower level of education seems to
inform the book banning movements in many school districts that appear to be
fueled by literary fundamentalism. For example, Twain's *Adventures of Huckleberry Finn* has been targeted for censorship throughout its publication history
for "racism," most specifically, the use of the "N-word."[50] Overlooked is the fact
that the novel centers on the innately moral Huck who intuitively perceives the
human worth of the runaway slave, Jim, and works to free him despite the mores
of his society, ultimately deciding to lose his soul rather than betray the slave. The
fundamentalist reading of novels at the most literal level of individual words
rather than a consideration of the values conveyed in the work is the basis for most
attempts at book banning, and the situation with *The Catcher in the Rye* is similar.

The major complaints against *The Catcher in the Rye* focus on Holden's
language, with charges ranging from "vulgar" to "filthy and profane."[51] Ignored
is the fact that Holden is mainly concerned with how to be a moral person in the
adult world he is experiencing, and in fact, the worst language in the book is
written on the side of a building, and Holden wipes it away lest children see it.
Holden speaks the teen argot of the 1960s, a language peppered with "crap, lousy,
and phony" as its major epithets, with "goddam" functioning as a ubiquitous
adjective. As with the language in Huck Finn, this is a situation in which it is
necessary to the verisimilitude of the novel. Both books are first-person narratives, and Twain and Salinger are using the vernacular appropriate to their adolescent narrators. Yet it is also true that for many evangelical Christians, the use of
profane language is deeply offensive and is, de facto, "un-Christian." Interestingly, in 2003 *The Catcher in the Rye* was named by *Time* magazine as one of
the 100 best English-language novels published since 1923. It is described by
Time's critic as "a permanent reminder of the sweetness of childhood, the hypocrisy of the adult world, and the strange no-man's-land that lies in between."[52]

This dichotomy between one view of *The Catcher in the Rye* as undermining morality and another that considers its moral world instructive is at the heart of the conservative/liberal split in American religion today. One contemporary writer attributes conservative reading of literature to the fundamentalist approach to Scripture. She comments, "Since they haven't learned to read the Bible and notice when it was metaphoric, when it was literal, when it was poetry, when it was history; they can't bring that kind of flexibility to other books."[53] Whatever the reason, the split that sociologists observe between liberals and conservatives in religion that cuts across denominational lines is even stronger among readers. Unfortunately, as we will see in subsequent chapters, this division, pitting one side against the other, prevents either from seeing the beam in its own eye.

The 1972 novel, *My Name is Asher Lev,* by Chaim Potok blends all three phases of Gunn's categories to offer the story of American religion in microcosm. The title character is a youth who belongs to an orthodox Jewish community, the Hasidim, in Brooklyn, New York. Initially, the Jewish experience is portrayed as normative, reflecting the complementary phase when literature assumed the presence of religion and supported its values. However, Asher Lev is a talented artist, and Judaism is an anti-iconographic religion for the most part; it opposes the making of any human image as a form of idolatry. Thus, there is a basic conflict between Asher Lev's drive to develop as an artist and the religious traditions of his community. Modern literature, a product of a post-Enlightenment culture, presupposes the priority of the individual. And thus, when there is a tension between the individual and the received traditions of religion, literature will be oppositional toward religion, valorizing individual self-determination. In the novel, this oppositional stance is reflected in Asher Lev's conflict with his parents. His father believes that the gift of art comes from Satan, and should be repressed. Fortunately, the community's spiritual leader, wiser than Asher's parents, nurtures the incipient artist. Even among such a traditionally cohesive group like the Hasidim, Potok juxtaposes the more educated, liberal response of the rabbi with the conservative reaction of Asher's father.

Studying painting, Asher becomes immersed in the traditional art of Europe, notably images of the Madonna and the Crucifixion. In doing so, he is not breaking any Jewish law so long as he does not paint such images for worship. However, in the tension between Asher's art and his religious tradition, the narrative metaphorically reflects the tension in literature's oppositional attitude toward religion, as Asher struggles to be faithful to both his religion and his art. Finally, he chooses to image his mother's suffering in a painting using the Crucifixion metaphorically for its power as a symbol of suffering. Asher knows that the Hasidim will be offended, but he also knows that if he censors himself now, there will be future challenges that he will need to face. Predictably, his conservative community interprets the painting literally rather than metaphorically, and they are horrified by his crucifixion imagery. He is expelled from the Hasidim, and the narrative then metaphorically reflects the alternative stage of literature as a substitute for religion, as Asher Lev derives meaning from his art more than from his religion. Potok deftly presents this transition in the narrative by describing Asher's art with the mystical and transcendent qualities that should be associated with religion, whereas the world of religious observance is conveyed with mundane and dispiriting imagery.

The conservative religious mind that thinks only literally and not metaphorically is a central problem in the novel and in our world today. *The Catcher in the Rye* and *Adventures of Huckleberry Finn* are banned, as are many other classic novels, because they are deemed offensive in some minor details, while the central message of the texts remains unheard. In *My Name is Asher Lev,* Chaim Potok's subject is the clash of cultures, the destruction that results when conflict between two well-meaning parties cannot be resolved amicably because one or both cannot understand the perspective of the other. Since the publication of Potok's novel in 1972, such conflicts have increased, as the chasm between conservatives and liberals has become a major feature in the landscape of the United States, as we will see in Chapter 3.

However, before examining the current situation, another novel can provide insight into the contemporary moment and help gloss the current religious antagonisms in our culture. Dan Brown's *The DaVinci Code* is a novel that has engendered controversy that seems to have involved all segments of the American religious community. It is thus an appropriate vehicle for an overview of the contemporary situation and is the focus of the next chapter.

Notes

1. Joe Gash, *Priestly Murders* (New York: Penguin Books, 1984), 89.

2. Richard Land, "How Religion Defines America" for BBC program *What the World Thinks of God,* February 25, 2004, http://news.bbc.co.uk/1/hi/programmes/wtwtgod/3518221.stm (accessed July 15, 2005).

3. Ibid.

4. For example, Robert Wuthnow, *The Restructuring of American Religion: Society and Faith Since World War II* (New Jersey: Princeton University Press, 1988), 5; and Mary Ann Glendon, "The Church and Popular Culture," *CCICA Annual* 14 (1995): 2.

5. The post–Vatican II phenomenon of "cafeteria Catholics" who pick and choose among Church teachings they follow is well documented—in fact, the term is so pervasive in popular culture that it can be found in the online encyclopedia, *Wikipedia,* http://en.wikipedia.org/wiki/Cafeteria_catholic (accessed July 20, 2006).

6. John Shea, *Stories of Faith* (Chicago, IL: Thomas More Press, 1980), 42.

7. Paul's conversion is described in Acts 9:1–31. All quotations from Scripture used in this book are from *The New Oxford Annotated Bible with the Apocrypha,* Revised Standard Version, ed. Herbert G. May and Bruce M. Metzger (New York: Oxford University Press, 1977).

8. Giles Gunn, *The Culture of Criticism and the Criticism of Culture* (New York: Oxford University Press, 1987), 182–3.

9. Wuthnow, *The Restructuring of American Religion,* 242.

10. Robert N. Bellah and others, *Habits of the Heart: Individualism and Commitment in American Life* (New York: Harper & Row Publishers, 1986), 220.

11. Ibid. Bellah is citing Perry Miller's famous study, *Errand Into the Wilderness* (Cambridge, MA: Harvard University Press, 1956).

12. Bellah, "Civil Religion in America," reprinted from *Daedalus, Journal of the American Academy of Arts and Sciences* 96, no. 1 (1967), http://hirr.hartsem.edu/Bellah/articles_5.htm (accessed July 15, 2005).

13. Anne Bradstreet, "Verses upon the Burning of our House," http://www.annebradstreet.com/verses_upon_the_burrning_of_our_house.htm (accessed June 21, 2006).

14. Gottesman and others, *The Norton Anthology of American Literature,* vol. 1 (New York: W.W. Norton Company, 1979), 4.

15. Bellah, "Civil Religion in America," 5–6.

16. Ibid., 10.

17. Francois Furstenberg, "Spinning the Revolution," *The New York Times,* July 4, 2006, A15.

18. Ibid.

19. As Gottesman and others, *The Norton Anthology of American Literature,* 576, point out, it is important to note that this group of writers knew each other "often intimately" or knew about each other, creating a very strong bond among them.

20. Ibid., 735.

21. Ibid., 1588.

22. Ibid.; italics his. While the religious establishment would be scandalized by such sentiments, Thoreau is reflecting a very prophetic understanding of spiritual development with *his* emphasis on the importance of personally appropriating the basic tenets of the faith rather than blindly following convention. This will not become commonly understood until the 1981 publication of James Fowler's *Stages of Faith: The Psychology of Human Development and the Quest for Meaning* (San Francisco: Harper & Row Publishers).

23. Quoted in Gottesman and others, *The Norton Anthology of American Literature,* 2078.

24. Dickinson's poems are quoted from Gottesman and others, *The Norton Anthology of American Literature,* 2349 ff.

25. Bellah, "Civil Religion in America," 7.

26. Richard Wightman Fox, "The President Who Died for Us," *New York Times,* April 14, 2006, A21. Also Bellah, "Civil Religion in America," 8, cites Lincoln's law partner W.H. Herndon who made the same association of Lincoln with Christ. Bellah notes, "With the Christian archetype in the background, Lincoln, 'our martyred president,' was linked to the war dead, those who 'gave the last full measure of devotion.' The theme of sacrifice was indelibly written into our civil religion."

27. Gottesman and others, *The Norton Anthology of American Literature,* 2265–66.

28. Samuel Langhorne Clemens, *Adventures of Huckleberry Finn* (1885; repr., New York: W.W. Norton, 1961), 168. Italics his.

29. Gunn, *The Culture of Criticism and the Criticism of Culture,* 184.

30. Bellah and others, *Habits of the Heart,* 223. In using the term "feminized," Bellah cites the seminal study by Ann Douglas, *The Feminization of American Culture* (New York: Knopf, 1977).

31. Ibid., 226.

32. For a discussion of the Modernist period in American literature, see Gottesman and others, *The Norton Anthology of American Literature,* 1016.

33. T. S. Eliot, "The Waste Land," 1.430, *T.S. Eliot, Collected Poems, 1909-1962* (London: Faber and Faber, Ltd., 1974), 79.

34. Cited in Gottesman and others, *The Norton Anthology of American Literature,* 1490.

35. Jay Dolan, *The American Catholic Experience* (New York: Doubleday and Company, Inc., 1985), 318.

36. Ibid., 127.

37. Ibid., 248.

38. Wuthnow, *The Restructuring of American Religion,* 144.

39. Paul R. Messbarger, *Fiction with a Parochial Purpose: Social Uses of American Catholic Literature, 1884-1900* (Boston: Boston University Press, 1971), 20.

40. Flannery O'Conner, *Mystery and Manners,* ed. Sally and Robert Fitzgerald (New York: Farrar, Straus, and Giroux, 1969), 180.

41. Wuthnow, *The Restructuring of American Religion,* 189.

42. Bellah and others, *Habits of the Heart,* 325.

43. Wuthnow, *The Restructuring of American Religion,* 182.

44. Will Herberg, *Protestant-Catholic-Jew: An Essay in American Religious Sociology,* 2nd ed. (Garden City, NY: Anchor Books, 1960), 31.

45. Philip Roth, "Defender of the Faith," in *Goodbye, Columbus and Five Short Stories* (New York: Vintage Books, 1959), 161–200.

46. Wuthnow, *The Restructuring of American Religion,* 145.

47. Ibid., 147–48.

48. Ibid., 189 and 218. This point about the cleavage within denominations is one of the main points of Wuthnow's book.

49. At the time of this writing, this issue is a continued story in the news. See, for example, Neela Banerjee, "Church Urges Its Dioceses Not to Elect Gay Bishops," *New York Times,* June 22, 2006, A18.

50. Nicholas J. Karolides, Margaret Bald, and Dawn B. Sova, *100 Banned Books: Censorship Histories of World Literature* (New York: Checkmark Books, 1999), 337.

51. Ibid., 367.

52. *Time,* http://www.time.com/time/2005/100 books/0,24459,the_catcher_in_the_rye,00.html (accessed July 6, 2006).

53. Doris Betts, "Learning to Balance," in *Of Fiction and Faith: Twelve American Writers Talk about Their Vision and Work,* ed. W. Dale Brown (Grand Rapids, MI: William B. Eerdmans Publishing Company, 1997), 26.

2

The Da Vinci Phenomenon

And Priests in black gowns were walking their rounds,
And binding with briars my joys & desires.

—William Blake

An American in Europe finds himself embroiled in an apparent religious conspiracy involving a secret society with information about the historical Jesus that can have extraordinary consequences for Christianity. It sounds familiar, but this is not a synopsis of *The Da Vinci Code,* Dan Brown's phenomenal best seller, published in 2003. Instead, it's a description of a 1972 best seller, Irving Wallace's thriller, *The Word.* Yet despite the similarities between these two novels, Wallace's book did not approach the incredible popularity of *The Da Vinci Code,* nor did it set off the firestorm of rebuttals that Brown's novel has provoked. The difference is not in the details of the two books but in their times. Because of the specific confluence of circumstances in American culture today, *The Da Vinci Code* is far more than a best seller; it is approaching iconic status and has become a touchstone in America's culture wars.

It is not difficult to be convinced that Dan Brown's thriller, *The Da Vinci Code,* has become an artifact of popular culture, given the attention it has received in the media: the plethora of puzzles, games, and DVDs inundating the market, and, perhaps the ultimate tribute in contemporary American culture, its own diet book.[1] That this popular novel in the action/suspense mode has even enticed the intellectual elite was evident when the judge in a copyright infringement case brought against Brown and his publisher included a *Da Vinci*-like coded message in his seventy-one–page decision ruling in favor of Brown.[2]

By the time the movie version appeared in May 2006, there were 60.5 million copies of the novel in print, and it had been translated into forty-four languages

and produced roughly $400 million in revenue in worldwide sales.[3] If this reli-
giously themed thriller is a publishing blockbuster in terms of sales, it has also
engendered a concomitant avalanche in terms of vehement opposition in a multitude of articles, web sites, and full-length books, all of which seem to consider the
novel a threat to Christianity. This phenomenon, the novel's enormous popularity
and the assault it has evoked, clearly indicates that this is more than a simple best
seller. Popular fiction reflects its culture, and the impact of *The Da Vinci Code* can
provide a distinctive insight into the contemporary culture of American religion.
To understand this phenomenon, it will be useful to look at both aspects—the
sales and the opposition generated by this book.

The Best Seller and Its Readers

It is axiomatic in the study of literature that no book becomes a best seller
simply because of its artistry—or lack thereof.[4] To appeal to the millions of
readers involved, a best-selling novel must tap into the *Zeitgeist,* the intellectual
and cultural climate of the times. That *The Da Vinci Code* has touched the contemporary *Zeitgeist* is evident in the sheer magnitude of its sales. Thus, an analysis of
the novel's appeal will help identify the lineaments of this contemporary cultural
climate.

The controversial content of the novel would not, in itself, account for its
incredible sales, since the revisionist religious history at the heart of this thriller
is not original but an amalgam of various nonfiction sources, all of which had
already been in print for some time—and unnoticed by most readers—before
Brown found them. Nor is the novel's theme of institutional venality on the part
of the Catholic Church very original, as evidenced by the two lawsuits claiming
copyright infringement. One lawsuit was brought by two of the authors of *Holy
Blood, Holy Grail,* one of Brown's acknowledged sources for the major conspiracy at the heart of his novel. The second was by Lewis Perdue, the author
of a novel, *Daughter of God,* published in 2001. Perdue's novel has not elicited
the vociferous condemnation accorded *The Da Vinci Code,* although it has
an equally provocative plot that indicts the Catholic Church—the murder of a
second, female Messiah by the early Church to protect its developing power,
and the Vatican's subsequent chicanery, including violence and murder, to keep
her existence secret and preserve its patriarchal hegemony. It is tempting to
assume that Mr. Perdue brought his lawsuit in an attempt to participate in the
Da Vinci firestorm and thus draw some readers to *his* historical conspiracy,
so noxious is his view of the Church and yet so unnoticed by its supporters clam-
oring to censure Dan Brown.

One of the provocative theological issues of *The Da Vinci Code* is also not
unknown. The idea of a married Jesus has been a topic of speculation for some
time, and made its way into print well before *The Da Vinci Code.* In the 1970s,
William E. Phipps posed the question in his book's title, *Was Jesus Married?*,
with the subtitle *The Distortion of Sexuality in the Christian Tradition,* and the

work was reprinted in a 1986 paperback. A more affirmatively titled book, *Jesus Was Married* by Ogden Kraut, was published in hardcover in 1970 and reprinted in paperback in 2003.[5] Moreover, Dan Brown makes no claims for originality in his historical speculation, listing on his web site a variety of sources that he says contributed to the development of the novel. Thus, the key issue in the incredible sales of *The Da Vinci Code* is not its provocative content per se, since almost all the ideas in the novel were already in print in other sources. However, in putting together his novel, Dan Brown created an amalgam that is unique in its appeal to a vast number of readers. And those readers, in turn, reflect contemporary American religious culture.

Almost twenty years ago, the sociologist Robert Wuthnow wrote of a "serious degree of polarization" that could have "sweeping ramifications for the future of American religion."[6] His concern was for the liberal/conservative chasm that he saw as the major division in religion, a division that cut through individual denominations.[7] Whereas at one time the major differences in American religion were between denominations, now the division is within those churches, and the like-minded are united across denominations. For example, historically, conservative evangelicals in the United States would see Roman Catholics as a heretical cult. Today evangelicals are allied with conservative Roman Catholics on many social issues, including abortion and homosexuality. And liberal Roman Catholics would be at odds with their more conservative fellow parishioners on many issues and be more in agreement with liberal Episcopalians. On the issue of the ordination of women, conservative Catholics and Episcopalians are much more likely to be in accord, for example, than with the liberal worshippers beside them in the pews. As the chasm between liberal and conservative cuts through denominations, it causes problems within churches, as in the question of ordaining homosexual bishops that more recently threatens a schism within the Episcopal Church.[8]

One reason for *The Da Vinci Code*'s popularity is that it transcends that liberal/conservative chasm and can appeal to both types of readers. Wuthnow associates religious liberals with a higher level of education, as well as "self-conscious syncretism of symbolism from several of the world's religions, a more privatized form of religious expression," and "mixtures of social scientific and theological reasoning."[9] For this liberal reader, *The Da Vinci Code* offers its symbolic codes and conspiracy theory infrastructure, as well as the appeal of a thriller that not only provides the intellectual challenge of various puzzles to solve but arcane religious and historical information as well. On the other hand, for the religious conservative, characterized by a lower level of education in general, the genre of the thriller is appealing because it makes few demands on the reader, since it is plot driven and, ideally, an engaging "page turner." Brown's very brief chapters are another feature of the well-constructed thriller that absorbs the reader with a less-than-optimum attention span.

Since conservative Christians tend to seek religious subjects in their reading, as evidenced by the phenomenon of Christian publishing, they would be attracted to a book with a religious theme, especially one that offers information about the historical Jesus. In our reality-focused culture that is almost voyeuristic in its devotion to the docudrama, reality shows on television, and the intrusive tabloid, the lack of detailed information about the daily life of the historical Jesus is frustrating to conservative Christians whose faith expression is centered on Jesus as personal savior. To such Christians, Jesus is more than the savior of theology. As Wuthnow explains, "Jesus is the muscular older brother you always wanted to fend off bullies on the playground, the effusive spinster aunt who takes you in for milk and cookies after a bad day, the confidante you can e-mail for instant reassurance."[10] Thus, a novel that purports to provide information about the human life of this sacred figure, to humanize him, as it were, would be especially appealing to conservative Christians.[11]

More significantly, however, both liberals and conservatives are united in the pervasive individualism that informs their religious experience. This tendency, identified by sociologists in the 1980s, appears to have escalated in the intervening years. In the early 1980s, Robert Bellah and his colleagues gave an example of this individualism in "Sheilaism," the private religion of Sheila, a young nurse they interviewed. They quote her as saying, "I believe in God. I'm not a religious fanatic. I can't remember the last time I went to church. My faith has carried me a long way. It's Sheilaism. Just my own little voice."[12] Another study by Robert Wuthnow, published in 2005, identifies religious individualists as a major category in American religious life, naming them "spiritual shoppers." And he quotes one such "shopper," a forty-year-old schoolteacher who describes her religious preference in this way:

I've made it my business to sort of look into a number of different faiths and pick bouquets from them, including ancient pagan beliefs and Christianity and laws and codes that overlap in a lot of different Muslim/Buddhist/Christian-Judaic laws to live by.[13]

This religious individualist is an ideal reader for *The Da Vinci Code,* with that novel's blend of traditional religion, suppressed goddess worship, and a secret society with arcane rituals. But lest one assume that these are rare individuals who only appear in sociological studies, note the following incident.

There is a local radio program in the New York City area that airs early Sunday mornings called "Religion on the Line," hosted by a Catholic priest and a Jewish rabbi. The clergymen discuss topical issues related to religion and like most of talk radio, invite calls from listeners. One particular morning (August 28, 2005), there was a call from a man who identified himself as "a Christian who does not belong to any church." One of the clergy hosts cautiously asked, "Why do you not belong to a church"? And the caller blithely replied, "I haven't found any church that agrees with my interpretation of Christianity." Neither of the hosts challenged that assertion, and the conversation moved on to the reason for the man's call. When I heard the caller's unselfconscious assertion of primacy in the interpretation of Christianity and the clergymen's tacit acceptance of this man's personal religion, I was astounded at how perfectly it illustrated the pattern described by these sociologists, affirming Wuthnow's conclusion that this phenomenon of the individualistic Christian is fairly ubiquitous in the United States today and a major change in what it means to be a religious person.[14]

It is important to add that even among ostensible adherents to a specific denomination, religion is more often a matter of personal experience than theology or dogma.[15] Even in hierarchical religions, most participants believe what they wish regardless of church teaching. For example, despite the Roman Catholic prohibition of divorce, by the mid-1960s, only about one Catholic in three in the United States considered divorce wrong.[16] The way that religion blends with culture is evident in the manner in which the rugged individualism and self-reliance that characterized those who settled and founded this nation has become a hallmark in its religious expression.

Thus, a novel that contains an alternative view of religious history and promises to be an "easy read" would have strong appeal for the individualists who construct their own religious cosmology. Moreover, the villainous institutional church in the novel taps into the criticism of institutional religion that is a strong element in American religion from the time of the Transcendentalists and so prevalent among religious individualists.[17] And perhaps most significant for the appeal of *The Da Vinci Code* is the fact that its villainous institutional religion is the Catholic Church.

While it is commonplace to note that the horrific child molestation scandals in the Catholic Church and the evidence of administrative lapses in managing those situations, revealed shortly before the publication of *The Da Vinci Code,* would help readers of the novel accept the Vatican as a villain, the Church's negative image is more complex and more deeply felt in contemporary American society. Although for much of American history Catholicism was marginalized in the dominantly Protestant culture, the country experienced a brief romance with the Church during World War II and its aftermath. Beginning in 1944, Bing Crosby portrayed Father "Chuck" O'Malley in films of casual clerical competence, *Going My Way* and its sequel, *The Bells of St. Mary's,* movies that conveyed a sense of innocence and hope to a society reeling from the recent Depression and World War.[18] This popular image reflected the rehabilitation of Catholicism in American social life throughout the 1930s and 1940s. As Jay Dolan notes in his history of the American Catholic experience, "By the end of the 1950s, Catholicism in the United States had clearly come of age. More accepted by the Protestant majority, Catholics entered the 1950s more confident about their place in American society."[19] The subsequent election of the first Catholic President in 1960 seemed to secure that place. Then came *Roe v. Wade.*

Religious leadership in the Civil Rights Movement had brought American religion into the political realm in the late 1950s and early 1960s. As other social issues claimed attention, religious leaders continued to be deeply involved in the country's social and political life.[20] And when the abortion issue gained momentum in the late 1960s, the Catholic Church was identified by abortion proponents as its principal opponent, the major reactionary voice against women from their perspective. Describing the policy of the National Abortion Rights Action League in the years immediately preceding *Roe v. Wade,* one commentator explains,

The strategy was simple: convince the media and the public that this was a case of the Catholic hierarchy attempting to impose its will on America. Portray all opposition from Catholics to legalized abortion as a power play by the Church with the laity marching in lockstep to its clerical overlords. Accuse the Church of abusing its tax exemption for a political power-grab. Secure the right to unlimited access to abortion by painting the pro-life position as a peculiarly Catholic notion with no rights in a pluralistic society. Pull out all the old anti-Catholic canards and focus the debate as a church-state issue.[21]

Thus, the Catholic Church was imaged as the antithesis of modern America. And it is thus hardly surprising that the Church has retained that negative image, since it appears to oppose the contemporary cultural value of inclusiveness with its continued refusal to ordain women or married men, as well as its rejection of homosexuality as an alternative lifestyle. Since the late 1960s, the Catholic Church has had increasingly negative image in the press in the United States due to its position on these social issues. In 1996, the head of the Catholic League cited as an example of the media's contempt for the Catholic hierarchy this comment about Pope John Paul II:

"There are 60 million Catholics in America," explained the *Washington Post* writer Henry Allen, "and for many of them the Pope also speaks with the voice of a conservative crank when he stonewalls on abortion, married priests, women priests, and so on."[22]

The appellation "conservative crank" conveys a disdain for the Papacy that is surprising in a newspaper of the stature of the *Washington Post* and reflects the strongly negative attitude toward Catholicism among liberals that is reflected in the media. In 1995, a commentator noted that "the negative relationship between the Catholic Church and the mass media is increasingly the focus of comment by Church leaders," citing Cardinal Keeler's address to the National Conference of Catholic Bishops the preceding year.[23]

Popular fiction is a sensitive register of the culture, and this negative image of the Catholic Church became apparent from the mid-1980s in one of the most formulaic forms of fiction, the detective novel. Despite the popularity of the British priest-sleuth, Father Brown, created by G.K. Chesterton, there was no priest-detective in American crime fiction until 1977 when Father Roger Dowling began solving crimes in Ralph McInerney's *Her Death of Cold.*[24] He was soon joined by William Kienzle's Father Robert Koesler, who began his sleuthing career in the 1979 *The Rosary Murders,* and in 1985 Father Andrew Greeley introduced his Msgr. Blackie Ryan in *Happy Are the Meek.* Since the detective is the hero in the convention of detective fiction, these three fictional priests, all of whom enjoyed serial success, reflect the last vestiges of the positive image of Catholicism in American culture. In some ways, they were their Catholic authors' attempt to prolong Americans' romance with Catholicism and keep at bay the negative image that was developing.[25] But just as Greeley's priest-detective began his career, a much less positive image of the Catholic priest emerged in the American crime novel in Joe Gash's *Priestly Murders* in 1984, an image that was more consonant with the developing perceptions of the Church fostered by the media.

In formulaic fiction like the crime novel, the archetypal story patterns (the conventions) and departures from those patterns reflect authorial intention. In *Priestly Murders,* a priest is shot and killed while in the process of distributing communion at Mass. The priest initially appears to be the conventional victim of the novel, and the murder of a clergyman suggests a particularly dastardly crime. However, as the novel progresses and detectives investigate, they learn that the murdered priest had been a substitute for a colleague, Father Bill Conklin, who wanted time to pursue his academic career, teaching criminology at the local university. One of the detectives had taken a course from Father Conklin and, asked about him, responds,

A bastard....And a phony. I passed the course, but it was a waste of time. He wrote a book; actually, he's written a few of them. He's all over the wall. He doesn't know anything about what he writes about.[26]

When it appears that Father Conklin may have been the intended victim, the detectives interview the priest at his luxurious apartment. He is arrogant and condescending, refusing to provide any information about his students, one of whom, the police suspect, may be the murderer. He spars with the police several times in the novel, always trying to use his superior knowledge of criminology to establish dominance. When the murderer is finally identified, he turns how to be a rather pathetic, mentally unstable individual named Victor DeLeo, who is killed in a confrontation with the police.

As the novel ends, the principal detective asks his lieutenant, "How come I feel sorry for DeLeo?" And his boss responds, "Because you don't feel sorry for Bill Conklin."[27] The latter, we soon discover, has acquired a book contract to write about his experience of almost being murdered. Thus, Gash deftly turns the intended victim into the novel's villain, the least admirable character in the fiction. Lest the reader miss this indictment of Catholicism, there's a final note about the Church that appears prophetic in light of the subsequent behavior of the Catholic hierarchy in the molestation scandals. On the final pages of the novel, two detectives are discussing the recently ended investigation and the efforts of a detective named Margolies:

Remember when Margolies asked him [the Cardinal] if the Church had gotten any threats....A couple of days ago, he found out the chancery office had been threatened

ten times in the past two years, individuals and institutions, and they never let us know
about it.

Why?

They want to keep secrets.[28]

In manipulating the conventions of the crime novel formula, Gash calls attention
to the venality of the Church by indirection and reinforces the increasingly
negative image of Catholicism in American society.

A few years later, another crime novelist similarly manipulates the conventions
to indict a priest; this time the clergyman is both victim and villain. Ed McBain's
series of police procedural crime novels of the 87th Precinct are well respected in
the genre, and McBain was a prolific master of the form. His 1990 novel *Vespers*
begins with the murder of a young, charismatic priest, Father Michael, brutally
stabbed in the rectory garden. After a series of false leads and an intricate subplot,
the murderer is revealed as a thirteen-year-old girl, one of the schoolgirls actively
involved in the parish. When she confesses, she describes how she had inadvertently observed the priest having intercourse with a woman in the rectory office.
Scandalized by the priest's behavior, she confronts him, and he denies it. Enraged
by both the sin and the lie, the child, overcome by hysteria, stabs him to death. As
the hardened detective listens to the teen's recitation of her crime, he muses,
"'Thirteen,' he was thinking, 'she's only thirteen.'"[29] Thus, the reader loses any
sympathy for the priest victim who has, in effect, precipitated his own murder
by scandalizing the young girl and thereby destroying her life. In McBain's masterful manipulation of the conventions of the crime novel, the murderer becomes
the novel's true victim, and the murdered priest is cast as the villain.

These novels by both Gash and McBain, appearing while the priest-as-
detective-hero was in its prime, effectively ended the reign of those sleuths,
reflecting the escalating disapproval of the Church in American culture. The problems with the image of the Church that developed from its antiabortion position
were magnified by its seeming intransigence to postmodern issues of diversity
and inclusiveness involving women and homosexuals. It is important to note
that a significant part of the problem in sociopolitical discourse is that the
Church views its positions on these issues as moral or sacramental, whereas most
Americans, including many American Catholics, see these same issues as purely
social and open to modification.[30] Neither side really understands the context of
the issues from the other's perspective, and the divisiveness deepens.

Thus, *The Da Vinci Code*'s demonizing of the Catholic Church would resonate
with most American readers, especially since publication coincided with the
worst scandal in American Catholic history in the multitude of cases of priests
accused of molesting children and the subsequent discovery of how the hierarchy
had ignored the problem over the years. The reader of *The DaVinci Code* would
be inclined to believe (and relish) any villainy attributed to Catholicism. Moreover, the novel's premise that the Church was guilty of suppressing the worship
of the Goddess to promote its patriarchal culture would resonate as the prequel

to contemporary misogyny in its intransigent attitude toward ordaining women priests. The villainy of the Church in the novel replicates the current social scene so perfectly that it would not only attract readers but contribute to the believability of Brown's conspiracy theory.

Another aspect of *The Da Vinci Code* that would appeal to readers across the spectrum in American society is Brown's exaltation of sex, presented in a way that would attract both liberals and conservatives. For the liberal reader, he affirms the value of sexual experience, an unqualified good in contemporary society that is often denigrated in orthodox religion, as he provides sex with a religious dimension in the ritual of the *hieros gamos,* the coupling that is a path to religious ecstasy. At the same time, Brown excludes sexually explicit scenes that are the stock in trade of most contemporary pot boilers and would offend conservative readers. The fact that the book takes place in a brief span of hours and the protagonists spend most of that time fleeing the police makes the exclusion of sexual activities realistic without denying their value in human experience. Thus, the theoretical affirmation of sexual experience and its virtual absence in the reality of the novel would tend to attract both liberal and conservative readers and alienate neither.

Finally, in the novel's protagonist, Professor Robert Langdon, Brown has created a hero who is attractive to both liberal and conservative readers, religiously committed or not. Again, the brief time span of the novel allows the reader to either assume or deny that Langdon has any specific religious affiliation. Liberal readers can appreciate someone who appears to be unaffiliated with organized religion but who is more knowledgeable about religious symbols and history than most clerics, while conservative readers are affirmed by someone who obviously belongs to the dominantly liberal academic establishment but who also respects and appreciates religion. Above all, Langdon is presented as the disinterested scholar, without apparent ideology, who is drafted into the novel's action. In fact, the most provocative theories in the novel are voiced, not by Langdon, but by the Grail scholar, Leigh Teabing. Langdon is the mythical knight rescuing the damsel in distress, while simultaneously he is also the unjustly accused victim of the police's rush to judgment who is aided by that damsel in establishing his innocence.

The fact that Langdon has almost precisely the same role in the novel that introduced his character, *Angels and Demons,* offers insight into why *The Da Vinci Code* was so much more appealing to readers than its predecessor in the Brown canon. Both novels are well-plotted thrillers involving religious themes and interchangeable protagonists. In Langdon's first adventure, his female companion is Vittoria, whose expertise as a physicist complements his talents in the particular challenges of that novel, much as Sophia's mastery of cryptology helps in *The Da Vinci Code.* Indeed, the similarities between the novels of Robert Langdon's adventures would suggest a similar expectation in terms of sales. This was not the case. If the readers' comments on Amazon.com are a reliable indicator, most people read the novels in reverse order, having come to know Langdon in

The Da Vinci Code, they looked for more about him in his first incarnation in *Angels and Demons.*

Although *Angels and Demons* is also replete with religion, the central tension of the novel, between science and religion, is too theoretical and arcane to attract conservative readers. Their interest in religion is more inclined to the concrete conspiracy plot of *The Da Vinci Code* and its focus on the historical Jesus. On the other hand, the liberal reader is less inclined to be captivated by a thriller that shows such obvious signs of the low-level pot boiler that *Angels and Demons* signals with its series of very grisly murders. In addition, although the plot of *Angels and Demons* is propelled by Langdon's need to solve a series of clues, as in *The Da Vinci Code,* the puzzles are less complex and intriguing in the earlier novel, and thus less likely to captivate the more educated reader.

The author himself has claimed to be "stunned" by the enormous sales of *The Da Vinci Code,* remarking that his themes "obviously resonate with a great many people."[31] It is not simply the themes, but the way that the various elements in the novel appeal to the entire spectrum of American religious culture, liberals and conservatives alike, that accounts for its spectacular sales. That universal appeal is also responsible for the barrage of detractors attacking the novel.

The Opposition

On Sunday, April 30, 2006, parishioners who arrived for Mass at a small Roman Catholic parish church in rural Orange County, New York, were greeted by an announcement in that week's church bulletin inviting them to a local lecture on Dan Brown's *The Da Vinci Code* scheduled for the following week. The lecturer was identified as Dr. Nancy de Flon, co-author of *The DaVinci Code and Catholic Tradition,* and the message advised, "If you have read the book or plan to see the movie, here is the place to ask your questions and receive clear scholarly answers."[32] This approach was replicated in countless churches across the country, as both Catholic and conservative Christian churches left no stone unturned in their efforts to defuse the effect of *The Da Vinci Code* on their congregants. The issue was less the content of the novel than the number of readers who devoured it.

The reaction to Brown's novel by the Christian establishment is well documented in published books, web sites, and even lectures at the local parish level. And, revealingly, this opposition comes almost exclusively from the conservative element, uniting both evangelicals and Roman Catholics in this effort to discredit *The Da Vinci Code.* The tone of these reactions is often dismissive, citing every imaginable error to challenge the novel, including geographical confusion about places in Paris. Both tone and content of these attacks suggest that these apologists are confronting a major heresy rather than a best-selling work of fiction that has religious speculation at its core. An examination of this focus on the "errors" in the novel provides additional insight into the contemporary culture of religion in the United States.

A key issue is reflected in the novel's dialogue when the Grail scholar Leigh Teabing is explaining his theories to Sophie, and ends with the smug statement, "I've written several books on the topic." To which Sophie responds, "And I assume devout Christians send you hate mail on a daily basis? 'Why would they?' Teabing countered. 'The vast majority of educated Christians know the history of their faith.'"[33] Teabing's response may simply reflect his own arrogance, or it may suggest some limitations in Brown's understanding of religious culture.[34] Teabing (or his creator) makes two errors here. His comment in the context of a response to Sophie suggests that the "vast majority" of Christians are educated and, as sociologists have noted, level of education is the primary distinction between the liberals and the conservatives among Christians. So a reference to "educated Christians" is not responsive to Sophie's question, since she is speaking of the general response, and he immediately refers to the "educated." In addition, he asserts that "educated Christians" know the history of their faith, but, as scholars agree, many people, regardless of their general level of education, participate in religious practices at an emotional and personal level without a clear understanding of doctrine and dogma or the history of their religion.[35]

Although level of education is a critical distinction in the analysis of sociologists, theologians identify a more useful way to understand the reaction to *The Da Vinci Code*. As James Fowler has shown in his study of *Stages of Faith*, just as level of maturity does not necessarily correlate with chronological age in some people, the "stage" of a person's faith may have little to do with that individual's age or commitment to a particular church. In Fowler's schema, the critical stages of spiritual development are three and four. Stage 3 faith is associated with adolescence but also comprises "a significant number of adults."[36] People in Stage 3 may be deeply committed to a religion's "images and values," but their commitment remains a "tacit system," a term Fowler uses for the fact that the beliefs involved are accepted as promulgated by authority but remain unexamined by the individual. As he explains, "A person in Stage 3 is aware of having values and normative images. He or she articulates them, defends them and feels deep emotional investments in them, but typically has not made the value system...the object of reflection."[37] This is an unexamined or conventional faith in which the individual follows the precepts of his or her religious tradition, often without fully understanding their meaning or significance. It is important to note that the stages of faith relate not only individuals but, in Fowler's model, faith communities as well. Indeed, a person's stage of faith can be strongly influenced by the stage of the community in which that person claims membership.[38]

The earliest faith stage of adulthood (spiritual maturity) is Stage 4, which entails critical reflection on one's identity and the values to which the individual is committed. For this stage to occur, according to Fowler, there must be some "interruption of reliance on external sources of authority."[39] This does not necessarily mean abandoning one's religious heritage; it means, however, that the individual does not blindly accept the principles and practices of a religion but reflects on those principles and practices and either recommits to that heritage from a per-spective of personal authority or embraces another system that the individual regards as more congruent with his or her personal values and beliefs. What makes this transition difficult is that institutional religion tends to foster the dependence characterized by Stage 3 faith, effectively promoting a spiritual adolescence among its members.[40] In pre-Vatican II Catholicism, the axiom that parishioners were called to simply "pray, pay, and obey" is indicative of this type of Stage 3 institution.[41]

Thus, it is revealing that the "corrections" to *The Da Vinci Code* have princi-pally come from those with a conservative, authoritarian religious affiliation, the type of religious institution most characteristic of Stage 3. Without reflection, it is impossible to dialogue, which explains why the focus has been on simple ref-utation. If the goal is to allay the concerns of troubled congregants in a Stage 3 church community, then this refutation of Brown's novel would suffice because the reliance on authority at this stage would be satisfied, regardless of the content of the refutation. However, given the strong strain of individualism among Americans, one problem is that anyone who tends to believe that *The Da Vinci Code* is reliable would not have the resources to tell who is correct when faced with competing versions of history.

It is a mark of Stage 3 faith experience to be unable to get beyond the perceived threat of ideas inconsistent with one's belief. Unable to reflect or dialogue, the person must either fully accept the propositions in Brown's novel or fully reject them, and the popularity of the book becomes a significant factor. How can one dismiss a book that has been read by so many millions of people? Thus, the less docile member of a Stage 3 congregation is just as likely to embrace the theories in *The Da Vinci Code* as to agree with its critics. Indeed, how the individual responds would depend on who was regarded as more authoritative, the debunker of the novel or *The Da Vinci Code* itself. If the novel causes an individual to question his or her religious heritage, as its opponents seem to fear, that actually can initiate a salutary process, according to Fowler's principles, since the movement from the adolescent faith of Stage 3 to a more mature faith in Stage 4 requires an abandonment of reliance on the authority figures of Stage 3.

Moreover, in a Stage 4 community, the leadership would be more inclined to use people's interest in the novel to aid reflection and growth in faith. This appears to be a response from more liberal communities. On his web site, Brown asserts that he gets some positive responses from institutional religion. "While many of them disagree with some of the ideas in the novel, they are thrilled that their parishioners are eager to discuss religion."[42] He then quotes a typical response from an Episcopalian priest eager for such dialogue with his parishio-ners. This type of response is an illustration of a Stage 4 community, one that would promote its members' reflection on the central issues of faith, using the novel as an occasion to deepen their experience. Here's how another pastor wrote to her congregation, inviting discussion of *The Da Vinci Code*:

The truth is, there are a lot of ideas out there that we need to begin discussing at church, ideas that are challenging, ideas that stretch the limits of our comfort and security, ideas that would reshape and redefine what it means to be a Christian in a modern setting.[43]

Sociologists agree that the vitality of American religion is to some extent due precisely to its flexibility, as this pastor has expressed it, its willingness to adapt to a more complex society.[44] But such adaptability requires the capacity—and willingness—to reflect, qualities more characteristic of Stage 4 faith and thus not available to those whose faith is Stage 2 or 3.

However, the motivations of those who write in opposition to *The Da Vinci Code* are not unworthy. From a Stage 3 perspective, this novel can confuse the faithful and is certainly a threat to the authority of institutional religion. The less educated, literal reader of conservative Christianity who focuses on the language in *Adventures of Huckleberry Finn* and *The Catcher in the Rye* and fails to appreciate the novels' value statements is the same reader who may fail to understand the context of *The Da Vinci Code*. This is popular fiction designed to entertain with a fast-moving plot and intriguing details. It should not be read as religious history. But fiction can be seductive, and the less sophisticated reader can easily be convinced by a masterful author with an implicit thesis. The fact that the novel's ostensible villain (for much of the reading) is the Vatican, already demonized in American culture, may incline naïve readers to view *The Da Vinci Code* as less oppositional to religion than complementary, as they believe they are learning a "truth" that has been suppressed, one that they believe will enhance their personal faith experience. When fiction skirts the edge of reality so closely, especially with issues of current concern, readers are more likely to absorb its ideas as nonfiction. So the concerns of *Da Vinci* critics are understandable.

To have a corrective available at the local Christian bookstore or a local speaker who can debunk the novel is important to maintain spiritual harmony in a Stage 3 community. Moreover, in its cultural context, *The Da Vinci Code* takes on a significance that belies its reality as a religiously themed thriller. Having unleashed the zeal of religious conservatives, similar to the way in which the movie version of *The Last Temptation of Christ* aroused their ire in the late 1980s, *The Da Vinci Code* is another chapter in the continuing polarization of American religious culture. We can get more insight into that culture by looking more closely at the novel and its detractors.

Fact or Fiction?

One difficulty in *The Da Vinci* controversy is that on many points, both sides have some credibility. For example, most of the objections to the religious ideas in the novel are countered by the assertion that it's "only fiction." But if we look at the literary genre, the typical reader, and the culture of today, it's apparent that fiction has the power to convey the illusion of truth.

The contemporary thriller has its roots in the American "dime novel" of the nineteenth century. Those fast-paced adventure stories were generally based on events of American history—the fighting of the Revolution or the Civil War, forging the frontier, or sometimes the life of a famous individual, such as Buffalo Bill Cody.[45] Thus, from its origins, the contemporary thriller was grounded in actual events that were fictionalized to appeal to the reader. The element of reality was always part of the fiction. In addition, the novel as a genre is characterized by verisimilitude, the appearance of actuality in the use of actual places and objects, thus enhancing the illusion of reality. *The Da Vinci Code* not only takes place in real geographical places, but the history it recounts has just enough factual information to be plausible. For example, Constantine *was* the emperor at the time of the Council of Nicea, and Jesus's divinity *was* proclaimed as an article of faith at that council. It is only a minor addition to claim that Constantine orchestrated the proclamation of Jesus' divinity for political purposes. And in the context of the "real" historical facts, that minor addition can appear "real" as well. If a reader is naïve enough to assume that a novel is presenting authentic history, how can the detractors convince that reader that it is not entirely true?

And critics of *The Da Vinci Code* who are allied with mainline denominations are undercut in the novel when Teabing, in expounding his theories to Sophie, explains that his version of history is not in conventional sources because "history is always written by the winners." He adds, "By its very nature, history is always a one-sided account."[46] Since Teabing's theories include some accepted facts, it is difficult to challenge his alternative version of religious history. The rationale for doubting the orthodox version would be that it was the history "written by the winners" rather than an accurate history that merits belief.

The naïve reader today would be even more inclined to accept the revisionist history of a novel as factual, since the boundary between fact and fiction is so blurred in contemporary culture. How many Americans rely on Oliver Stone's movie *JFK* for their "knowledge" of the Kennedy assassination? Given an unsophisticated reader, it is more than likely that the religious ideas promoted in *The Da Vinci Code* would be accepted as valid theories, if not the truth of history.

The entertainment resources of the paranoid message are unrivaled. It offers puzzles, drama, passion, heroes, villains, and struggle. If the story-line can be tied to an historical event, especially one that involves romantic characters and unexpected death, then fiction, history, and popular delusion can be joined in the pursuit of profit.[47]

This is not a comment on *The Da Vinci Code*. It comes from an academic paper dealing with the movie *JFK* and the facts of the Kennedy assassination. The authors go on to explain that "Films are not simply entertainment; they are also cultural, intellectual, and political influences."[48] Change the first word to "popular novels," and the statement is equally accurate. And the influence is especially powerful among those least capable of discriminating between fact and fiction. As the many *Da Vinci* detractors note, Brown makes (or copies from his sources) so many obvious errors that anyone who knows the general history of Christianity would not be persuaded by the novel's theories. However, since even the errors are tinged with fact, the naïve reader, a product of contemporary culture, would be influenced to accept the theories proposed.

Thus, from the perspective of institutional religion, discrediting *The Da Vinci Code* is as imperative as combating any heresy. This is especially true for evangelicals whose religious experience is rooted in the Bible and who are emotionally invested in the person of Jesus, not only as Savior but also as intimate friend who will help resolve every human problem.[49] Any deviation from the stories of Jesus that they know would be the worst blasphemy, and thus the claim that this is fiction would be irrelevant. It is the audacity of appropriating the story of Jesus that is reprehensible, much as in *The Last Temptation of Christ.* This is why the conservative Christian press has quickly stocked Christian bookstores with one or more of the books that claim to expose the "hoax" of *The Da Vinci Code.* The difficulty, of course, is that just as with the Kennedy assassination, there's something in the American psyche that loves a conspiracy. And since the opposition to *Da Vinci* is simply confrontational for the most part, one authority challenging another with dueling versions of history, the naïve reader is as likely to side with Brown as with any of his opponents. Since the *Da Vinci* opponents are mainly associated with the church in some way, the prevailing suspicion of institutional religion would shift credibility to *The Da Vinci Code* for many individualists, a type quite prevalent in contemporary American religion.

It is doubtful that Dan Brown intended to cause such a crisis. We should not forget that behind *The Da Vinci Code* is an authorial process very similar to his *Angels and Demons.* Hoping to write a best seller and, in the true spirit of American capitalism, make a lot of money, Brown engaged in research to find a plot for his thriller, preferably one involving a secret society, along with some issue requiring urgency to propel his narrative. Unfortunately, in both novels, Brown's understanding of the history and culture of Christianity is demonstrably very weak, resulting in glaring errors. Such ignorance may be the cause of the condescending tone of many of his critics. Most of Brown's detractors have probably not read the earlier novel because if they had, they would understand that his grasp of Catholicism is so very limited that he is clearly controlled by his sources because he would be unable to evaluate their accuracy, even if he wanted to do so.

In *Angels and Demons,* for example, a Cardinal announces that he was the "Devil's Advocate" at the time of the election of the recently deceased Pope and had thus learned the Pontiff's secret, a key to the novel's plot.[50] The office of Devil's Advocate was abolished by Pope John Paul II in 1983, but it would not be unusual for someone to be unfamiliar with that fact. What is remarkable is that Brown would be unaware of the fact that the Devil's Advocate was involved in investigating candidates for canonization, not candidates for the Papacy. Although the process of Papal selection is often referred to as an "election," it is not comparable to a presidential election in the United States. "Electing" a pope is believed to be a process of discerning the will of God in choosing the successor to Peter by invoking the Holy Spirit and praying for enlightenment.

Thus, investigating the backgrounds of the most viable Papal candidates, as described in the novel, would be contrary to the spiritual nature of the selection process. Granted, there are always political intrigues involved, since this is a process conducted by human beings. However, it is difficult to understand how any educated person can fail to know that the use of the Devil's Advocate was part of the canonization process, since this is not arcane knowledge but would probably be encountered in any undergraduate survey course in Western culture. And were Brown unsure, the role of the Devil's Advocate could be researched in any Catholic encyclopedia—or by a simple internet search.[51]

Even more revealing is Brown's apparent inability to understand the spiritual basis for Church discipline. The plot key in *Angels and Demons* is that a priest and a nun had a child, a scandal that causes much of the chaos in the novel because of the belief that the couple violated their vows. However, it is later revealed that although the couple were very much in love, they respected their vows; the nun became pregnant by artificial insemination, using the priest's sperm. She then left the convent to raise the child with the emotional support of the father who remained in the priesthood. But she dies when the child is only ten years old, so the priest, by now a Bishop, takes charge of the boy and raises him without identifying himself as his biological father. When the boy reaches adulthood, he learns the facts of his birth, but he is assured that his parents "were both virgins" and had "kept their vows to God," with parenthood made possible by the "miracle of science."[52] From a Catholic perspective, the errors in this fable are mind-boggling.

The fact that the Church forbids any artificial means of procreation is so well known that Brown's apparent ignorance on this issue is simply incredible. The idea that the priest and the nun would assume that this procedure would be less sinful in the eyes of their church than sexual intercourse defies belief. The major error, however, provides even more insight into the author's ignorance of Catholicism. He totally fails to understand the theological basis for the vow of celibacy for Roman Catholic clergy and religious. It is not based on some denunciation of human sexuality, as implied in the novel's scenario. Celibacy signals the fact that the individual sacrifices both spouse and children for the sake of the Kingdom of God. That is, priests and religious dedicate themselves to ministry as their sole focus, sacrificing the creation of a family of their own. Hence, the creation of a child would be a violation of their vows, regardless of the procedure used in procreation. It is only if one assumes that celibacy is enforced solely as a negation of sex that the facts of the novel make any sense at all. Brown's apparent inability to understand the nature of Church teaching in *Angels and Demons* helps in understanding the errors in *The Da Vinci Code.*

In writing *The Da Vinci Code,* Brown appears to have accepted the theories promoted in the texts he used to develop his plot without any awareness of their limitations. The most glaring example is when Teabing explains that the concept of Jesus's divinity was first broached at the Council of Nicea and implies that the declaration was purely political maneuvering on the part of the Emperor Constantine.[53] Anyone with a modicum of understanding of church history knows that most declarations of doctrine were based on centuries of common understanding and oral tradition and were only made "official" as the church grew and became an institution. As with the proclamation of Jesus's divinity, many of these doctrines were promulgated to counter various heresies that developed over the course of time. This process is particularly easy to understand in the case of Jesus's divinity, since the earliest New Testament writings, Paul's letters, confirm that the first generation of Christians considered Jesus the Son of God and divine.[54] The Christology established at Nicea was grounded in an understanding of the Christology believed by Christians from earliest times and documented in Paul's letters.

Dan Brown's ignorance of both Catholic doctrine and church history left him unable to critique his sources, even if he wished to do so. However, it is also apparent that he wasn't attempting to write nonfiction; he was simply looking for a good conspiracy that might fuel a best seller. And in that goal, he was eminently successful, since he managed to select from among his sources the ideal elements for tapping into the contemporary American *Zeitgeist.* And the result is not only a glimpse of the lineaments of our culture but also a sense of its current crisis.

The Crisis

Religious culture in the United States today is so polarized because the two sides are operating from competing paradigms, and neither can appreciate the perspective of the other. In a 1987 essay, an academic theologian referred to a "cultural transition" in religion, commenting on what he termed an "unproductive response," an effort to

stop the process, to turn the clock back—indeed to turn it back to pre-Enlightenment times, to traditional bases of authority and conventional forms of religious belief. The resurgence of conservative and evangelical Christianity in recent years (at least in America) is symptomatic both of the magnitude of the experienced threat and of the deep desire to recover stable ethical and religious foundations in a topsy-turvy age.[55]

The author then proceeded to describe the opposite response which "arises from the postmodernist sense of 'irrevocable loss and incurable fault,' which has the possibility of issuing in a radical relativism for which nothing is known, believed, or acted upon."[56]

What is evident here is the failure of Christianity to respond to the secularizing forces of the Enlightenment with a vision of church that would be consistent with its heritage but also consonant with its adherents' experience of the modern world. The stance of conservative and evangelical Christianity in seeking to revert to a pre-Enlightenment ethos is understandable (if ultimately futile) in light of the "radical relativism" into which the more liberal churches appear to have slipped. The proliferation of spiritual seekers or shoppers who are not affiliated with any specific religious denomination reflects the failure of churches on both the right and the left. Conservative spiritual seekers may reflect the failure of the pre-Enlightenment paradigm to which they are philosophically wedded to address the issues encountered in a post-Enlightenment world. While for liberals, an individualistic approach to religion may reflect the failure of more liberal churches to offer a viable model of modern Christianity in this post-Enlightenment world that they can see as faithful to Christianity's heritage and values.

The conservative and evangelical response to *The Da Vinci Code* is consistent with their response to social movements that they see as threatening their core values and political actions that appear to marginalize Christianity. What liberals see as "imposing religion on others" in a pluralistic society, conservatives view as an attempt to preserve the nation by maintaining the values on which it was founded. Note for example, how the Catholic bishops of the United States invoked neither the Bible nor Papal decrees when expressing the Church's opposition to abortion; instead, they use the rhetoric of American democracy. In testifying before congress in 1981, the bishops' representative stated:

Our Declaration of Independence recognizes the right to live as inherent and inalienable from the first moment of each human being's existence when it proclaims that "all men are created equal" with respond to this right. The Fifth Amendment to our Constitution states that no person shall be deprived of life or liberty without due process of law.[57]

Conservatives and evangelicals, drawing on the tradition of the United States' founding as a religious mission, believe that the nation's deviation from traditional values and moral principles breaks faith with the God who guides that mission. That's the thinking behind Rev. Jerry Falwell's unfortunate remarks following the terrorist attacks of September 11, 2001. Excoriated for his comments that liberal civil liberties groups, feminists, homosexuals, and abortion rights supporters were partially responsible for the attacks, Falwell explained further but did not recant:

"I put all the blame legally and morally on the actions of the terrorists," he said. But he said America's "secular and anti-Christian environment left us open to our Lord's [decision] not to protect. When a nation deserts God and expels God from the culture… the result is not good."[58]

For Falwell, and most of his fellow evangelicals, the secularization of the nation, its failure to live by the Christian principles that guided its founding, will inevitably lead to its destruction. In true, Old Testament spirit, Falwell saw the attacks as a warning from God. Thus, while the liberal faction in society sees the conservatives as imposing their religion on others, the conservatives view themselves as keepers of the flame of democracy by reminding the nation of its foundational principles. It is interesting to note that *The Da Vinci Code* has been banned in Iran because of protests by Christian clergymen in that country, even though Iran is a nation of 69 million Muslims and only about 100,000 Christians.[59] It is the fundamentalist theocracy of Iran that liberals fear is the agenda of America's Christian right.

The inability of one group to understand the thinking of the other speaks to the failure of religious leadership in our society. As Robert Bellah and his colleagues concluded almost a generation ago, for some time mainline Protestantism has lacked a significant intellectual voice; "they have failed to produce a Tillich or a Neibuhr who might become the center of fruitful controversy and discussion."[60] That the conservative side is unable to exert viable leadership is apparent from its responses to the imagined threat of the *Da Vinci Code*. The reliance on dogmatic assertion might persuade Stage 3 followers who rely on strong authority for meaning, but such dogmatism does not convince independent thinkers. Thus, the situation in American religion today is a stalemate between the liberals and the conservatives who are incapable of the dialogue that can help close the chasm. What is needed, as theologians have been reporting for more than a generation, is a process whereby the essential truths of faith are revealed in a way that is consonant with the post-Enlightenment world.[61]

Without the leavening of a creative intellectual focus, the quasi-therapeutic blandness that has afflicted much of mainline Protestant religion at the parish level for over a century cannot effectively withstand the competition of the more vigorous forms of radical religious individualism, with their claims of dramatic self-realization, or the resurgent religious conservatism that spells out clear, if simple, answers in an increasingly bewildering world.[62]

Unfortunately, since the evangelical churches understand their role in terms of moral urgency, with the future of the United States at stake, they cannot remain silent. The Biblical prophets are a model for them—speaking out against moral decay.[63] And the liberals meet that voice protesting against their values by demonizing the conservatives, thus deepening the chasm between them. One result of the tension between these competing paradigms is that those with a religious affiliation will retreat into the "safe community of like-minded believers."[64] So significant is this crisis that we will trace its development in our next chapter to see how we have arrived at this bifurcated culture.

Notes

1. Stephen Lanzalotta, *The Diet Code: Revolutionary Weight Loss Secrets from Da Vinci and the Golden Ratio* (New York: Warner Wellness, 2006).

2. Sarah Lyall and Ed Marks, "Broken: The Code in the 'DaVinci Code' Ruling," *New York Times,* April 28, 2006, A8.

3. Julie Bosman, "'Da Vinci' As a Brand: From Soup to Nuts," *New York Times,* May 20, 2006, C8.

4. The most artistic fiction typically appeals to a smaller audience, so there is a tendency among the literati to dismiss any novel with significant sales as merely pulp for the masses. This attitude has a long history.

5. In the interest of full disclosure, I should also mention that in a graduate class in the New Testament that I attended in the mid-1980s at a Jesuit college, our professor explained the scholarly basis for the speculation that Mary Magdalene may have been Jesus's spouse from a Scriptural perspective.

6. Robert Wuthnow, *The Restructuring of American Religion: Society and Faith Since World War II* (New Jersey: Princeton University Press, 1988), 315.

7. Ibid., 220.

8. Laurie Goodstein, "Episcopalians Shaken by Division in Church," *New York Times,* July 2, 2006, 10. Another article (Michael Luo, "Leaning Left, But Not When Topic at Hand Is Gay Bishops," *New York Times,* July 17, 2006, B1) highlights the conflict in one specific New York City parish that is described as "a mix of political liberalism and theological orthodoxy."

9. Wuthnow, *The Restructuring of American Religion,* 305.

10. Wuthnow, *America and the Challenges of Religious Diversity* (Princeton and Oxford: Princeton University Press, 2005), 176.

11. Note that I am referring to the general reader. The official response to the novel by evangelical Christianity has been no less strident than that of official Catholicism, but the attempts to debunk the novel are precisely because of the number of readers of *The Da Vinci Code* among the religion's adherents.

12. Robert N. Bellah and others, *Habits of the Heart: Individualism and Commitment in American Life* (New York: Harper & Row Publishers, 1986), 221.

13. Wuthnow, *America and the Challenges of Religious Diversity,* 125.

14. Ibid., 107.

15. Wuthnow, *The Restructuring of American Religion,* 144.

16. Ibid., 156.

17. Bellah and others, *Habits of the Heart,* 234.

18. Anita Gandolfo, *Testing the Faith: The New Catholic Fiction in America* (New York and Westport, CT: Greenwood Press, 1992), 3–4.

19. Jay Dolan, *The American Catholic Experience* (New York: Doubleday and Company, Inc., 1985), 417.

20. Wuthnow, *The Restructuring of American Religion,* 145.

21. Robert P. Lockwood, "NARAL, Anti-Catholicism and the Roots of the Pro-Abortion Campaign," http://www.catholicleague.org/research/naral.htm (accessed July 22, 2006).

22. William A. Donohue, "The Media War on the Catholic Church," *Catalyst,* April, 1996, http://www.catholicleague.org/research/media_war.htm (accessed July 22, 2006).

23. Michele Dillon, "Church Rhetoric and Popular Culture," *CCICA Annual* 14 (1995): 145.

24. Gandolfo, *Testing the Faith,* 71.

25. This may not have been a conscious effort, but Greeley is a well-known priest and sociologist, Kienzle is a former priest, and McInerny is a Catholic layman, a professor at the University of Notre Dame. All would be well aware of the threat to Catholicism in American culture and the need for rehabilitation of its image.

26. Joe Gash, *Priestly Murders* (New York: Penguin Books, 1984), 43.

27. Ibid., 160.

28. Ibid., 161.

29. Ed McBain, *Vespers* (New York: William Morrow and Company, Inc., 1990), 328.

30. Dillon, "Church Rhetoric and Popular Culture," 147.

31. Brown makes these statements in response to questions posed on his web page at http://www.danbrown.com/novels/davinci_code/faqs.html (accessed July 23, 2006).

32. Quoted from the parish bulletin of St. Joseph's Roman Catholic Church, New Windsor, NY, Sunday, April 30, 2006.

33. Dan Brown, *The Da Vinci Code* (New York: Doubleday, 2003), 233–34.

34. As early as *Angels and Demons,* it was apparent that Brown has significant limitations in understanding the nuances of church teaching and church history, as will be evident in the analysis that follows in this chapter.

35. Bellah and others, *Habits of the Heart,* 226; Wuthnow, *The Restructuring of American Religion,* 144; and Dolan, *The American Catholic Experience,* 231. A good example of this dichotomy can be seen in American Roman Catholics' response to the changes of Vatican II. Those changes were not of doctrine or dogma but principally involved pious practices and the liturgy, theologically scarcely significant. Thus, the hierarchy was unprepared for the chaos that ensued, not understanding that their people's experience of liturgy and other pious practices was the essence religion for them.

36. James W. Fowler, *Stages of Faith: The Psychology of Human Development and the Quest for Meaning* (San Francisco: Harper & Row Publishers, 1981), 161.

37. Ibid., 162.

38. Ibid., 161.

39. Ibid., 179.

40. Ibid., 178.

41. This axiom, familiar to the author as a lifelong Catholic, is confirmed in the academic analysis by Dolan, 225.

42. From http://www.danbrown.com/novels/davinci_code/faqs.html (accessed July 23, 2006).

43. Rev. Jennifer Fey of the United Church of Christ, June, 2006, http://www.occhurch.net/ppage.html (accessed July 24, 2006).

44. Wuthnow, *The Restructuring of American Religion,* 305.

45. Northrop Frye, Sheridan Baker, and George Perkins, *The Harper Handbook to Literature* (New York: Harper & Row Publishers, 1985), 145.

46. Brown, *The Da Vinci Code,* 256.

47. Robert S. Robins and Jerrold M. Post, "Political Paranoia as Cinematic Motif: Stone's 'JFK,'" presented at the August/September, 1997 meeting of the American Political Science Association. Washington, D.C., http://mcadams.posc.mu.edu/robins.htm (accessed July 27, 2006).

48. Ibid.

49. Wuthnow, *America and the Challenges of Religious Diversity,* 176.

50. Dan Brown, *Angels and Demons* (New York: Pocket Books, 2000), 542.

51. It is unlikely that Brown made this error deliberately as a form of "poetic license" to advance his plot because there are many logical ways in which the Cardinal could have learned the secret that would have not been difficult to work into the plot without resorting to such a gaffe.

52. Brown, *Angels and Demons,* 543–45.

53. Brown, *The Da Vinci Code,* 233.

54. See, for example, Philippians 2:5–7 and Colossians 1:15.

55. Peter C. Hodgson, "Ecclesia of Freedom," *Theology Today,* 44, no. 2 (July 1987), http://theologytoday.ptsem.edu/jul1987/v44-2-article1.htm (accessed July 28, 2006).

56. Ibid. In this comment, Hodgson is quoting Mark C. Taylor, *Erring: A Postmodern Altheology* (Chicago: University of Chicago Press, 1984), 6.

57. National Conference of Catholic Bishops, "Submission to the Senate Judiciary Committee's Constitution Subcommittee," *Origins* 11 (1981): 363, cited by Dillon, "Church Rhetoric and Popular Culture," 148.

58. John F. Harris, "God Gave U.S. 'What We Deserve,' Falwell Says," *Washington Post,* September 14, 2001, C03.

59. "'Da Vinci Code' Banned," *New York Times,* July 27, 2006, E2.

60. Bellah and others, *Habits of the Heart,* 238.

61. Walter Kasper, *Jesus the Christ* (New York: Paulist Press, 1976), 44.

62. Bellah and others, *Habits of the Heart,* 238.

63. Wuthnow, *The Restructuring of American Religion,* 203.

64. Wuthnow, *America and the Challenges of Religious Diversity,* 185.

—— 3 ——

Competing Paradigms

Men living in democratic times are therefore very prone to shake off all religious authority. . . .

—Alexis De Tocqueville, *Democracy in America*

While sociologists agree that the years following World War II involved major changes in American religion, the era began well for those who believed that religion was the bulwark of American democracy. Among statesmen, the notion that religion was a positive force was normative. A hero of the war and later President, Dwight D. Eisenhower is quoted in a 1946 address:

Without God, there could be no American form of government, nor an American way of life. Recognition of the Supreme Being is the first—and most basic—expression of Americanism.[1]

It is difficult to conceive any political leader making such a statement today, so ingrained is the avoidance of any association of the government with religion in our pluralistic society. However, as Robert Wuthnow points out in his study of American religion, such sentiments were routinely expressed by political leaders in post–World War II America.[2] Eisenhower was in the mainstream in his time, and, of course, as President was responsible for the addition of the phrase "under God" in the Pledge of Allegiance, the words that have been the center of much controversy in recent years. How we, as a country, transitioned from acceptance of a public declaration of the Deity's leadership of our nation in our Pledge of Allegiance to the recent attempts to remove the phrase "under God" is the story of a progressively bifurcated nation whose contemporary "culture wars" provide the title to more than one study.[3]

In any controversy, the terms used are significant. In the last chapter, I used the "conservative" and "liberal" terms of Bellah and Wuthnow to denote the polarized factions in American society. James Davison Hunter has argued persuasively to substitute the terms "orthodox" and "progressive." For him, the former terms, conservative and liberal, are too closely associated with politics, with the concomitant danger that "one can easily forget that they [the polarities] trace back to prior moral commitments and more basic moral visions."[4] While I fully agree with Hunter that it's important to see this division as not simply political, I think that his terms present yet another problem. The label "progressive" seems to give more value to that position in light of the valorization of "progress" in American culture. Nevertheless, Hunter's main point that these divisions are deeply rooted in our identity as Americans is important for any discussion of contemporary religion and politics. He helpfully explains, "I define cultural conflict very simply as political and social hostility rooted in different systems of moral understanding."[5] These "different systems" are, I believe, concerned with more than just "moral understanding"; they encompass a total worldview.

My preference would be to see the conflict as one of competing paradigms, the classical vs. the modern, to use the concept expressed by Thomas Kuhn in his *The Structure of Scientific Revolutions.* As Kuhn himself notes, his concept of paradigm shift is as applicable to social change as to change in science. And he defines paradigm as "the entire constellation of beliefs, values, techniques, and so on shared by members of a given community."[6] In other words, what makes the current bifurcation of American public discourse so problematic is that the two sides have fundamentally different ways of looking at life. Thus, whether we use the term "conservative," "orthodox," or "classical," that perspective is well explained by Hunter as "the commitment on the part of adherents to an external, definable, and transcendent authority." And the competing paradigm, whether called "liberal," "progressive," or "modern," is one in which "moral authority tends to be defined by the spirit of the modern age, a spirit of rationalism and subjectivism."[7] Often these polarities are considered the "Pre-Enlightenment" vs. the "Enlightenment" perspectives.

The Enlightenment is commonly considered the watershed in this change in Western society. Just as the Copernican Revolution removed the earth from the center of the universe and replaced it with the Sun, the philosophy of the Enlightenment removed God from the pinnacle of the Great Chain of Being, putting the human person there instead. All was possible, not with divine intervention but through human reason. We saw the effects of the Enlightenment in Chapter 1 with the Deists, who were the principal thinkers at the founding of the nation, as well as the writers who forged our own American literature. And, as noted, the Deists did not reject God so much as express skepticism of institutional religion, since they valued the individual's own rational approach to the Creator.

That was an immediate effect of the Enlightenment on those raised in the classical world who confronted this new way of thinking. However, Enlightenment thinking has had an erosive effect over the years, and in the aftermath of the World War II, the United States experienced a major eruption of its secularizing power in the era known as The Sixties. The celebration of individualism in that era intensified the differences between those who adhere to the "classical" as opposed to the "modern" paradigms, resulting in the bifurcation that currently exists in our culture.

It is important to note that these are not differences among the religious and irreligious, but divisions that cross denominational lines. Hunter makes the point that to the extent that the progressives or moderns identify with a religious tradition, they are similar to the individualists identified by Bellah; that is, they tend "to resymbolize historical faiths according to the prevailing assumptions of contemporary life."[8] For example, as noted in the last chapter, although the official doctrine of the Roman Catholic Church proscribes divorce, surveys indicated that by the mid-1960s when divorce was no longer a scandal in American society, only approximately one Catholic in three thought divorce was wrong, regardless of church teaching.[9] The struggles within Episcopalian congregations over women's ordination in the past were similarly contested among the orthodox and progressives, as is the contemporary conflict over the ordination of homosexual priests. This bifurcation within religions reflects the competing paradigms that conflict on most social and political issues. To better understand the current moment, it's useful to trace the development of this bifurcation.

Religion in Society

As Robert Bellah and his associates pointed out, "the place of religion in our society has changed dramatically over time."[10] Despite the centrality of religion in many of the early colonies and in the daily lives of the colonists, the effect of disestablishment was to move religious practice gradually into the private sphere, where it eventually became a haven from the harsh and cruel world as society became more complex and competitive.[11] However, religion maintained a "public face" in our civil religion, with our trust in God minted on our coinage and the public benedictions that preface ceremonial events. This American pattern of privatizing religion while, at the same time, allowing it some visibility via public symbols worked well throughout the nineteenth century and well into the twentieth. However, since religion, like other social institutions, is affected by change within the culture, it is hardly surprising that the vast changes in American society following World War II had dramatic effects in American religion.

How we got from the rhetoric of Eisenhower and other leaders in the late 1940s and early 1950s to the current conflict wherein the progressives seek to eliminate religion from the political realm provides an interesting example of how religion is influenced by its cultural context. If 1972 was the *annus horribilus* for Catholics with the decision in *Roe v. Wade,* for evangelicals and other conservative Protestants, it was 1962 and the Supreme Court's decision in *Engel v. Vitale*—the elimination of school prayer. To use the title of Thomas Hardy's famous poem about the sinking of the Titanic, this was a "convergence of the twain"; two forces had been developing that met and clashed, changing forever the landscape of American religion.

Two Cultures

The years immediately following World War II were a time of remarkable growth in evangelical Christianity.[12] The evangelicals had prepared for this by creating a national organization, the NAE (National Association of Evangelicals) in 1943, a group that, though small, provided a centralized platform to unite varied efforts to promote evangelical values.[13] Following the war, the crusades of Billy Graham attracted large audiences as well as national recognition to the evangelical movement. In addition, the Campus Crusade for Christ was an extremely timely ministry, given the expansion of higher education in the postwar years, helping conservative Christians maintain their faith during their college years as well as recruiting members among college students developing their faith life. Moreover, evangelical preachers were among the first to experiment with the new medium, television, and by the end of the 1950s, Oral Roberts and Rex Humbard has established popular television ministries, as did Billy Graham whose "Hour of Decision" was one of the first religious programs in prime time.[14] By the end of the decade of the 1950s, evangelicals were well established as a significant influence in American religious culture.

However, during these same postwar years, there was a democratization movement in American society, reflected in the proliferation of ethnic literature noted in Chapter 1. The children and grandchildren of immigrants not only had access to higher education in unprecedented numbers, but they were subject to the secularizing influences of higher education at the same time and were forging a unique, personal identity in American society. Thus, at a time when Dwight Eisenhower could openly equate religion with Americanism, the secular impulse to privatize and depoliticize religion was also growing—gradually and unnoticed. And so it happened that a group of parents in the liberal New York suburbs brought suit against a nondenominational prayer that had been instituted in the pubic schools of the state in the late 1950s. It is important to note that the dominant tone of the culture at this time was more consistent with Eisenhower's impulses than with this lawsuit. In fact, the prayer itself was a similar casual linking of religion and country without reference to any religious denomination. It read, "Almighty God, we acknowledge our dependence upon Thee, and we beg Thy blessings upon us, our parents, our teachers and our Country."[15]

A sign that American culture at the time was dominantly in favor of school prayer can be seen in fact that the suit was rejected in two lower courts before the parents brought it to the Supreme Court, the case of *Engel v. Vitale*.[16] As further evidence of the cultural climate at the time, during this process the Attorneys General of twenty-two states supported the constitutionality of the prayer, so widespread was the practice of school prayer and so ingrained in the culture of American schools. New York did not arbitrarily decide to insert a prayer in a secular environment; acknowledging God was a standard practice in most public schools, and Bible readings regularly prefaced school assemblies. In fact, a major reason that the Catholic people had made the costly commitment to their own parochial schools was not because of any perception that the public schools were too secular but the belief that they promoted a dominantly Protestant piety.[17] Ironically, had the lower courts found in favor of the parents, the prayer would only have been eliminated in the public schools of the State of New York. However, in reaching the Supreme Court, the ultimate decision would be binding not only in New York but throughout the United States.

Thus, when the 1962 decision upheld the claim of the parents and ruled the prayer unconstitutional, that decision not only affected prayer in schools throughout the United States; it was a dramatic clashing of the two cultures that reverberates today as those cultures have become increasingly confrontational. When we look at this decision from our perspective today with our current awareness of religious pluralism and the importance of inclusion, those who opposed the Supreme Court decision may appear to be extremists. But this was a judicial decision well in advance of the culture. People's investment in school prayer was much more emotional than logical, and it is important to understand how significant this decision was to the politicization of evangelicals who naturally united against this enemy of religion—the U.S. Supreme Court.

Let me offer an analogy. In another study, I wrote of Catholic literature following the Second Vatican Council, and there are interesting similarities between the school prayer decision and the church's actions in the early 1960s. The changes of the Vatican Council were similarly unsought by the people in the pews, and there was no consensus on any need for change. Moreover, from the hierarchy's perspective, the changes were minor, not in doctrine but primarily in liturgy and pious practices. Out went the Latin Mass and the requirement to abstain from meat on Fridays, for example. However, as every sociologist of religion affirms, for the typical worshipper, religion is primarily experiential and unrelated to theology or doctrine. And for American Roman Catholics, religion consisted of their experience of liturgy and other pious practices, experiences that they had grown up with and that they regarded as the essence of their religious identity.

So although "fish on Friday" was a practice that was compulsively observed, for most Catholics in the United States it was also a way of reinforcing their identity in a land where they were the minority. The fact that Catholics had "made it" in the United States could be seen from the newspaper supermarket ads that proclaimed specials on fish for Fridays and during Lent. Thus, on the first Sunday in Advent, 1966, when Catholics were told they could now choose whether or not to abstain from meat on Fridays, American Catholics did not wholeheartedly welcome this unsought permission. It was just one of a host of changes that were taking their culture from them.[18]

Similarly, in 1962, conservative Christians viewed the Supreme Court decision regarding school prayer as "taking their culture from them." After all, these were people who had grown up with school prayer, which was as natural to them as reciting the Pledge of Allegiance. Indeed, it could be argued that the "prayer" in question did not violate the establishment clause but was simply another manifestation of our country's civil religion, and that was the argument of the lone dissent by Mr. Justice Stewart who wrote,

I think the Court has misapplied a great constitutional principle. I cannot see how an "official religion" is established by letting those who want to say a prayer say it. On the contrary, I think that to deny the wish of these school children to join in reciting this prayer is to deny them the opportunity of sharing in the spiritual heritage of our Nation.[19]

Thus, it is hardly surprising that the ruling in *Engel v. Vitale* immediately sparked reaction among religious conservatives. And the organizational structure that had slowly developed throughout the previous decades made possible a protest at the national level. Beginning in the decision year of 1962, there were hearings, prayer initiatives, or bills in Congress every few years designed to override the Court's decision with a constitutional amendment for school prayer. But the pull to the left in American society in the era known as The Sixties deepened the chasm between the orthodox and the liberals, and when the Court ruled in *Roe v. Wade* a decade later, the orthodox could clearly see the government as an enemy. In 1987, a writer for the journal *Christianity Today* summed up the sentiment of conservative Christians with the comment that many believers felt that "the lifeblood of our religious freedom is slowly being sucked from our constitutionally protected veins."[20]

It is impossible to overemphasize the sense of dislocation experienced by Americans who believe that the courts have betrayed them. We commonly refer to ourselves as "a nation of law," and as early as his nineteenth century visit, Alexis deTocqueville commented, "In America, then, it may be said that no one renders obedience to man, but to justice and to law."[21] Assured that the law will rectify any injustice, people naturally feel disenfranchised when the courts decide against their position, a position to which they are strongly committed. In her 1978 novel *Final Payments,* Mary Gordon describes the reaction of traditional Catholics to the changed world of Vatican II as feeling, "like someone's broken into their home and stolen all the furniture."[22] That sense of violation and desolation is analogous to how evangelical Christians felt in the wake of *Engel v. Vitale.* The system designed to insure their freedom and prosperity had turned against them.

Conservative Christians' feeling that the tide of American culture had changed and was moving swiftly away from their values was reinforced by the radical changes in popular fiction. The romance novel, a standard in post–World War II popular fiction, was typically the chaste, idealized romance inherited from the nineteenth century. It was a novel that could be read without qualms of conscience by evangelical women, and the readership was vast. However, as a result of the women's movement, in the 1970s, publishers believed that their readers wanted more explicit sex in the romance, and the genre changed accordingly.[23] Moreover, the new, more "realistic" teen novel emerged at the same time with S.E. Hinton's *The Outsiders* (1967) and Judy Blume's *Forever* (1975) leading the way. Both novels are frequently banned by local school boards, a practice that intensified, as conservative Christians tried to protect their children from what they considered the vulgarization of American society. It was easy to imagine a causal relationship. That is, take prayer out of the schools, and you have profanity and drug use (*The Outsiders*) along with premarital sex among teens (*Forever*). Both socially and politically, evangelicals were stripped of the comforting American culture they had experience in the 1950s.

Into the Public Forum

While the orthodox entered into political life to mobilize against the abhorrent decision of *Engel v. Vitale,* religious progressives also entered fully into American political life at about the same time via the Civil Rights Movement. Although many of the mainline churches were involved in influencing public policy for racial equality in the years following World War II, there was a turning point in 1963 with Martin Luther King, Jr.'s March on Washington, the event that fully brought white church leaders into the movement.[24] From policy papers and official pronouncements, they moved into overt social activism to join the Rev. King and his followers in the effort to achieve racial equality in the United States. The Vietnam War soon offered another focus for their activism, and the privatization of American religion was at an end, as religious leaders were increasingly vocal and visible in the political process.

However, although liberal church leaders supported Dr. King and opposed the Vietnam War, they have played merely a supporting role in subsequent liberal causes involving pornography, abortion, and homosexuality, so it often seems as though conservatives are the only ones politically, and from a liberal perspective, inappropriately, engaged in political action. As the opponents of liberal causes, Christian conservatives have been demonized, much like the Catholic Church in response to its unalterable opposition to abortion. This has primarily been due to the negative images of conservative Christians conveyed by the dominantly liberal media. The legal scholar Stephen Carter cites three studies of "the attitudes of media and entertainment elites, as well as of television news programming and newspaper coverage of various social issues and political events," all of which concluded that there is "a fairly strong and consistent bias toward a liberal and progressivist point of view."[25] It seems evident that the public's opinion is strongly influenced by the media. As one article explains,

Ordinary citizens' only contact with the political world is the "pictures in their heads" put there by news accounts or other public-affairs media presentations. As a result of this dependence, it is inevitable that what people think about politics is subject to considerable media influence.[26]

It is important to note that the emphasis on a "bifurcated America" can be misleading. In his study, *Culture War? The Myth of a Polarized America* (2004), the political scientist Morris P. Fiorina uses polling data and argues that the country is less polarized than we are led to believe. He contends that it is closer to an ambivalent nation forced to take sides when presented with highly polarized positions. Ironically, this helpful view is actually consistent with that of James Davison Hunter in his book *Culture Wars.* That is, Hunter argues that the public forum is dominated by intellectuals and other elites who control the rhetoric, they "create the concepts, supply the language, and explicate the logic of public discussions."[27] Thus, the differences of opinion among Americans on social issues are magnified by the inflated rhetoric used in the public forum. And Hunter essentially agrees with Fiorina, emphasizing his point in italics, *"Without doubt, public discourse is more polarized than the American public itself."*[28] Nevertheless, while the "culture wars" may be conducted principally by the intellectual elites who dominate the public forum, the liberal bias of the media plays a major role in influencing and forming the opinions of relatively ambivalent Americans on many social issues.

The nature of public discourse is also interesting in terms of how we've arrived at this state of competing paradigms. Unfortunately, the chasm between the competing paradigms, orthodox and progressive, deepened as the level of discourse lowered, when religion was once again influenced by changes in the culture. In the early 1960s, when religious denominations on both the left and the right became involved in political issues, the intellectual leadership in all denominations were schooled at universities and seminaries, contributed to scholarly conferences, and published in academic journals.

This intellectual leadership was capable of reasoned, tolerant discourse, and for a time, it seemed as though rapprochement rather than divisiveness would be the trend.[29] Unfortunately, the extreme evangelicals had already discovered the medium of television. The more educated, scholarly, and moderate evangelicals were drowned out by the "more strident voices of the religious right" on television.[30] As the public forum shifted to the popular media, it became less concerned with reasoned discourse. As Hunter explains, "the shrill pitch of harsh moral criticism and blunt commentary is much more likely to sell newspapers, build audience ratings, or raise money. The net effect of loud, sensational clamor, however, is to mute the more quiet and temperate voices."[31]

Moreover, as Hunter notes, this "loud, sensational clamor" fails to present a truly coherent perspective on the issues. Instead, he argues, "what actually exists in public discussion are, very often, nothing more than jumbled accumulations of pronouncements, accusations, appeals, and partisan analyses."[32] The talking heads of television political shows degenerated into shouting heads more often than not. This makes it far more difficult for the average American to fully understand the complexities of the issues involved and come to a reasoned opinion. Instead of substantive moral reasoning, the public forum consists principally of "reciprocal bellicosity."[33] Thus, the average citizen is forced to choose a side, as it were, often affiliating with the position with which he or she identifies most closely, whether or not the individual fully believes in all the details involved in that position. In this way, the polarizing nature of the public forum tends to polarize the populace.

On the subject of the place of religion in public life and the metaphoric wall of separation between church and state, the competing paradigms are clear. Interestingly, both sides believe that they are fighting to preserve their First Amendment rights. The orthodox or conservatives identify with the free exercise clause and fear an encroaching government that will gradually deny them their freedom to worship as they wish. In addition, they fear a general degeneration of moral values in society as a whole that will hamper their ability to transmit their moral views to their children. And the progressives or liberals identify with the establishment clause and fear that the other side's goal is the creation of a theocracy that will, Taliban-like, put women back into figurative burkas and eliminate the civil liberties of all minority groups. Unfortunately, there are sufficient examples of radicalism on both sides to support the fears of each group. The absence of reasoned dialogue between these groups results in a continuation of bellicosity in the public forum that exacerbates the division.

One reason I prefer to concept of competing paradigms is that in the adherence to a specific paradigm, an individual is unable to perceive the particulars of the other. And that is especially true in the polarities involved in contemporary American culture. The orthodox perspective is essentially the pre-Enlightenment, classical worldview of Western civilization, that commitment to an external and transcendent authority; whereas, the progressive view is a post-Enlightenment perspective that values human reason as the ultimate authority. Although a strictly chronological perspective on history would prioritize the progressive view, as Stephen Carter comments with ironic understatement, "not everyone agrees that the Enlightenment project of replacing divine moral authority with the moral authority of human reason was a good idea."[34] He cites a 1989 Gallup survey that reported "79 percent of American adults believe that 'there are clear guidelines about what's good and evil that apply to everyone regardless of the situation.'"[35] This belief in universal principles that supersede the individual suggests that the majority of Americans actually embrace the pre-Enlightenment or classical perspective at heart, although their expressed opinions may not be consistent with that view. The strong tendency toward individualism in American culture tends to mask that classical perspective. In addition, proponents on both sides are usually unaware of the philosophic basis for their opinions.

As noted earlier, the nature of the rhetoric in the contemporary public forum does not lend itself to the formulation of clearly reasoned viewpoints, so it's difficult to know whether people fully ascribe to the principles they profess. For example, the major premise of Stephen Carter's The Culture of Disbelief is how the progressives or liberals trivialize religious devotion in an attempt to banish religion from politics. He takes delight in pointing out that while liberals heartily embraced the goals of the Civil Rights Movement, they chose to ignore not only the fact that the major support for the movement was from the churches but also that Martin Luther King spoke from classical principles. Carter notes that King's "Letter from Birmingham City Jail" is "an overtly and unapologetically religious document," and one that is rooted in the pre-Enlightenment paradigm.[36] King's assertion that "A just law is a man-made code that squares with the moral law or the law of God" is, as Carter claims, "classic natural law theology, and could have been lifted word for word, from the more recent pastoral letter of the Roman Catholic bishops on abortion."[37] Thus, it seems hypocritical to support the role of religion in the Civil Rights Movement but to insist that religion has no place in political realm when the issue is abortion or homosexuality. It is also illogical to accept Dr. King's reasoning on the issue of civil rights but reject similar reasoning when the issue is abortion.

So long as both conservatives and liberals rely on polarizing rhetoric, it is doubtful that either side will develop coherent, reasoned perspectives on the issues they so hotly debate. Slogans dominate. Absent reasoned discourse, the tendency is to simply discredit the opposition, and thus political "dialogue" degenerates into name-calling, denunciation, and intolerance.[38] It is ironic that in an era of advanced education in America, it is so difficult to achieve reasoned, tolerant discourse in the public forum. One educator, C. John Sommerville, contends that although a century ago American universities sought to exert cultural leadership, they have become "increasingly marginal to American society," having ceded influence to popular culture.[39] The fact is that even the highly educated in American society appear unable to bridge the chasm between the competing paradigms to achieve true dialogue. One example of this failure is in a recent article by the historian Garry Wills.

In an opinion essay for the *New York Times,* Garry Wills argues forcefully for the avoidance of religion in politics.[40] He is writing from the premise that the Democrats want to challenge the Republicans' monopoly of religion in politics by claiming that Jesus is really on *their* side, and he is urging them to abandon this approach. It is difficult to know who he envisions as his audience because although the essay's thesis *seems* to address liberal Democrats in an attempt to warn them against involving themselves in religion, Wills' rhetorical strategy, citing Scripture, seems to be more suited to an audience of conservative Christians, who would be more inclined to value Biblical evidence. And Wills's claim that the Jesus of the Gospels would have nothing to do with politics, either in ancient Israel or contemporary America, is unsubstantiated except for his basic assertion. For Wills, the "Gospels are scary, dark and demanding," and he bemoans the fact that people seem to want to make them into "generic encouragements" to provide solace and support for their lives.[41] What Wills seems not to understand is that such "generic encouragements" are precisely what most Americans, Christians or not, want from religion.

In a recent book, the sociologist of religion Robert Wuthnow describes how contemporary Christians have modified the concept of salvation:

Christians talk about personal fulfillment and happiness...more than they do about life beyond death, defining salvation as the key to a prosperous life more than to a heavenly kingdom. Salvation of the kind that Jonathan Edwards preached about has been replaced by self-realization, while Christian therapy, dieting, and self-expression have apparently become more urgent than redemption from divine retribution.[42]

However, this orientation is not limited to Christians alone. It is not so very different from the perspective Wuthnow observes among "spiritual shoppers," those individualists who seek religious experience in a variety of ways. Theirs is not a "quest for coherent set of beliefs," he explains, but for "experiences that serve as affirmations of the goodness and meaningfulness of life."[43] Both groups would fail to be engaged with Wills's perspective on the Gospels as "scary, dark, and demanding," as well as his assertion that the "Jesus of the Gospels is not a great ethical teacher...." In a focus on this life rather than salvation in the next, the contemporary interest is precisely in Jesus as an ethical teacher. That's the basis for the "WWJD" (What would Jesus do?) phenomenon among conservative Christians.[44]

What Wills seems to fail to appreciate is the fact that his own perspective is strongly colored by his high level of education in history and theology, as well as his personal heritage of traditional Roman Catholicism. While his portrait of Jesus is not incorrect, it would also be foreign to the concept of Jesus held by most contemporary Christians. Thus, although this essay eschews invective and other unpleasant characteristics of confrontational political discourse, Wills's triumphal attitude of knowing the "true" Jesus actually belongs to "the politicized 'I win—you lose' stakes of public confrontation" that is so characteristic of contemporary discourse.[45] Moreover, Wills's opening salvo, "There is no such thing as a 'Christian politics,'" is much more debatable than his dogmatic tone would allow. Although Garry Wills is an experienced writer, his lack of attention to audience in this essay perfectly illustrates the difficulty for those in one paradigm to communicate with those who embrace the competing paradigm.

Despite the persistent liberal claim that religion is intrusive in American politics, the sociologist James Davison Hunter argues for its integral relationship. Since politics is an expression of culture, and religion is at the heart of culture, the two are inextricably involved.[46] To vote for a candidate or a proposition based on personal moral values inherent in one's religious affiliation is not to "impose" religion on others, as is often charged. As New York's former Governor Mario Cuomo famously stated in a speech at the University of Notre Dame in the 1980s, "That values happen to be religious does not deny them acceptability" in terms of support for public policy.[47] Thus, religion as a part of an individual's way of making meaning in this world cannot be isolated and eliminated from that individual's public persona. It is significant that even someone as highly educated as Garry Wills appears to be unable to develop a reasoned argument to engage other Americans on the topic of religion and politics. In his essay, Wills's rhetorical strategy seems to be limited to pure assertion. And this is consistent with research studies that conclude that neither side seems capable of entering into discourse with the other.[48]

In the view of most sociologists of religion, the watershed in the current controversy over religion and politics (and thus the driving force behind Garry Wills's essay and other attempts to argue that religion is inimical to politics) was the Supreme Court decision in *Roe v. Wade*. Conservative Christians, already mobilized by the issue of prayer in public schools, were now joined by Catholics, and, as Stephen Carter explains, there was a seismic shift that reverberates even today:

And so the public rhetoric of religion, which from the time of the abolitionist movement through the era of the "social gospel" and well into the 1960s and early 1970s had largely been the property of liberalism, was all at once—and quite thunderously, too—the special province of people fighting for a cause that the left considered an affront.[49]

It is interesting to note why the left considered opposition to *Roe v. Wade* an "affront," as this illuminates the dichotomy between the two conflicting paradigms. The pro-choice movement is aptly named, since the modern or progressive paradigm valorizes individual choice as an ideal. This is part of its heritage from the Enlightenment that so highly values personal freedom and is opposed to any constraint on an individual's freedom of choice, which is identified with its rejection of absolutism. The left, then, is affronted by all those who limit choice, which is how they view all opposition to abortion.

Catholics and evangelicals who view abortion as a violation of an absolute moral code belong to a paradigm epistemologically foreign to liberals. For the latter, any effort to limit individual choice is an example of the pre-Enlightenment, monarchical world that has no credence in a democratic society. However, to classical thinkers of the pro-life side, abortion violates that same "law of God" that Martin Luther King invoked in his "Letter from Birmingham Jail." What one side sees as an issue that can be resolved by adapting law to human need, the other side views as an unalterable principle. Thus, for pro-choice advocates, the opposition is simply intransigent, and for the pro-life group, those who allow abortion are violating a principle that is part of the natural law that guides all human interaction. That neither side seems capable of understanding the reasoning of the other is distressing, and the result is continued conflict.

Conservative Christians in American Society

Thus, it is not the use of religion in politics that is problematic, but the causes that are supported in the name of religion. As Stephen Carter has pointed out, the support of churches and prominent clergymen for the Civil Rights Movement and the anti-Vietnam War movement elicited no comparable uproar about separation of church and state. The activism of religious leaders was considered appropriate in such demonstrably moral crusades. From this, Carter concludes that "the religious voice is required to stay out of the public square only when it is pressed in a conservative cause."[50] What Carter overlooks is the fact that from the liberal perspective, current conservative causes—such as abortion and same-sex marriage—are considered ones that limit choice and are thus inconsistent with the Enlightenment values on which this nation was established. As James Davison Hunter notes, the liberals have difficulty tolerating positions that appear "choice-restrictive" and therefore intolerant.[51] Such positions would seem to contradict our country's founding in toleration as a prime value.

Of course, from the orthodox or conservative perspective, individual choice is controlled by a higher law which may be church teaching or simply accepted principles of one's religious heritage. For religious conservatives who firmly hold that the United States was not only founded on Judeo-Christian principles but with a divine mandate to conform itself to those principles, their perception of a progressively antireligious tenor in our society is confirmation that the nation is in decline and must be returned to its heritage. Thus, the fundamental problem is conflicting paradigms, the basic *Weltanschauung* of each group, each faction unable to perceive the perspective of the other.

In his *The Culture of Disbelief,* Stephen Carter's thesis (and subtitle) concerns "how American law and politics trivialize religious devotion," and he complains,

In contemporary American culture, the religions are more and more treated as just passing beliefs—almost as fads, older, stuffier, less liberal versions of so-called New Age—rather than as the fudaments upon which the devout build their lives.[52]

What he is describing is a viewpoint with which he disagrees, but one which has validity to those who participate in the progressive paradigm. As noted earlier, this inability of the two groups to communicate their perspectives effectively to each other is a product of our society's current engagement with popular media, a form that prioritizes the sensational over the substantive, the sound bite over the reasoned argument. And in the media, it is the modern paradigm that dominates.

A 2004 survey showed that three-quarters of all evangelicals report that they feel part of mainstream American society, but three-quarters of all evangelicals *also* believe they are "a minority under siege and must fight for their voices to be heard."[53] Almost half of those surveyed (46%) believe that evangelical Christians are "looked down upon" by other Americans. This is not paranoia, since 35% of *nonevangelicals* believe that Americans look down on evangelicals.[54] Since public opinion is so strongly influenced by the media, this sense of marginalization of evangelicals by other Americans is understandable. Ironically, this sense of being marginalized in a dominantly secular culture may be at the heart of the "power" of evangelical Christians that so disturbs liberals, as the 2004 Presidential election indicates.

Many Americans were astounded by the reelection of George W. Bush in 2004, considering the widespread dissatisfaction with the administration's handling of the Iraq War and the resulting low approval ratings for the President. Two factors that are unobserved in conventional political analysis may account for this. Robert Wuthnow notes that in the past, court rulings have led conservative Christians to "believe that their basic rights are imperiled." And he further comments that religious conservatives are more organized politically than liberals.[55] The 2004 election campaign also featured the issue of same-sex marriage, an issue that was on the ballot in many states. Thus the association of a critical issue for conservatives on the ballot during a Presidential election would tend to mobilize the conservative Christian vote nationally.

Moreover, Stephen Carter speculates that Americans who feel marginalized because of their commitment to religion may be inclined to support politicians who use religious rhetoric and thus appear to be committed to similar concerns.[56] He cites the support for Ronald Reagan by many religious people as an example of this phenomenon, but he was writing well before the advent of George W. Bush who clearly used language designed to appeal to conservative Christians. Thus, the strong sense of exclusion felt by evangelicals, a sense promoted by their negative treatment by the media, may have inadvertently resulted in their "power" in the 2004 presidential election, as they voted in large numbers to combat a social situation they deplore, and they voted for the candidate they believed most sympathetic to their perspective on other moral issues.

Marginalized Conservative Christians

While both evangelicals and Catholics have a notably negative image in contemporary media, influenced by the predominance of liberal writers and commentators, the Protestant minister has not suffered a transition to negative imaging in popular fiction comparable to that of the Catholic priest, as described in Chapter 2. This may be due to the fact that the fallible Christian minister has been a consistent character in American fiction from Hawthorne's Rev. Dimmesdale through Sinclair Lewis's Elmer Gantry (1928), and including Barbara Kingsolver's Nathan Price in her remarkable novel, *The Poisonwood Bible* (1998). The strong strain of individualism in American religion that regards the institutional church with suspicion is reflected in its literature and the portrayal of Protestant clergymen. And the evangelical preacher has always been outside the mainstream and thus an easy target for the anti-institutional impulse. However, in Kingsolver's complex novel, her characterization of the Baptist missionary Nathan Price suggests that this portrayal is very much influenced by the current moment in American religion.

When Nathan Price leads his wife and four daughters into the Congo, he initially seems to be a typical zealous missionary who has ignored warnings that this is neither the time nor the place to launch a mission with his family. We soon learn that he is a more specific type of Christian, one who is so assured that he is doing God's work that he presumes that he is equally omniscient. The Rev. Price is incapable of being shaken from his certitude on any issue. As his beleaguered wife explains, "For him, our life was as simple as paying in cash and sticking the receipt in your breast pocket: we had the Lord's protection, he said, because we came to Africa in His service."[57] Like the archetypal "ugly American," Price insists on trying to impose both his religion and his culture on the Congolese. Even his least insightful daughter, Rachel, understands his problem, and as an adult at the end of the novel, she explains, "Father's mistake, see, was to try to convert the whole entire shebang over into just his exact way of thinking."[58] Her more perceptive sister, Leah, noticed her father's disposition when she was only fourteen, "Watching my father, I've seen how you can't learn anything when you're trying to look like the smartest person in the room."[59] In the character of Price, Kingsolver images the dissatisfaction of those in the modern paradigm with the advent of Jerry Falwell and his Moral Majority in the 1980s, moral certitude combined with an inability to engage in dialogue.

In a telling scene, the Price family is visited by their predecessor at the mission, Brother Fowles, who was relieved of his responsibilities for consorting too closely with the natives. He arrives with his Congolese wife and children, and immediately the reader knows this man is the antithesis of Nathan Price. Fowles has the flexibility to understand the essence of the Gospel message and to live it as a witness to its values without demanding that others adhere to his version of it, as Price does. When Nathan begins to challenge Fowles by spouting Scripture, Fowles astounds him by not only citing chapter and verse but also defusing the challenge by beginning an academic discussion of translations and interpretations. Price, unable to respond to such an intellectual argument, says loftily, "Personally I've never been troubled by any such difficulties with interpreting God's word." [60] The reader understands that he has "never been troubled" because he uses Scripture primarily as a weapon to demand obedience to his way—from his children, from the Congolese, and even from his wife.

Later when Fowles mentions that some of his monetary support comes from a Baptist mission, Mrs. Price is surprised because their own stipend from the Baptists had been suspended when Nathan refused to leave the Congo when all missionaries were advised to do so just before the state proclaimed independence. Her exclamation, "But we're Baptists" is a cry of distress that the denomination is not supporting them but is offering help to Fowles. His quiet response is telling, "there are Christians and then there are Christians."[61] Many years later, the adult Leah recalls these words when she thinks of the aid and assistance provided to the struggling Congolese by Fowles and others like him over the years, assistance that proved far more valuable than her father's empty rhetoric.[62]

Initially, in the character of Nathan Price, *The Poisonwood Bible* seems to belong to the category of oppositional literature that challenges the value of religion in the modern world. As Price's overbearing character fades to a single note in the complex tale of his daughters and the Congo itself, the novel appears more complementary, belonging to that category of literature that provides "a form for the exploration, articulation, and revivification of religious conceptions and sentiments by displaying their fusion with contemporary social, political, and aesthetic beliefs."[63] The reader understands that it is not Christianity that is indicted by the author with the character of Nathan Price, but a particularly vehement and self-righteous type of individual, a mirror of the activist evangelists in American politics. The novel as a whole invites reflection on the meaning of Christianity in the modern world, and it offers a variety of exemplars for such reflection.

Unfortunately, our media does not invite either reflection or reasoned argument, and the Nathan Prices of Christianity become the "Christians" of popular culture. In a bifurcated society, the opposition must be a single entity, and thus every thought or argument based in the classical paradigm is quickly labeled "Christian" as a means to discredit that thought or argument. Interestingly, Monique El-Faizy, in her study of contemporary evangelicals, points out that although most Americans associate conservative Christians with "the Moral Majority and the pushy fundamentalists of the 1980s," there has been a radical shift, and today's evangelicals "take a much softer line of attack and have carefully broadened their appeal."[64] Unfortunately, the tendency to label has triumphed, and "Christian" has become a synonym for "intransigent."

It is ironic that in a nation professedly Christian, the word has become a negative epithet. In an interview, the novelist Frederick Buechner mentioned that he does not publicize the fact that he is an ordained Presbyterian minister because he fears that will prejudice readers against his fiction and, at the same time, he avoids the designation of "Christian writer" because he knows that will also negatively affect readers' perceptions of his work.[65] The scarlet letter seems to have been changed from an "A" to a "C."

The effect of the perceived marginalization of Christians is evidenced more clearly in the alternative culture that conservative Christians, particularly evangelicals, have established in reaction to their belief in an increasingly secular American society. Sociologists and political scientists have documented the various ways that conservative Christians, both evangelicals and Catholics, have mobilized political and social resources in reaction to their perceived marginalization in secular American culture. This is especially notable in the complex network of electronic media, television and radio stations, established throughout the country.[66] More important, for the purposes of this study, is the "billion-dollar book industry" of evangelical publishing houses and bookstores, developed in response to a de facto censorship of Christian literature.[67]

This de facto censorship occurs when major magazines and newspapers either refuse to review conservative Christian literature or deliberately omit best-selling titles from their lists of best sellers. For example, as early as the 1970s, when Hal Lindsey's *Late Great Planet Earth* was the top nonfiction seller in America for the entire decade, it was neither reviewed by the literary establishment nor did it appear on best-seller lists, until it was later issued by a mainstream publisher.[68] Although the phenomenal success of contemporary Christian books like Rick Warren's *The Purpose Driven Life* and the famed Left Behind series have received attention from the mainline press because of their record sales, most

Christian books, if reviewed at all, are still treated with disdain as something less than "literature." For example, in *Of Fiction and Faith,* a book of interviews with twelve writers known for the Christian orientation of their lives and work, every one disdained the description "Christian writer," a label that they believe would convey an erroneous impression of their work, so established is the epithet "Christian" in our culture. This situation is as much a product of the political climate discussed in this chapter as it is a misguided notion of the nature and purpose of fiction, and we will explore this phenomenon in the next chapter.

Notes

1. Quoted in Robert Wuthnow, *The Restructuring of American Religion: Society and Faith Since World War II* (New Jersey: Princeton University Press, 1988), 67.

2. Ibid., 66–7.

3. For example, James Davison Hunter, *Culture Wars: The Struggle to Define America* (New York: Basic Books, 1991); Morris P. Fioina, *Culture War? The Myth of a Polarized America* (Longman, 2004); Bruce Wilson, *Disarming the Culture War: How the Silent Majority Can Break the Stalemate* (iUniverse, Inc., 2005); Don S. Browning, *From Culture Wars to Common Ground* (Westminster John Knox Press, 2000); Paul A. Cleveland, *Understanding the Modern Culture Wars: The Essentials of Western Civilization* (Boundary Stone, LLC, 2003); Peter Kreeft, *How to Win the Culture War: A Christian Battle Plan for a Society in Crisis* (InterVarsity Press, 2002).

4. Hunter, *Culture Wars: The Struggle to Define America,* 46.

5. Ibid., 42.

6. Thomas Kuhn, *The Structure of Scientific Revolutions* (Chicago: University of Chicago Press, 1970), 175.

7. Hunter, *Culture Wars: The Struggle to Define America,* 44.

8. Ibid., 44–5; italics his.

9. Wuthnow, *The Restructuring of American Religion,* 156.

10. Robert N. Bellah and others, *Habits of the Heart: Individualism and Commitment in American Life* (New York: Harper & Row Publishers, 1986), 219.

11. Ibid., 220 and 223.

12. Wuthnow, *The Restructuring of American Religion,* 173. For the purposes of this study, I will only identify some of the major influences in this development. For a detailed account, see Wuthnow's Chapter 8, 173–214.

13. Ibid., 174.

14. Ibid., 184.

15. Quoted at http://www.religioustolerance.org/ps_pray.htm, June 25, 2002 (accessed September 2, 2006).

16. Ibid.

17. Jay Dolan, *The American Catholic Experience* (New York: Doubleday and Company, Inc., 1985), 263.

18. Anita Gandolfo, *Testing the Faith: The New Catholic Fiction in America* (New York and Westport, CT: Greenwood Press, 1992), 14.

19. Quoted from *Engle v. Vitale,* http://www.nationalcenter.org/cc7252.htm (accessed September 5, 2006).

20. Terry Muck, "The Wall That Never Was," *Christianity Today,* July 10, 1987, 16, as quoted by Robert Wuthnow, *The Struggle for America's Soul* (Grand Rapids, MI: William B. Eerdmans Publishing Company, 1989), 57.

21. Alexis de Tocqueville, *Democracy in America,* ed. Richard D. Heffner (New York: Signet Classics, 1984), 70.

22. Mary Gordon, *Final Payments* (New York: Random House, 1978), 101.

23. Janice Radway, *Reading the Romance: Women, Patriarchy, and Popular Literature* (Chapel Hill: University of North Carolina Press, 1991), 30–1.

24. Wuthnow, *The Restructuring of American Religion,* 145–6.

25. Stephen L. Carter, *The Culture of Disbelief: How American Law and Politics Trivialize Religious Devotion* (New York: Basic Books, 1993), 227.

26. Shanto Iyengar, "Public Opinion," in *Grolier Multimedia Encyclopedia* at http://ap.grolier.com/article?assetid=0238240-0&templatename;=/article/article.html (accessed November 3, 2006.

27. Hunter, *Culture Wars: The Struggle to Define America,* 59.

28. Ibid., 159. For a recent discussion of this issue, see "Is There a Culture War?" This panel discussion that included Hunter, as well as some of the nation's leading journalists, took place in May 2006, and a transcript is available at http://pewforum.org/events (accessed November 6, 2006).

29. Wuthnow, *The Restructuring of American Religion,* 194.

30. Wuthnow, *The Struggle for America's Soul,* 35.

31. Hunter, *Culture Wars: The Struggle to Define America,* 160.

32. Ibid., 107.

33. Ibid.,170.

34. Carter, *The Culture of Disbelief,* 225.

35. Ibid.

36. Ibid., 228.

37. Ibid.

38. Hunter, *Culture Wars: The Struggle to Define America,* 136.

39. Peter Steinfels, "Beliefs," *New York Times,* July 8, 2006, A14. This column is a discussion of Sommerville's book *The Decline of the Secular University.* According to Steinfels, Sommerville's thesis is that in driving religion out of academe, the contemporary professoriate is unable to provide (or consider) answers to questions about the nature of humanity or the basis of morality.

40. Garry Wills, "Christ Among the Partisans," *New York Times,* April 9, 2006, WK12.

41. Ibid.

42. Wuthnow, *America and the Challenges of Religious Diversity* (Princeton and Oxford: Princeton University Press, 2005), 174.

43. Ibid., 120.

44. The evidence of cultural phenomenon is surely in having its own web site, http://www.whatwouldjesusdo.com/, as well as an entry in the online encyclopedia Wikipedia, http://en.wikipedia.org/wiki/What_would_Jesus_do%3F (accessed November 6, 2006).

45. Wuthnow, *The Struggle for America's Soul,* 64.

46. Hunter, *Culture Wars: The Struggle to Define America,* 57.

47. Quoted by Carter, *The Culture of Disbelief,* 112. Governor Cuomo's speech, "Religious Belief and Public Morality: A Catholic Governor's Perspective" was published in the *Notre Dame Journal of Law, Ethics, and Public Policy* 1 (1984): 13, 19.

48. Wuthnow, *The Struggle for America's Soul,* 44.

49. Carter, *The Culture of Disbelief,* 58.

50. Ibid., 64.

51. Hunter, *Culture Wars: The Struggle to Define America,* 154.

52. Carter, *The Culture of Disbelief,* 14.

53. A March 2004 poll by Greenberg Quinlan Rosner Research Inc., for *Religion & Ethics Newsweekly* and *U.S. News & World Report,* http://www.pbs.org/wnet/religionan dethics/week733/release.html, April 13, 2004 (accessed September 12, 2006).

54. Ibid.

55. Wuthnow, *The Struggle for America's Soul,* 54–5.

56. Carter, *The Culture of Disbelief,* 54.

57. Barbara Kingsolver, *The Poisonwood Bible* (New York: Harper Perennial Modern Classics, 2005), 96.

58. Ibid., 516.

59. Ibid., 229.

60. Ibid., 251.

61. Ibid., 255.

62. Ibid., 435.

63. Giles Gunn, *The Culture of Criticism and the Criticism of Culture* (New York: Oxford University Press, 1987), 182.

64. Monique El-Faizy, *God and Country: How Evangelicals Have Become America's New Mainstream* (New York: Bloomsbury, 2006), 8.

65. W. Dale Brown, ed., *Of Fiction and Faith: Twelve American Writers Talk about Their Vision and Work* (Grand Rapids, MI: William B. Eerdmans Publishing Company, 1997), 32, 34.

66. Hunter, *Culture Wars: The Struggle to Define America,* 229.

67. Ibid.

68. Ibid., 244.

4

A Literature of Their Own

From airport newsstands to *Newsweek,* Christian fiction continues to grow in popularity, resonating with readers looking for both faith and fiction.

—ACFW (American Christian Fiction Writers)

In July 2006, the publishing world took notice of the fact that Multnomah Publishers, a modest-size, Oregon-based, evangelical Christian publishing house, had been put up for sale. Multnomah is notable for being the publisher that started a renaissance in Christian publishing in 2001, when its book, Bruce Wilkinson's *The Prayer of Jabez,* sold more than 8 million copies and became the best-selling book that year—not the best-selling religious-themed book, but *the* best-selling book of the year.[1] There was speculation from the trade magazine *Publishers Weekly* that the mainline publisher Random House was the likely buyer of Multnomah. Although not confirming the rumor, a spokesman for Random House commented, "We've long been committed to the Christian book market and are interested in growing in this area."[2]

That interest is surely sparked by the phenomenal market for Christian books. The emergence of best-selling nonfiction books like Wilkinson's *The Prayer of Jabez* and Joel Osteen's *Your Best Life Now* has demonstrated the tremendous market for Christian books and brought religious publishing into prominence in the publishing industry. Both Wilkinson and Osteen are purveyors of the "prosperity" gospel that advises Christians that God wants them to have riches in this world, a gospel that however untraditional an interpretation of scripture, is certainly well suited to the materialistic culture of the United States, as these authors' sales figures indicate. Although the recent blockbuster Rick Warren's *The Purpose Driven Life* does not promote the prosperity gospel, he is not immune from a materialistic impulse. In the readers' reviews on Amazon.com, one reader, who self-identified as "a believer," commented that Warren's book, "is largely a piece of advertising." The reader goes on to explain,

Throughout the chapters, Warren discusses a point and says something like, "if you want more help with that topic, see my other book" or "see the resources of mine listed at the back" which you can purchase. Just about every other chapter contained at least one plug for one of Warren's resources which can be purchased.[3]

The reviewer concludes, "Though this may not be the original intent of the author, the self-promotion throughout the book leaves a reader pondering Warren's true intentions."[4] And Amazon.com's traditional listing of "Customers who bought this book also bought" tends to confirm this reader's view, since the five books listed as commonly purchased along with *The Purpose Driven Life* are all ancillary to that book. In 2005, *Business Week* reported that *The Purpose Driven Life* had sold more than 23 million copies and was the "fastest-selling nonfiction book of all time."[5] Sales escalated in March 2005 when the book received national attention in the news media after a hostage crisis in Atlanta. The woman who had been held hostage reported that she had calmed her captor and eventually convinced him to surrender by sharing some passages from *The Purpose Driven Life.* However, some months later, she admitted that sharing her crystal meth with the man may have also been somewhat responsible for his relatively docile surrender.[6]

Although Rick Warren may not share Joel Osteen's focus on the prosperity gospel, he shares with Osteen the practice of using business marketing techniques to "sell" church membership. *The Purpose Driven Life* was preceded by Warren's *The Purpose Driven Church,* a manual for building up church membership that is as influential with many evangelical pastors as *The Purpose Driven Life* is with individuals. Both Warren and Osteen are pastors of "megachurches" (defined as those that attract at least 2,000 weekly worshippers—although Osteen was drawing about 30,000 each week, and that was before he renovated and moved into the Compaq Center in downtown Houston, the former home of the NBA's Houston Rockets).[7] The marketing savvy of megachurch pastors has drawn worshippers from traditional churches that adherents deem more stodgy; mainline Protestant churches have been described as "the religious equivalent of General Motors Corp. today."[8] Indeed, because of the growth of evangelical megachurches, pollster George Gallup, who has long studied religious trends in America, describes evangelicals as "the most vibrant branch of Christianity."[9]

This vibrancy of evangelical Christianity both fuels and is fueled by the publishing phenomenon in contemporary Christian fiction. Unlike their nonfiction counterparts, reliable sales figures for Christian fiction are difficult to ascertain, since many of the best sellers in this genre do not appear on mainstream best seller lists. However, in 2004, 2,200 titles were published in the category of Christian fiction, and Bethany House, a major publisher of this fiction, reported that number to be an increase of more than 80% from the 1,200 titles published just a decade earlier.[10] This development of Christian fiction has not gone unnoticed in the secular world. Christian books are increasingly found in mainline stores. For example, the ECPA (Evangelical Christian Publishers Association), in announcing its 2006 Christian book award winners, noted that "Barnes & Noble will be featuring all six winners in selected stores during August 2006."[11]

Like Christian nonfiction, the distinguishing characteristic of Christian fiction is that it is agenda driven, designed to conform to specific guidelines to insure orthodoxy. Every author is influenced by his or her worldview, but in this type of fiction, that worldview determines the text. Thus, prayer is a central part of the life of the characters in a Christian novel, and they can be expected to uphold the social values associated with Christians, an emphasis on fidelity in marriage and eschewing premarital sex, for example. And characters speak without profanity. This standard excludes many well-known writers whose fiction deals with religious values or principles. For example, in a conversation about the novelist John Updike, Garrison Keillor identified the essence of the perspective that permeates Christian fiction. Commenting on the strong theological understanding that pervades Updike's fiction, Keillor said, "He's a very Christian writer. No one would consider him one because he writes about adultery as if he might have committed it himself."[12] And the novelist Frederick Buechner, who is also an ordained minister, has noted that readers who devour Christian fiction would be "horrified" by his work. "After all, my books have bad words in them and people do naughty things."[13] The focus of this chapter is this specific, prescriptive fiction that is written to promote the values of conservative Christians. These are the books that at one time were sold exclusively in conservative Christian bookstores but because of the magnitude of their sales, many are now available on mainstream shelves in places from Borders to Wal-Mart.

In many ways, this contemporary Christian fiction is analogous to the Catholic novel of the nineteenth and early twentieth centuries. That earlier fiction was similarly concerned with promoting a specific religious worldview, and the needs of the Catholic community that fueled that fiction are also relevant to the current preponderance of conservative Christian fiction. In the nineteenth century, Catholics were not only a minority in a dominantly Protestant culture, their ethnicity was very much tied to their religious identity. Becoming American while retaining their unique heritage was a challenge to these immigrants as well as to the Catholic hierarchy.[14] While the local parish evolved as the social center for these immigrant groups, they formed various ethnic enclaves within the dominant culture.

As Will Herberg pointed out in the 1950s, Americans are able to be both secular and religious simultaneously because religion is not simply a faith expression but a form of cultural identity.[15] In the 1950s, there were clear denominational distinctions, and Americans tended to identify themselves as Protestant, Catholic, or Jew, rather than by any reference to the country from which they or their parents immigrated. Catholic identity was reinforced by the various practices of devotional Catholicism, such as fish on Friday and Mass every Sunday, but there was additional reinforcement in the various diocesan newspapers and devotional magazines that flourished in the second half of the nineteenth century. And Catholic novels soon followed as another medium for reinforcing Catholic identity and promoting orthodoxy.[16] This was a fiction specifically designed "to give metaphoric reinforcement to ideology."[17] Since the novel as a literary form is especially attuned to realism, it creates an alternative reality in which the marginalized group's ethos is dominant. As in all escapist fiction, such religious fiction enables readers to experience a world fully attuned to their particular values and beliefs.

The disappearance of the parochial Catholic novel coincided with Catholicism's integration into American culture, a process that was reflected in the sales of the 1950 novel, *The Cardinal* by Henry Morton Robinson, which was not only a best seller but made into an equally popular movie produced by Otto Preminger. In this clerical Horatio Alger story, a poor Boston youth, Stephen Fermoyle, ascends to the College of Cardinals, thus embodying the American Catholic immigrant ideal of success in religion. However, the fact that this novel, permeated with orthodox Catholic doctrine, could be a best seller in Protestant America illustrates the success of Catholicism in overcoming Protestant enmity and assimilating into mainstream culture, a process that would culminate in the election of the Catholic Kennedy to the Presidency a decade later. The success of *The Cardinal* in 1950 also reflects how attuned mainstream American values were with those of the Church in the years immediately following World War II. For example, in a pitiful scene in the novel, Stephen, then a young priest, refuses to allow a physician to save the life of his adored younger sister because it would involve aborting her child. Within twenty-five years, *Roe v. Wade* would not only change the average American reader's attitude toward this scene but change the image of Catholicism in popular literature as well.[18]

However, although the contemporary evangelical Christian novel stems from the same impulse to bolster parochial values as the Catholic novel of years past, there are some significant differences. Catholics were a marginalized minority in American society, and their need to bolster identity and orthodoxy of their members through fiction is obvious. The paramount question is why Christians, the dominant religion in American society, appear to have a need for such alternative fiction. Especially today, when the old hostilities between Protestants and Catholics, and even Christians and Jews, have considerably lessened and the cultural focus is on tolerance and applauding diversity, it seems odd to find this emergence of a distinctly Christian subculture of Christian schools, bookstores, and literature, usually the mark of a marginalized group. But, as indicated in the preceding chapter, conservative Christians are very much a marginalized group—or perceive themselves to be marginalized—in the culture of the United States today.

Why Christian Fiction?

Evangelical Christians have always been conscious of the secularizing forces in American society, and as a more educated public emerged after World War II, evangelicals began to develop their own media to counter perceived secularism with Christian values. For example, in 1956, the journal *Christianity Today* began as an alternative to "liberal theology, secularism, modernism, and the corrosive decay of scientism."[19] And, as noted in Chapter 3, evangelical preachers were among the first to exploit the new medium of television to expand their audience exponentially. As the Supreme Court decisions mounted, forbidding school prayer and legalizing abortion, conservative Christians saw themselves as marginalized in an American society that seemed to have the government's blessing in promoting non-Christian values.

The most obvious reason for the proliferation of Christian literature is to provide conservative Christians an alternative to the secularizing influences of the dominant culture. And I believe that it is not coincidental that the novel that is most often credited with initiating the development of this unique Christian fiction is a traditional, historical romance, Janette Oke's *Love Comes Softly,* originally published in 1979. While Oke's novel may not have been a *direct* response to a change in publishing in the mid-1970s, its immediate popularity was certainly due in large measure to that change. The romance novel, a form of popular fiction that is ubiquitous today, was not particularly promoted until the 1950s. At that time, publishers, noting a decline in their mainstay form of popular fiction, the detective novel, speculated that female readers, always a strong force in book buying, were not attracted to the hard-boiled detective novels of the Mickey Spillane style then in fashion.[20]

To try to attract women readers, one publisher reissued Daphne DuMaurier's *Rebecca,* originally published in 1938 and a consistent favorite in the previous generation. It was a success, and publishers discovered other female writers who were producing similar chaste romances. This type of romance novel, known as the "gothic," became a staple of popular fiction.[21] A characteristic of the gothic romance is the absence of explicit sexual scenes, and conservative Christian women would have found such fiction acceptable. However, as the Women's Movement developed in the early 1970s, some publishers felt that their female readers expected more explicit sex in the romance novel, and the genre changed accordingly.[22] Is it only coincidental that *Love Comes Softly,* published soon after the romance genre became more sexually explicit, found a receptive audience among Christian readers? Oke provided a novel that met their expectations for romance, a genre they had been reading, while preserving the decorum they had experienced with the gothic romance. Thus, the overwhelming sales of *Love Comes Softly* indicated that the Christian novel already had a receptive and eager audience, very likely also including nonevangelical conservative Christian women who had been alienated by the more sexually explicit romance novels.

I suggest this because not only the romance but also American popular fiction in general became much more explicit in its use of sexual scenes from the mid-1970s. Since popular fiction reflects the society that produces it, the riotous and permissive era we know as The Sixties was increasingly reflected in popular novels. Just as conservative Christians felt marginalized by the secular culture, as readers they felt disenfranchised by mainstream fiction that presented characters and situations antithetical to their values and beliefs. And Christian fiction has accordingly developed to provide these readers with "a literature of their own," to paraphrase Virginia Woolf. Just as Woolf identified the cultural issues involved in the absence of great female writers in her landmark, *A Room of One's Own,* the current market for Christian fiction is similarly fueled by the cultural situation in the United States today.

In a similar way, the second novel credited with the development of Christian fiction, Frank Peretti's *This Present Darkness,* originally published in 1985, had an equally receptive audience for this very different type of novel. Peretti's focus on spiritual warfare, the contest between angels, demons, and humans, can be attributed to his Pentacostal background, but his fiction is also similar in theme to those secular blockbusters of Stephen King, who, in the mid-1980s, was almost at the height of his career.[23] King's second novel, *Salem's Lot,* published a decade earlier (1975), is a similar tale of spiritual warfare. Interestingly, King originally titled his novel *Second Coming,* and he later changed it to *Jerusalem's Lot.* But the publisher, Doubleday, shortened it because they felt that the author's choice sounded *too religious.*[24] During the subsequent decade, King's other very successful forays into the realm of demons demonstrated that there was an audience for such intimations of the supernatural. Peretti's Christianized novel of spiritual warfare appealed to Christian readers who, like their secular counterparts, had a predilection for the supernatural horror mode of fiction popularized by King. And surely Peretti has been continually popular because fiction of spiritual warfare would resonate, albeit most likely at an unconscious level, with Christians who felt themselves at war with the "demons" of secular culture.

As an indication how far we've come from Doubleday's fear of a title sounding too religious in 1975, in September 2006, a news item reported that the Hollywood movie studio 20th Century Fox announced a new division, FoxFaith, that will focus on religious-oriented films, with a plan to release up to a dozen each year.[25] That this plan owes something to the robust market for Christian fiction is reflected in the fact that the first film to be released is based on a novel by Janette Oke, who was not only a pioneer in Christian fiction but also has become one of its most prolific authors.[26] I mention this because this development in film is analogous to what has happened in fiction. The enormous sales of Christian fiction influenced mainstream publishers to create their own religious divisions, just as movie studios are now doing. For example, among the seven 2006 Christy Award winners for excellence in Christian fiction, two novels are not from specifically Christian publishers but from mainstream firms that have established separate divisions specifically for Christian novels.[27] The immense popularity of

Christian fiction seduces the secular market to adapt to its standards in order to benefit from its profitability. And Christian readers, like Christian moviegoers, are similar to other American readers and moviegoers except for the content of the books and movies they prefer.

The eminent literary critic Cleanth Brooks, in the last collection of essays before his death, *Community, Religion, and Literature,* refers to the value of literature in giving us our sense of community, letting us "know what it feels like to be a certain sort of person or to hold a certain faith."[28] Thus, the development of a "Christian" literature is a natural result when Christians find their values subverted by the dominant culture. It is, as Robert Wuthnow explains, a retreat into "a safe community of like-minded believers."[29] Wuthnow suggests that such Christians also have a desire to "expand their horizons," and a literature of their own can create that illusion of openness to new experiences while keeping adherents safe from the secularizing influences of the dominant culture.

Appeal to Readers

It is important to note that the contemporary Christian novel is primarily what is known as popular fiction. It's the type of "light read" that makes few, if any, demands on the reader and can thus be a form of relaxation rather than study and concentration. And since the current Christian fiction market includes every type of escapist fiction found in secular publishing—from horror through action/suspense to traditional romance and family saga—it appeals to a broad spectrum of readers. It is hardly surprising that the market for Christian fiction is so strong, since popular fiction is a big seller in mainstream publishing as well, and Christian fiction, like its secular counterpart, offers readers a variety of subgenres to accord with individual tastes. Christian readers are no different from their secular counterparts except that they expect their novels to include details that conform to their community values and exclude those that do not. A look at the subsequent career of Janette Oke, which is not dissimilar to that of other popular Christian novelists, indicates another reason for the volume of sales in this fiction.

Oke's first novel, *Love Comes Softly,* credited with confirming the market for Christian fiction, was a pure romance, but although it evolved into a series of eight novels, Oke initially wrote it as a stand-alone, single novel. As she recounts in the preface to a 2003 edition of the novel, it was the volume of reader requests, combined with her publisher's marketing acumen, that led to the continuation of the characters' lives in a series. She also noted that so involved were readers in the lives of the fictional Davis family of the novel, that one reader mentioned actually praying for them. In addition, when Oke finally closed the story at the end of the eighth novel, readers continued to ask for more information about the family, begging her to at least tell them what happens even if she wasn't going to write any more novels about them. Readers responded as though the Davis family had actually existed in nineteenth-century California, as though Oke, who had deliberately chosen to end the series before the death of the initial couple, had not composed a fictional account of imaginary characters but recounted a segment of an actual family's history.[30]

The romance novel reader's identification with fictional characters as "real" is not unlike television soap opera viewers who similarly identify with characters as though they are friends in what is termed "para-social relationships."[31] In Janice Radway's study of the romance novel, she points out that the limited vocabulary and syntactic simplicity in these novels promotes easy comprehension and visualization for readers. Moreover, since the simplicity of language and directness of presentation requires minimal interpretation, the reader's energy can focus on more emotional involvement in the story, thus lending the illusion of reality.[32]

Following the example of *Love Comes Softly,* the practice of generating a series of novels featuring the same characters has become common among the better known Christian fiction writers and is certainly a factor in the volume of sales produced by the loyalty of readers. Interestingly, Radway notes that her interview subjects, readers of secular romance novels, expressed the wish that more writers would develop sequels so that they could follow the lives of characters with whom they become involved. As Radway notes, such a practice tends to increase the identification of the fictional world with the real-life world of the readers.[33] This identification with the idealized fictional world appears to be exceptionally strong in Christian fiction, since the novel series is so normative, and it indicates that this fiction may play a significant role in the spiritual lives of readers. In Christine Camella's study of soap opera viewers, she notes that theorists argue that these "para social" relationships, strong identification with fictional characters, can "in some cases be life changing and personality molding, but definitely life impacting."[34] Many of the best-selling Christian authors have readers' letters on their web sites, testifying to the impact of the novels on their lives. The evidence of para-social relationships in the intensity of readers' engagement with this fiction tends to lend credence to its power to affect the lives of its readers.

The Fiction

To sample Christian fiction beyond *Love Comes Softly,* I used Amazon.com's practice of publishing readers' own lists of favorites. I correlated several of these lists of favorite Christian fiction to identify novels that were common preferences among many readers, and the five writers whose work I explored are sisters of Oke in many ways. All were women, and although there are significant male writers of Christian fiction, the genre is dominated by female authors, just as its readers are dominantly female. And despite the variety among the novels—contemporary, historical, and suspense—they are all principally romance novels. It's predominately boy meets girl, one of whom is typically not a Christian, and the tension in the novel is not only how the pair will get together but also how the unchurched member will come to Jesus.

This fictional world is an idealized Christian one. Since the purpose of Christian fiction is to reinforce values and provide succor, the romance is its ideal expression. The development of the group known as American Christian Fiction Writers reflects the dominance of romance in this field. It was organized in 2000 as American Christian *Romance* Writers, but the name was changed in 2004 "in response to the diverse needs of the membership who write across many genres."[35] Despite the various types of fiction currently being written, romance still predominates, either explicitly or as the underlying structure in many of these novels.

Ironically, this Christian romance can reduce the concern that many readers of secular romances express about their indulgence in reading novels. In Radway's study of romance readers, women spoke of feeling that their "escape" into fiction was self-indulgent, and they felt that their husbands believed that this reading wasted both time and money. However, since the Christian romance is promoted as inspirational and "life-changing," reading this fiction becomes dutiful rather than indulgent.[36] Readers can claim it as a form of spiritual reading. Even in Biblically based faiths in which members regularly read the Bible, it is difficult for the average person to be inspired by the often difficult and obscure texts without the aid of a Bible study group or pastoral exegesis. However, a novel that is especially easy to comprehend, as is the typical romance, can convey the essence of Biblical truths to the reader in a more accessible fashion.

A good example of how fiction can enhance appreciation of the Bible can be seen in the contrast of the Book of Hosea with Francine Rivers' novel *Redeeming Love,* which is based on that text. So complex is Hosea that most Bibles have a multitude of footnotes to explain the often obscure references, since so much of this text is metaphorical. The fact that the marriage of the prophet to the prostitute is a complex analogy of the relationship of God to his people Israel can be extremely confusing to the less-skilled reader who tends to read much more literally than metaphorically. However, the essence of the Book of Hosea, the expression of God's redeeming love, is so superbly presented in Rivers' novel that the average Christian, relying on reading alone, would be more likely to be inspired by the novel than its Biblical source. The absence of the need to interpret in the romance novel enables the reader to be more affectively involved in the narrative.

While *Redeeming Love* is necessarily a stand-alone novel, given its source in Scripture, part of the selling power of Christian fiction is the development of the serial novels that prolong the plot and characters through five, six, or more separate novels, following the development of Oke's pioneering *Love Comes Softly.* These novels of Christian romance are the ultimate wish-fulfillment fantasy; the protagonist finds true love and God at the same time. The writing varies, based on the experience of the author. Some Christian authors have been successful writers in the secular realm, as was Francine Rivers, who wrote eleven romance novels before her conversion to Christ and subsequent career in Christian fiction. Others have a strong background in writing or journalism.

But some have little experience, having been avid readers of the fiction they decide to try to write. Thus, the prose in these novels varies from the fluent, "page-turner" of good popular fiction to the less felicitous prose of the sincere but limited writer.

The theology in many of these novels tends to be simplistic but is perhaps consistent with the genre. That is, romance novels are not intended to be realistic portrayals of human experience but idealized versions of the reader's world. Thus, the fact that characters not only frequently ask for God's guidance but receive it almost instantly, and often audibly, may seem to be a reductive description of the religious practice of discerning God's will—a practice that can be challenging for even the most spiritually mature. But this simplified version of spirituality can be understood as religious wish-fulfillment, consistent with the fantasy of the romance novel. In many ways, it is also consistent with the evangelical perspective. One former evangelical has made the significant point that those of us who have no experience of evangelical religion would have difficulty understanding the immediacy of the evangelical's spiritual experience in which "God is a living, tangible, and daily presence."[37] Thus the evangelical spiritual experience is both idealized and reinforced through these Christian romances. The five authors whose fiction I sampled based on readers' recommendations offer insight into this genre and the variety it offers to accommodate the preferences of readers. The work of these writers also indicates why Christian fiction is so enormously popular.

The novel that was most frequently praised and recommended in the sources I consulted was Francine Rivers' *Redeeming Love,* published in 1997. And it is easy to appreciate why this novel is so often listed by readers. This is Christian fiction at its best, and its excellence is not unrelated to the fact that Rivers was a published author prior to her first foray into Christian fiction. She is an experienced and accomplished novelist. In fact, Rivers notes in her preface that this is the "redeemed" version of the novel that she first published with Bantam in 1991. It is a significant reflection of her talent as a writer that she has been able to create this historical romance, set in nineteenth-century California during the Gold Rush and based on the Biblical Book of Hosea, in a form acceptable to a Christian audience. For like the Hosea of the Bible, her protagonist, Michael Hosea, takes a prostitute, named Angel, as a bride in accord with his discernment of God's will for him. Rivers is able to convey the horror of Angel's life, both as a child sold into sexual slavery and as a young woman who is trapped in a life of prostitution, without resorting to extremely lurid details or salacious images that would violate the conventions of Christian fiction. Yet the dreadfulness of Angel's existence is eminently clear to the reader, so deftly has Rivers fashioned this novel. For the average reader, this novel would convey a more powerful sense of God's redeeming love than the actual book of Hosea because of the latter's technical difficulties.

Redeeming Love also illustrates why this genre is so often called "inspirational" fiction. The tension between Angel, whose psychic wounds prevent her from accepting Michael's unconditional love, and Michael, who is driven by his need to reflect God's redeeming love, is the epitome of the religious romance, a story that can communicate the essence of relationship with the Divine to its readers. It is not surprising that according to Francine Rivers' web site, *Redeeming Love* has sold more than half a million copies and was among the top twenty on the Evangelical Christian Publishers Association's fiction best sellers list four years running.[38] And, as in Oke's *Love Comes Softly,* there is an absence of didacticism in this fiction. In both novels, the female protagonist comes to know God principally from the example of the male and his unspoken prayers for her. The emphasis is on Christian living as a witness that can facilitate the action of God's grace in others. There is also a generosity toward the initially nonbelieving female in both novels insofar as her life experiences have not exposed her to same opportunities as the Christian protagonist.

Francine Rivers continued her career in Christian fiction primarily by focusing on the historical romance and novels featuring Biblical protagonists. A novelist of this caliber easily can become a "brand," an author whose books are sought out by readers who want every book she publishes. So it was inevitable that she would publish novels in a series. However, unlike other series that continue the story of a group of characters from one novel to another, Rivers' series novels are primarily thematic, as in the Lineage of Grace series that focuses on Biblical women. This development of a series by popular authors was especially important for sales in Christian fiction when these novels in the past were often not considered for the nationally known best-seller lists nor stocked by mainstream bookstores. The development of Christian fiction is due primarily to its acumen in meeting the needs of its readers, disenfranchised from mainstream popular novels, and the quality fiction of writers like Oke and Rivers who satisfied those needs. Even today, the author's "brand" or reputation among readers is a significant factor in sales.

Perhaps the queen of branding is the best-selling Karen Kingsbury, another author who came to Christian fiction with writing experience. She has also perfected the "series" novel; even her separate series are often intertwined. For example, when I read the first volume of the "Firstborn" series, *Fame,* I soon realized that there must be a prequel somewhere, so frequent were allusions to events involving the characters in the recent past. I eventually discovered the five-volume Redemption series that chronicles the story of the Baxter family. The Firstborn series focuses on the romance of Katy Hart and Dayne Matthews, but the Baxters continue throughout that series in ancillary plots as well. In fact, Dayne Matthews is inextricably connected to the Baxters, a fact neither party is aware of for some time, and so the ongoing narrative of this family weaves in other characters and their stories to propagate Kingsbury's fiction. Thus, the reader's experience is more of virtual reality than simply reading a novel, as the various novels of the intertwined series create a virtual world that the reader enters—and is soon impelled to learn more about by devouring the pertinent novels.

Kingsbury's prose has the characteristic simplicity of romance fiction, creating a strong, visual experience for the reader, almost as though watching a televised soap opera. And plots in the series novels develop at a glacial pace similar to that of the soap. As each novel ends, the reader is already anticipating the next one, much as the soap opera viewer is looking forward to Monday's show at the close of every Friday's episode. And the prolific Kingsbury does not disappoint, each subsequent novel of the series appearing without keeping the reader waiting too long.

To complement the reader's experience of Kingsbury's fiction, she has a complex web site that not only keeps her readers informed of projected publication dates and other Kingsbury news but also offers naming opportunities for characters in her novels (with proceeds going to charity), contests for readers, as one in which they vie to be selected to visit the Kingsbury family, a newsletter, a message board, and even a section where readers can submit prayer requests. Perhaps the most powerful part of this web site in terms of branding is Kingsbury's "Journal," a section on the web site where she promises to post "thoughts and happenings" in her professional and personal life. As she explains,

Sometimes I will share a Scripture that God is using to speak to me. Other times I'll tell you something funny Austin said or the details of a performance one of my kids gave, a performance that maybe brought tears to my eyes. Often this will be an area where I will share something special a reader told me or the victories and struggles I'm having with my current writing project.

In any case, it will be a look at my heart. I share this with you because I consider you my friends. If you read my books, you already know how my emotions work, now you can understand a little more about my daily life. You'll feel the connection, laugh with me and cry with me, and you'll know how you can pray for me and my family. Please know that I am always praying for you and yours![39]

By engaging her readers in this very personal way, Kingsbury draws them not only into the virtual reality of her novels but also into a pseudo friendship with the author herself. It's hardly surprising that she sells so many books. And this Journal is also a way to keep readers apprised not only of upcoming publication dates but also of her writing plans, as in the entry dated August 11, 2006, when she announced that although the Firstborn series was drawing to a close, the characters would continue in yet a *third* incarnation:

I'm well into the last book in the Firstborn Series. *Forever* will definitely give you the next piece of the Baxters' story, the next segment of the life between Katy and Dayne. But it won't be the end. That's the only reason I'm enjoying the writing it so much, because this series will springboard into the Sunrise Series.[40]

The virtual world created by the ten novels of Redemption and Firstborn will thus continue in Sunrise, for the readers' pleasure and author's profit.

Kingsbury doesn't only write series for these characters. She is extraordinarily prolific, with a September 11 series of two books, the Red Gloves series of four books, Forever Faithful with three books, a Women of Faith of two books, and the Miracle group of five books. In addition, she publishes stand-alone novels, and in the fall of 2006, she had seven novels in that group. This substantial production seems to affect the quality of her work. Between the second and third novels in the Firstborn series, for example, Kingsbury produced a stand alone, *Like Dandelion Dust,* that appeared in June 2006. The series novels may be easier to write quickly because of the ongoing characters and continuing plot because this stand-alone novel is much less polished than my sampling of the Firstborn series, *Fame.*

The prose of *Like Dandelion Dust* is pedestrian at best, and her characters function as elements in the plot rather than individuals. Perhaps this is partially due to the fact that two characters were developed from contest winners. People had bid to name characters, and Kingsbury obliged the winners by naming two characters in the novel in accord with the individuals designated by the contest winners. In addition, she attributed details from these people's lives to the characters, things like the number and names of their children or pets. The process of developing the novel in conjunction with a contest among readers appears to have negatively affected Kingsbury's writing process because the other characters in the novel are also extraordinarily flat, seeming more like plot elements than people. Her four-year-old protagonist, the pawn in a custody struggle between adoptive and birth parents, often speaks more like a wise forty-year-old than a child of four, although Kingsbury gives him some annoyingly "cute" features to remind the reader of his age, as his ending prayers with "Gee this name, Amen," an obvious rendition of hearing "In Jesus' name," since he has learned to pray from listening to his older cousin at prayer.

In this novel, realism is often sacrificed to the needs of plot. At a critical point in the book, the birth mother, a woman who neither attends church nor reads the Bible, is suddenly dipping into the good book. Of all the narratives involved, she not only comes across the story of King Solomon and the two women who claim to be the mother of the same child, so relevant to her personal circumstances, but she is also able to see the lesson for her in the Biblical tale without any assistance. However, despite the authorial lapses, the heart-rending plot of adoptive parents who are being forced to surrender the child they've raised from birth will captivate Kingsbury readers, as they hope to see how God will resolve this dilemma. So powerful is the Kingsbury brand that readers will devour her novels and be easily satisfied by the fiction of their "friend."

If I seem negative about Kingsbury, it is less because of any of her limitations as a writer than skepticism about the veritable industry she is creating with her fiction. When does marketing supersede fiction itself? Are there limits to branding? The expression "life-changing" is often used of inspirational fiction like that of Oke, Rivers, and Kingsbury, all three writers often quoting readers who testify to the power of the novels in their lives. Rather immodestly, Kingsbury has

trademarked the expression "life-changing fiction" to apply to her *oeuvre,* but
with this patent, it seems to apply to her novels alone. Nevertheless, in Kingsbury's ability to engage readers, she is surely a publisher's dream author,
and perhaps more so because of her ability, indeed her apparent joy, in actively
marketing her brand.

In her study of contemporary evangelicals, Monique El-Faizy describes the
incredible marketing plan that helped propel sales of Rick Warren's *The Purpose
Driven Life.*[41] Although sales of individual Christian novels don't approach that
behemoth, Warren's plan illustrates the fact that marketing to the evangelical
community is facilitated by their insularity. Since they tend to focus their social
lives around their church, whether it be the vast megachurches or relatively
modest-sized parishes, evangelicals are fairly centralized and thus easy to
reach.[42] In addition, as noted earlier, evangelicals were the first to grasp the
advantage of using technology in sharing their message, and Christian writers,
like Kingsbury, artfully employ the Internet to create web sites that offer a virtual
community for their readers. Jan Karon, another best-selling evangelical writer,
offers a similar virtual community for her readers focused on her fictional community of Mitford.[43]

All fiction that sells well resonates with readers in a variety of ways.
Kingsbury's novels not only stress Christian living but also incorporate details
that are well suited to the anxieties and concerns of evangelical readers. For the
contemporary conservative Christian who feels somewhat marginalized in
American culture, an emphasis on the value of being different is important, and
in various ways, this fiction provides support for that feeling of exclusion. For
example, in Kingsbury's Firstborn series, the heroine Katy Hart turns down a
chance to star in a movie, surely an ideal example of the contemporary American
dream, because she feels that the Hollywood environment is inconsistent with her
spiritual values. She is confident and strong in her spirituality, and part of that
confidence stems from her belief in her conservative Christian culture. In one
novel, Katy is confused about a specific line in Scripture, "You must be holy
because I am holy," but gains insight when "Pastor Mark" clears it up. "God
wanted His people to be holy, not perfect. Holiness for God meant perfection,
of course. But holiness for His people meant being set apart. Different."[44] Rather
than feeling marginalized, the Christian who reads Kingsbury is bound to feel
special, which is another appeal of these novels.

Kingsbury has moved the traditional romance novel in the direction of family
drama with her Baxters, committed Christian parents whose children all find
their own way to Jesus through personal struggles. This emphasis will certainly
resonate with her family-centered readers who are equally concerned with the
spiritual development of their own children. In her analysis of romance novel
reading, Janice Radway has identified the compensatory nature of reading
romance fiction.[45] And for the conservative Christian reader, identification with
this idealized Christian family, as well as other strong Christian families in the
Baxter's community, serves a support function similar to the way female readers

are encouraged by the strong, independent heroines of traditional romance novels. Of course, with the character of Katy Hart in the Firstborn series, Kingsbury also includes the strong, independent heroine of the romance tradition, thus providing an ideal Christian heroine for the traditional female romance reader.

Although Janette Oke was a pioneer in Christian fiction, Karen Kingsbury's work shows how Christian fiction, like religion itself, has evolved with the culture. Kingsbury's more contemporary narratives provide even easier access for those with limited reading experience, some of whom may be deterred by the unfamiliar setting of the historical novel. Kingsbury's emphasis on family and the contemporary setting within the romance genre is also characteristic of the popular Christian novelist Dee Henderson. Henderson is known for the unique combination of inspiration, mystery, suspense, and romance in her fiction. She writes series, initially "Uncommon Heroes" that had a military theme most reminiscent of Tom Clancy, but her subsequent "O'Malley" series offers an interesting permutation of the romance genre for contemporary Christian readers.

The six novels in Henderson's O'Malley series focus individually on the seven "siblings," men and women, unrelated by blood, who originally met as children in an orphanage and so strongly bonded that they came together as a family when they left the orphanage, each adopting the common surname "O'Malley" to signify their commitment to each other. Their occupations propel the details of the plots of their respective novels, although the same basic structure is common to all. Among the O'Malleys are a hostage negotiator, an emergency medical technician, a forensic pathologist, a firefighter, and a U.S. Marshall, all of whom are not yet Christians when their respective books begin. The seventh O'Malley, the first of the family to become a Christian, is a sister, a lawyer who is dying of terminal spinal cancer.

Henderson's predilection for action melodrama is certainly a factor in her fiction's appeal to readers, given the public's interest in both firefighters and EMTs in the wake of 9/11, and the contemporary fascination with the work of the FBI and forensic science as reflected in the popularity of television shows such as *CSI, Without a Trace, 24,* and similar dramas. In the O'Malleys, Henderson also provides the interest in family that's the staple of Kingsbury's fiction. The family is the background of the entire series, and each of the sibling's stories in the individual novels follows the basic romance pattern—meet potential spouse, who is already a Christian, and become involved in a dangerous situation that draws them closer together (to avoid having the Christian actually date the non-Christian—a taboo of the Christian fiction genre), the resolution of the dangerous situation, and the conversion to Christ of the non-Christian O'Malley, resulting in the happily-ever-after of the romance genre.

The sameness of the pattern is camouflaged by the change in gender from novel to novel. That is, Henderson begins with a female O'Malley who meets a male Christian, and since there are three siblings of each gender among the series' protagonists, she alternates between male and female O'Malley from novel to novel, thus changing the Christian potential spouse from male to female as well. In addition, since each novel in the series features the conversion of a different sibling, their various occupations determine the plot details of the novel, and so the books appear far different than they actually are in their basic romance structure. The variety of occupations among the O'Malleys also appeals to readers, often unconsciously. It's axiomatic that readers of popular fiction like books that appear to provide knowledge or information that is deemed practical. Radway observed this in her romance readers; the knowledge is considered valuable in itself but also as a way of expanding their horizons and ameliorating any guilt about spending time reading novels.[46] Henderson's fiction ably fulfills this desire for information with myriad details related to the high-interest careers of the O'Malley siblings.

This is especially important for conservative Christian readers who want to be part of the mainstream culture but without sacrificing their own values. In a series like the O'Malleys, Christian readers can enjoy the pleasure of the television action/adventure series and learn about forensics, law enforcement, and other topics of those shows without dealing with the violence, profanity, or other elements that they deem offensive. They can participate in the same interests as other Americans on their own terms. And much like television drama that continues to attract viewers because they get involved with the characters, the serialized novels of Christian fiction are equally engaging for readers who become similarly involved with the fictional characters. Moreover, with the equal time given the male protagonists and the mystery/suspense/action context, Henderson's fiction can appeal to male readers as well as females, as evidenced by one reader's explanation that he and his wife are "reading the whole O'Malley series together."[47]

Despite her focus on the action/suspense genre, Henderson actually engages her readers through the characters, as in most Christian fiction. Commenting on a stand-alone Henderson crime/mystery novel, *Before I Wake,* one reader wrote in a review on Amazon.com dated September 18, 2006, "The characters are people you just want to get to know! Plus you even get a few mentions of people from past books, which always makes me happy." Note how this same reader is also anticipating a sequel, commenting that "Henderson does not wrap up all the threads at the end of the novel. Hopefully there will soon be a follow up to this book!" Another reader commenting on *The Negotiator,* a novel in the O'Malley series, sums up the appeal of Henderson's fiction and the addictive nature of these series novels. In a review dated December 21, 2005, the reader described *The Negotiator* as "a well-written story with wonderful characters that draw you into their lives." Reviewing the same novel on May 9, 2004, another reader commented on having "ended up buying the whole series after reading this one." Novels of action/suspense usually draw readers with the plotlines rather than characters, but a consistent feature of Christian fiction appears to be engaging the readers with characters they identify with and care about, thereby increasing reader involvement—and sales.

Interestingly, a review of Henderson's fourth O'Malley novel *The Protector* in *Publishers Weekly* aptly terms her work "a familiar tale of Christian redemption set against a suspenseful backdrop and sprinkled with loving family ties," identifying the elements that readers always cite as important to them.[48] The same reviewer complains that the author's "terse, choppy writing style is too heavy on dialogue and short on descriptive narration," claiming that it "seems more suited to a mystery-of-the-week teleplay than a sustained, character-driven crime novel." This is an example of the type of criticism often leveled at Christian fiction—asking it to be something it doesn't want to be. The style is intentional. In an essay on "How to Write a Good Story," Dee Henderson explained, "I am not a descriptive writer. So my formula doesn't have an arrow for description. I write very terse and sparse."[49] And the complaint that the fiction reads visually, like a teleplay, ignores the fact that this fiction is intended to be similarly entertaining through its strong visual appeal.

The consistency of Christian fiction creates a fellowship among writers whose novels appear very dissimilar, and that's how the fiction of Beverly Lewis may seem in contrast to that of Dee Henderson. Worlds apart from Henderson's fast-paced, suspense fiction are Lewis's novels of bucolic family life among the Amish. Drawing on her Mennonite heritage and Lancaster County upbringing, Lewis, author of over seventy books for adults, teens, and children, creates family sagas that are in some ways an Amish version of the O'Malley clan or Karen Kingsbury's Baxters—family drama in the romance tradition of popular fiction.

The Amish also provide Lewis with a setting that attracts readers, since, as noted earlier, acquiring knowledge is a significant issue for many readers of romance and other popular fiction. Predictably, many of the reader reviews of Lewis's novels on Amazon.com cite learning about Amish culture as one of the significant satisfactions of reading Lewis's books. The Amish setting also creates an interesting parallel for Christian readers that may draw them to this fiction, albeit unconsciously. The Plain folk are famous for eschewing the dominant culture to remain apart, and contemporary conservative Christians may identify with that sense of separateness. Since the Amish separateness is self-imposed for religious purposes, this fiction may enable evangelical Christians to see their own separateness from the secular culture in similarly spiritual terms.

In addition, Lewis's fiction has the potential for exploring faith development with more complexity than is found in the typical romance of Christian fiction with its correlation of finding a spouse with finding God. Perhaps due to the fact that in the Amish culture, young people are expected to decide whether or not to continue in the community and make a commitment to their heritage in late adolescence, Lewis's novels are more focused on this issue of personal appropriation of one's heritage, consistent with the movement between Fowler's faith stages of 3 and 4, the transition between adolescent faith to maturity in faith. In two of her series, Annie's People and Abram's Daughters, she explores the tension among children of Amish families who often struggle in deciding whether to remain

with the Brethren or choose their own path apart from their heritage. Alas, the
tension remains at the most superficial level, and there is little sense of serious
reflection. Nevertheless, the question itself, whether or not to embrace one's
religious heritage, is a significant one, and Lewis's interest in this issue may be
due to the fact that she also writes fiction for young adults.

What appears odd in Lewis's serial novels is that in one novel at least, she dis-
penses with the illusion of a self-contained novel completely. In *The Covenant,*
the first in the Abram's Daughters series, there are several plot lines but not one
of them concludes in any way at the end of the novel. It's as though the author
simply stopped writing, a technique that violates the conventions of the novel
form. In their Amazon.com reviews, many readers comment on how unsettling
this was for them, even among readers who are aware that the story continues
in subsequent books. What is remarkable is that there are no complaints about
the lack of any closure to the novel. Readers simply note that Lewis appears to
have a unique type of serial novel. This suggests that readers are so thoroughly
engaged with the characters that they see the novel more as a representation of
the real world than as fiction, which reinforces the idea that readers of Christian
fiction often develop para-social relationships with fictional characters, lending
power to the ability of the fiction to affect readers' spiritual lives.

Lewis also has written two series of novels for young teens (ages 11–14), and
her adult novels could be easily given to young people from about age thirteen as
well, since the prose is undemanding and the situations are not inappropriate for
younger readers. In fact, the relative immaturity of Lewis's prose enables parents
to share some novels with their children, and there are comments about this in
reader reviews on Amazon.com. Her series Abram's Daughters involves the
development of five daughters from their teens (one actually from birth), and
more than one reader review on Amazon.com mentioned sharing the novels
either with children or among the entire family, both parents and children. This
would provide a positive forum for parent/child communication on serious
issues, certainly a value for Christians who are concerned with their children's
development in faith.

Using the Amish, Lewis metaphorically reflects the experience of all young
Christians who, if they are to develop spiritually, must make a personal commitment and not remain in the conventional Stage 3 that Fowler describes, adhering
to the practices that have been inculcated from birth without any personal appropriation of the values or doctrine involved. Beverly Lewis's novels may seem to
reflect a quaint lifestyle, but the separateness of the Amish and the challenges to
young people to personally appropriate their faith will resonate with conservative
Christian readers who may believe that they are reading about an exotic sect but
will be able to draw lessons for their own life from her novels. Overall, Lewis
draws readers to her novels in the same way as Kingsbury, Henderson, and other
Christian writers. In a October 5, 2004 review of *The Prodigal,* one of the novels
in the Abram's Daughters series that focuses on the Ebersol family, one reader
succinctly summed up that appeal, "The Ebersol family have become friends of

mine." Kingsbury's Baxters and Henderson's O'Malleys create similar friend-ships with their readers.

The ability to create such engaging characters sells far more books than mastery of the craft of fiction, as illustrated by the career of Robin Jones Gunn. Like Beverly Lewis, Gunn has published adult, young adult, and children's fiction. Basically a self-taught author with no prior experience in professional writing, Gunn appears to be a natural story teller whose career has tapped her life experience. She began writing children's books when her own children were young, and her two very successful young adult series, Christy Miller and Sierra Jones, stem from her work in youth ministry. Although the young adult fiction of both Lewis and Gunn appears to have naturally evolved in their careers, the pub-lication of Christian fiction for young people is also due to cultural changes that opened a market for such fiction, not unlike the shift in the romance novel that created a market for Christian romance.

The Christian young adult fiction market is another product of The Sixties. Although there was fiction that appealed to adolescent readers even in the nineteenth century, like *Treasure Island* (1883), the specific genre of young adult fiction burgeoned in the United States in the late 1960s. One suggestion for the sudden emergence of books for young adults is the 1965 Elementary and Secondary School Educational Act that provided funds for school libraries.[50] While that funding may have provided support for young adult fiction, the first novel of the new era, S.E. Hinton's *The Outsiders* (1967), published when the author was herself only seventeen, was inspired by the fact that there was no realistic fiction for young adults that mirrored her own high school experience.[51] But the realism of contemporary fiction in The Sixties produced novels that most conservative Christians would not want their children to read.

The striking difference between Beverly Cleary's *Fifteen,* a young adult romance published in 1956, and Judy Blume's young adult romance *Forever,* published in 1975, reflects the nature of the cultural changes wrought by The Sixties. The subject of *Fifteen* is a young girl's first crush. When the most popular boy in school asks the heroine, Jane, out on her very first date, her concerns are typical for her age and the culture of the 1950s. Will her parents let her date at fifteen? What if she makes a fool of herself? Will she know what to say? But by 1975, in Judy Blume's *Forever,* the heroine Katherine's major concern is responsible sex, since she and her boyfriend, both high school seniors, have decided that they are in love and are planning to have intercourse. Katherine visits a clinic and obtains a prescription for The Pill, the medical innovation of The Sixties that enabled young people to ignore the specter of unwanted pregnancy.

Given the spirit of reflecting the realism of The Sixties, it's hardly surprising that Judy Blume's young adult novels are regularly found on lists of banned books. In fact, the pioneers of realistic fiction for young adults, all perennial best sellers, are found regularly on lists of banned books. *The Outsiders* ranked 43rd on the American Library Association's One Hundred Most Frequently Chal-lenged Books from 1990 to 2000, a list that includes Paul Zindel's *The Pigman*

(1968); Robert Cormier's *The Chocolate War* (1974); and five young adult novels by Judy Blume, all popular and critically acclaimed young adult fiction.[52] Given conservative Christians' literal reading of novels that condemns Twain's *Huck Finn* and Salinger's *The Catcher in the Rye* without appreciating the overriding values in those books, it is hardly surprising that the young adult novels that feature typical adolescent profanity, sexual experimentation, and rebellion against parents are also censored. However, the novels of Hinton, Cormier, and Blume are exceptionally popular among young readers, and it is only natural that Christians try to counter their influence with Christian young adult fiction that more suitably reflects their own values. Evangelicals are not only concerned with the faith development of their teenagers, but they organize effectively to combat the dangers of the secular influences that their teens encounter.[53] The marketing of Christian young adult fiction is one aspect of that organization.

The market for Christian young adult fiction is evident in the success of both of Robin Jones Gunn's youth series. Since Christy Miller's birth in the 1988 *Summer Promise,* her series and that of Sierra Jensen have sold over 2.3 million copies.[54] Several other writers have developed young adult Christian series, including Judy Baer with her Cedar River Daydreams series and Laura Peyton Roberts with the Clearwater Crossing series. Another interesting series is Brio Girls, written mainly by Jane Vogel and Lissa Halls Johnson, but with various other writers authoring books in the series as well. The series is an outgrowth of *Brio* magazine, a publication of Focus on the Family for female teens aged twelve to sixteen, and that group publishes *Breakaway,* a magazine for male teens thirteen and older, as well as *Brio & Beyond* for young female Christians sixteen and older. The journal *Christianity Today* also publishes a magazine for Christian youth, *Campus Life.* Thus, meeting the needs of young adult readers is an important aspect of evangelicals' concern for their younger members, a reflection of the critical nature of the teen years in faith development.

The extension of Christian "brand items" to youth is further indication of the importance of the young adult market. The best-selling *The Prayer of Jabez* spawned *The Prayer of Jabez for Teens,* and the "Chicken Soup for the Soul" series added *Chicken Soup for the Christian Teenage Soul: Stories to Open the Hearts of Christian Teens.* And the fact that Christian fiction for teens has become a significant share of the market is reflected in the 2005 publication of *The Librarian's Guide to Developing Christian Fiction Collections for Young Adults* by Barbara J. Walker. Given the psychosocial challenges of adolescence, and the secular nature of contemporary American popular culture, including young adult fiction, it is hardly surprising that teen fiction has become a significant aspect of Christian fiction, given that genre's overarching purpose of providing its readers with succor and support in their religious lives. As with adult Christian fiction, the goal is to provide Christian teens with "a literature of their own."

In keeping with the virtual reality of series novels, Robin Jones Gunn segued from her best-selling teen series into adult romance fiction with her Glenbrooke series by populating those novels with various friends of Christy Miller who, as young adults, are concerned with finding true love and, of course, finding God as well. By linking her young adult series to its more adult romance successor through the aging of characters in the earlier series, Jones strengthens the virtual world of her fiction. Glenbrooke is a fictional town, which is described in each novel as "a quiet place where souls are refreshed." Each of the eight novels in the series involves a character who is renewed at Glenbrooke, sort of a spa for the soul. In this series, some of the literary flaws in Christian fiction are apparent. While Gunn has undeniable ability to spin a satisfying tale, especially for young adult readers, her romance fiction in the Glenbrooke series is obviously driven more by the message rather than any strong plot or well-developed characters.

Clouds, the fifth novel in the series, is typical. Its heroine is Shelly Graham who, as the novel opens, is returning to her hometown of Seattle after an absence of five years. She had left to become a flight attendant, based in California, and now has been transferred back to Seattle. However, in those five years, Shelly, raised a Christian, has become lax in her church going and prayer life. The reader later learns that when Shelly left Seattle, she had also abandoned Jonathan, a young man who had been her best friend from childhood and who had proposed marriage. It was not a lack of feeling for Jonathan but her need to be an independent person that impelled her departure and abandonment of boyfriend. Since her career also resulted in her lapse in religious observance, there's an underlying implication that women in pursuit of careers are at risk of losing their faith as well as their intended spouse.

And when Shelley finally connects with Jonathan again, that message is reinforced since he is engaged to someone else. Happily, Shelley's career as a flight attendant becomes precarious because of cutbacks in the industry; she takes a job at a conference center, is brought back to her Christian roots through a women's retreat at the center, and is suddenly asked to accompany her sister on a business trip. The destination just happens to be Glenbrooke. There Shelly, having returned to religion, now finds Jonathan sans fiancé and ready to resume their love. Shelly's soul is indeed refreshed in this idyllic town.

While it's easy to be critical of Gunn's simplistic plotting and trite situations, it's clear from responses to her novels that she knows her readers. Although the Glenbrooke stories feature older protagonists in situations appropriate to their ages, many of the readers who review the books on Amazon.com identify themselves as thirteen or fourteen, and others write as though they are of a similar age. This is understandable in light of Gunn's reputation in Christian fiction. A young person who has read all the Christy Miller and Sierra Jensen books would naturally seek out other novels by Gunn, and they aren't disappointed, as she has developed the series as an extension of the earlier teen novels. Writing about *Secrets,* the first novel in the Glenbrooke series that features Jessica and Kyle as protagonists, one reader summarizes the appeal of the book in this review dated June 12, 2000:

I am an almost-14-year-old girl who loves reading Christian romances, especially by Robin Jones Gunn. This book (and the rest of the Glenbrooke series) is great. I especially like Kyle. He's the ideal & perfect guy. I love how this and the rest of the Glenbrooke books are linked in certain ways to each other and the other books in the Glenbrooke series. It's cool because Christy Miller is mentioned, and you keep seeing people like Kyle and Jessica in the later books.

Note how the linkages between the books is through the characters, increasing readers' identification with these characters as "friends," as in other Christian fiction.

   With the Glenbrooke series completed, Gunn began another series for older readers by transitioning into the latest Christian fiction subgenre, chick lit, with her "Sisterchick" series. This is another example of Christian fiction responding to a popular genre in mainstream fiction. Fiction depicting the concerns of single women, à la *Bridget Jones's Diary* and older women as pals in the *Thelma and Louise* mode, is extremely popular. In a January 24, 2004 review of Gunn's first sisterchick novel, *Sisterchicks on the Loose,* note the reader's comments about mainstream secular chick lit: "all too many of the characters and plots involve myriad kinds of substance abuse (from caffeine to codeine and beyond) and self-loathing (cottage-cheese thighs, wardrobes lacking glamour, nasty boy-friends)." This reader explains that she finds Gunn's Sisterchick "a refreshing antidote to these other books." Jones's foray into chick lit will not only appeal to readers like this one who finds the mainstream genre distasteful, but it will also please Gunn's multitude of fans, as noted by this reviewer in her comments dated December 23, 2003: "Robin has a lot of teen fans who are growing into young adulthood and womanhood. Its great that she has moved into fiction for an older crowd so her fans can grow with her." And the Amazon.com listing of books that readers also purchased indicates that those who read one of the Sisterchicks series tend to buy the rest of them, as is standard with Christian fiction series.

   Apart from the natural appeal of the contemporary popular genre of chick lit, Gunn has wisely created Sisterchicks as a road series. Each novel takes her forty-something protagonists to one exotic location after another with titles such as *Sisterchicks Do the Hula* (Hawaii) and *Sisterchicks Down Under* (Australia), thus providing the appeal of information prized by so many readers of popular fiction. This is reflected in a reader's review dated April 30, 2004 of *Sisterchicks on the Loose,* which takes its protagonists to England and Finland: "This was a very interesting book, getting to read more about Finland and England, and about the people and their customs." The series also appeals to the fantasy aspect of traditional romance fiction insofar as one of the two friends on these journeys is always fabulously wealthy and willing to spend freely; there's no budget consciousness on these journeys.

   And at least one fellow author of Christian teen fiction has also moved into chick lit. Judy Baer's *The Whitney Chronicles* is described in a *USA Today* feature about Christian chick lit as "about a 30-year-old heroine who struggles with her weight, bad dates and meddling relatives who want to know why she's not married. Being active in her church doesn't preclude searching for Mr. Right."[55] One editor describes Christian chick lit as presenting "real-life situations that modern women of faith face without sacrificing strong morals and values: How do I live an authentic contemporary Christian life?"[56] And this is precisely how first-time novelists Anne Dayton and May Vanderbilt describe their fiction, which they call "good girl lit" and define on their web site:

Let's face it. Life is messy. And trying to live by faith only makes it harder. Good Girl Lit features contemporary characters dealing with modern life. It's about facing real issues with faith. It's about trying to live as God wants, and failing. It's also about the redeeming power of grace. It's Christian fiction for the real world.[57]

The *New York Daily News* pointed out the similarities between authors Dayton and Vanderbilt and their first heroine, Emily, as young Christian women trying to make their way in New York City.[58] In their first two novels, *Emily Ever After* (2005) and *Consider Lily* (2006), the pattern is similar; young Christian woman trying to find career and Mr. Right within a very secular culture while preserving her values and morals. Both Emily and Lily stumble along the way, but in keeping with her heritage in the romance novel tradition, the chick lit heroine finds Mr. Right along with a renewed sense of her faith and place in the world.

There is a hope among publishers that this subgenre of chick lit may be able to cross over to the mainstream market, something few other Christian publications have managed.[59] And this potential can be seen in the difference between Dayton and Vanderbilt's first two novels. Both have the type of sassy, modern cover art characteristic of mainstream chick lit fiction, covers that give no indication of the Christian emphasis in the novels. But *Emily Ever After* presents a heroine who is continually worried about the possibility of being "outed" as a Christian, whether to her friends at work or her employer, almost as though being fed to the lions would be the result of identification as a Christian. This rather isolationist attitude by the heroine may be the result of the authors' inexperience in this first novel, but it is also characteristic of Christian fiction that emphasizes a dramatic difference between Christians and other Americans. Indeed, although Katy Hart, the heroine of Karen Kingsbury's Firstborn series, lives and works in Bloomington, Indiana, home of Indiana University and thus a fairly diverse Midwestern city, Katy's associations are solely among similarly committed Christians; the tension in the series being between Katy's Christian world in Bloomington and the secular world of Hollywood. By locating her heroine in Bloomington, Kingsbury is suggesting that mainstream America is dominantly evangelical, with only the most notoriously secular cities responsible for the secularization of American culture.

Similarly, in *Emily Ever After,* the heroine's move to New York City is depicted as though this innocent young Christian has been relocated to a pagan society that is so threatening that she dare not reveal her identity as a Christian.

This separatist element in Christian fiction appeals to the sense of marginalization so common among evangelicals but limits the appeal of this fiction to other conservative Christians who want to emphasize their separateness. On the other hand, in their second novel, *Consider Lily,* the authors are much more inclusive. The heroine has a close friend, who is not Christian, as well as family members who do not share her faith. Lily is less parochial in her attitude toward non-Christians, though no less committed to Christian values. Among Lily's church friends, the authors present a variety of individuals, from the dorky through the sophisticated, reflecting the fact that Christians are as varied in personality as their secular counterparts. The various crises Lily experiences in the novel could be experienced by any young woman in American culture, Christian or not—establishing a life independent of family, dating, and finding Mr. Right—the basic challenges of chick lit in general. Lily's transformation from tomboy ugly duckling to trendy swan is a universal story that can cross over and be read profitably by Christian and non-Christian alike. Moreover, since Lily remains committed to her Christian beliefs but not obsessed by church, she is a heroine whose narrative can evangelize, inspiring both believers and nonbelievers. It remains to be seen whether this subgenre will provide evangelical publishers with their desired cross over to mainstream readers.

What's Wrong with Christian Fiction?

This most recent phenomenon in Christian fiction also offers an opportunity to reflect on the criticism of this genre, criticism that indicates a limited understanding of the history of literature. Frederick Buechner and other writers whose work is nourished by religious concerns eschew the label "Christian writer" because of prerequisites of the genre. What is disdained is the agenda-driven fiction that has long been characteristic of the Christian novel because didacticism is considered inimical to the novel as an art form. Buechner has commented, "I lean over backward not to preach in my novels, because that would make for neither good novels nor good preaching."[60] Buechner's comment is relevant because of his unspoken but clearly held definition of what makes a "good" novel.

As a literary form, the novel is the most familiar to contemporary readers, but in the history of literature, it is also the most recently established genre, a child of the Enlightenment that developed in English in the last half of the eighteenth century. And as a product of the post-Enlightenment worldview, the novel, like the society in which it developed, is considered a form fueled by reason and liberated from the tyranny of religion or any authority that seeks to dominate the individual. From this perspective, the term "Christian novel" would be a contradiction in terms. However, the novel as a genre is a product of a long tradition in narrative, story telling being the most ancient art form. And the initial purpose of narrative in society was to provide support for that society's beliefs. In fact, it took a while for the novel to be liberated from the demand that fiction provide instruction. For example, except for the name of the heroine, the title page of

Samuel Richardson's *Pamela,* published in 1740 and considered one of the earliest novels in English, could be used without any change on the title page of *Consider Lily*:

Pamela, or Virtue Rewarded—Now first published in order to cultivate the Principles of Virtue and Religion in the Minds of the Youth of Both Sexes. A narrative which has the Foundation in Truth and Nature, and at the same time that it agreeably entertains.[61]

Prior to the paradigm shift of the Enlightenment, literature was *expected* to promote "virtue and religion." In fact, the origins of drama in the English language are rooted in the medieval miracle and morality plays which were written to instruct the substantially illiterate populace in Christian doctrine (miracle plays) and behavior (morality plays) in a manner that was both entertaining and instructive.

Since the basis of Christianity is a belief in a reality that supersedes that of the individual, committed Christians participate in the traditional or classical paradigm rather than the modern one. It is thus understandable that their fiction would reflect that paradigm and seek to both entertain and instruct, to "cultivate the principles of virtue and religion" among readers. The enormous sales that this literature generates confirm that its readers are seeking literature that accords with their worldview. Thus, complaints that Christian fiction is too restrictive or dogmatic in its presentation of "reality" fail to consider that its reality is consistent with the life experiences of its readers. Perhaps Christian fiction engenders such antagonism because although it derives its meaning from the classical paradigm, its sales reflect success in the modern world. In fact, that very success seems to indicate that it has an appeal beyond conservative Christians and is read by those who are often identified as either individualists who do not belong to any church or "seekers" who dabble in a variety of religious traditions. Christian fiction may be providing succor for many Americans who long for the certitude of the classical paradigm and are uncomfortable with the dominant culture today.

However, the blockbuster in terms of sales in Christian fiction is a very different subgenre from the dominantly romantic fiction discussed in this chapter. The Left Behind series is an industry unto itself, and in the next chapter, we will consider the meaning of this phenomenon in contemporary American society.

Notes

1. "Profits From Christian Books Make Believers of Top Publishers," at http://www.bloomberg.com/apps/news?pid=20601088&sid;=aFZKuWjSOYmE&refer;=home, July 25, 2006 (accessed August 1, 2006).

2. Ibid.

3. Reader review from Amazon.com dated October 30, 2003 (accessed September 26, 2006).

4. Ibid.

5. William Symonds, Brian Grow, and John Cady, "Earthly Empires," *Business Week Online,* May 23, 2005, http://www.businessweek.com/magazine/content/05_21/b3934001_mz001.htm (accessed September 25, 2006).

6. This well-known incident is summarized at http://en.wikipedia.org/wiki/The_Purpose_Driven_Life.

7. Symonds, Grow, and Cady, "Earthly Empires."

8. Ibid.

9. Ibid.

10. Tyrone Beason, "Retailers are Riding the Wave of Popularity of Christian-Themes Books," *Seattle Times,* August 16, 2004, http://archives.seattletimes.nwsource.com/cgi-bin/texis.cgi/web/vortex/search?c=0&skip=0&query=Tyrone+Beason&zsectionID=099496800.=range&start_month=08&start_day=01&start_year=2004&end_month=08&end_day=30&end_year=2004&searchType=date&Search.x=24&Search.y=9 (accessed September 23, 2006).

11. Evangelical Christian Publishers Association, http://www.ecpa.org/pr/pr.php?id=76 (accessed August 24, 2006).

12. W. Dale Brown, ed., *Of Fiction and Faith: Twelve American Writers Talk about Their Vision and Work* (Grand Rapids, MI: William B. Eerdmans Publishing Company, 1997), 215.

13. Ibid., 35.

14. Jay Dolan, *The American Catholic Experience* (New York: Doubleday and Company, Inc., 1985), 127–8.

15. Will Herberg, *Protestant-Catholic-Jew: An Essay in American Religious Sociology* (Garden City, NY: Anchor, 1955), 39.

16. Ibid., 215.

17. Paul R. Messbarger, *Fiction with a Parochial Purpose: Social Uses of American Catholic Literature, 1884-1900* (Boston: Boston University Press, 1971), 20.

18. See Chapter 3 for an explanation of this change in the years following *Roe v. Wade.*

19. Robert Wuthnow, *The Restructuring of American Religion: Society and Faith Since World War II* (New Jersey: Princeton University Press, 1988), 185.

20. Janice Radway, *Reading the Romance: Women, Patriarchy, and Popular Literature* (Chapel Hill: University of North Carolina Press, 1991), 30–1.

21. Ibid., 31.

22. Ibid., 33–4.

23. From 1974 with his first novel *Carrie,* King published nine of his most famous novels in the years immediately prior to the publication of Peretti's *This Present Darkness* in 1985.

24. *Salem's Lot* at http://en.wikipedia.org/wiki/Salem's_Lot (accessed September 23, 2006).

25. Sharon Waxman, "Fox Unveils a Division for Religious-Oriented Films," *New York Times,* September 20, 2006, E1.

26. More direct evidence to Hollywood producers of the strong Christian market was the surprisingly huge success of Mel Gibson's *The Passion of the Christ* in 2004, a film that was so vociferously derided by the liberal press that Hollywood expected it to fail and could not help but be impressed by its success based in the support of conservative Christians.

27. Listing at www.christyawards.com (accessed September 18, 2006).

28. Cleanth Brooks, *Community, Religion, and Literature* (Columbia: University of Missouri Press, 1995), 212.

29. Wuthnow, *America and the Challenges of Religious Diversity* (Princeton and Oxford: Princeton University Press, 2005), 185.

30. Janette Oke, *Love Comes Softly* (1979; repr., Minneapolis, MN: Bethany House Publishers, 2003), preface.

31. Christine Camella, "Parasocial Relationships in Female College Student Soap Opera Viewers Today" at http://people.wcsu.edu/mccarneyh/acad/Camella.html (accessed September 30, 2006).

32. Radway, *Reading the Romance,* 195–6.

33. Ibid., 109.

34. Camella, "Parasocial Relationships in Female College Student Soap Opera Viewers Today."

35. From the ACFW (American Christian Fiction Writers) web site at http:www.acfw.com (accessed September 26, 2006).

36. The terms "inspirational" and "life-changing" are regularly encountered in promotions of this fiction, and one author, Karen Kingsway, has actually trademarked the term "life-changing fiction" for her work.

37. Monique El-Faizy, *God and Country: How Evangelicals Have Become America's New Mainstream* (New York: Bloomsbury, 2006), 7.

38. At http://www.redeeminglovenovel.com/ (accessed September 25, 2006).

39. Quoted from http://www.karenkingbury.com/karensJournal/ (accessed September 25, 2006).

40. Ibid.

41. El-Faizy, *God and Country,* 128–32.

42. Ibid., 132.

43. Jan Karon's web site is at http://www.mitfordbooks.com (accessed January 8, 2007).

44. Karen Kingsbury, *Fame* (Wheaton, IL: Tyndale House Publishers, Inc., 2005), 171.

45. Radway, *Reading the Romance,* 84.

46. Ibid., 111–2.

47. Quotations are from reader reviews posted on Amazon.com. I have found such reviews to be an excellent way to sample reader reaction to authors' work, especially since those who like the fiction are as likely to post reviews as those who dislike it. Many of these reviews are very specific in providing reasons for their preferences.

48. Quoted by Amazon.com in editorial reviews of Henderson's *The Protector.*

49. Dee Henderson, "How To Write a Good Story," April 26, 2001, http://www.likesbooks.com/sb30.html (accessed September 27, 2006).

50. "Young Adult Literature" at http://en.wikipedia.org/wiki/Young_adult_literature (accessed September 29, 2006).

51. S.E. Hinton, http://www.sehinton.com/ (accessed September 24, 2006).

52. American Library Association, "The 100 Most Frequently Challenged Books of 1990–2000," http://www.ala.org/ala/oif/bannedbooksweek/bbwlinks/100mostfrequently.htm (accessed January 11, 2007).

53. Laurie Goldstein, "Fearing the Loss of Teenagers, Evangelicals Turn Up the Fire," *New York Times,* October 6, 2006, A1 and A20. In this article about a survey indicating that evangelicals may be in danger of losing a larger percentage of their teenagers, a leading sociologist, Christian Smith of the University of Notre Dame, counters that the reality

is that "when it comes to organizing youth, evangelical Christians are the envy of Roman Catholics, mainline Protestants and Jews."

54. From http://christymillerandfriends.com/author.aspx (accessed September 29, 2006).

55. Deidre Donahue, "Publishers put their faith in churchified 'chick lit,'" *USA Today,* http://www.usatoday.com/life/books/news/2003-10-29-church-lit_x.htm (accessed September 26, 2006).

56. Ibid.

57. Anne Dayton and May Vanderbilt, http://www.goodgirllit.com/Good%20 Girls.html (accessed September 26, 2006).

58. Krista Eccleston, "Onward Christian Chick Lit," *New York Daily News,* June 26, 2005, http://www.nydailynews.com/entertainment/v-pfriendly/story/322225p-275411 c.html (accessed September 26, 2006).

59. Ramona Richards, "Redeeming 'Chick Lit,'" *Christianity Today,* http://www.christianitytoday.com/tcw/2004/005/3.50.html (accessed September 28, 2006).

60. Quoted in William Zinsser, ed., *Spiritual Quests: The Art and Craft of Religious Writing* (Boston: Houghton Mifflin Company, 1988), 13.

61. Original front page reproduced in Samuel Richardson, *Pamela or, Virtue Rewarded,* ed. T.C. Duncan Eaves and Ben D. Kimpel (Boston: Houghton Mifflin Company, 1971).

5

The Left Behind Phenomenon

Would you know how to discern these signs, there are myriads of books upon the market today which will help you.

—Sydney Watson

Christian fiction is not only populated by the competent novels of Janette Oke, Francine Rivers, and other writers discussed in the preceding chapter, it is a mecca for the amateur. The ACFW (American Christian Fiction Writers) is a group that exists, in part, to nurture fledgling authors; as they explain in their mission statement, the rise of this genre has "birthed" many new writers.[1] Frank Peretti, who, along with Janette Oke, is credited with affirming the viability of the Christian fiction market, represents that type of author, and his immediate success with his first novel suggests that artistry is not a requirement for a high volume of sales in this market. As with any best seller, the book primarily has to appeal to a significant number of readers.

Peretti's *This Present Darkness* apparently took Christian readers by storm and helped usher in the current vogue for Christian fiction.[2] However, the novel reflects the work of the amateur writer, not uncommon in Christian fiction, and exhibits all the warts of his inexperience. Interestingly, although Christian fiction has significantly improved, *This Present Darkness* continues to be lauded by readers on Amazon.com, most of whom give it five stars, the highest rating, and enthuse about its excellence. Yet the novel surely is the type of fiction that evangelical publishers have been trying to surmount for some time, filled with turgid prose, stereotypical characters, and plodding narration interspersed with scenes of violent battles. Since it's a novel about spiritual warfare, of the suspense/thriller subgenre, the awkwardly constructed narrative is especially problematic, as this is a subgenre that relies on a coherent and fluent narrative for its success with readers.

The excellent sales of *This Present Darkness* despite its literary flaws illustrate some important points about both best sellers and Christian fiction. Peretti's success indicates that believers will accept poorly written novels if the books meet their personal needs, and a key to the sales of *This Present Darkness* is enabling evangelicals to read a type of fiction that would be proscribed if authored by the master of the genre, Stephen King. The theme of spiritual warfare enables Peretti to transcend the strictures of evangelical fiction, allowing his readers to wallow in brutality, violence, and tales of rape and incest because they are related to "spiritual" warfare. Thus, conservative readers who would be affronted by King's novels of the supernatural can assuage their thirst for horror and suspense with fiction that carries the evangelical imprimatur.

As is standard in the classic horror novel, the fiction taps into its readers' fears. It is commonplace to observe that in the classic horror novel of nineteenth-century English literature, Bram Stoker's *Dracula,* the dreaded vampire arriving from Transylvania is a metaphor for the Victorians' social and political anxieties, among them a concern about the industrialization of society and the effects of the Age of Reason.[3] Hence, while *This Present Darkness* is apparently concerned with the spiritual war with Satan, his human minions have embraced New Age Spirituality which, at the time of the novel's composition, was the trendy choice for many spiritual seekers. This association of New Age Spirituality with the forces of darkness is natural for evangelicals, since the New Age movement developed as a critique of Christianity. Evangelicals would have a natural antipathy toward New Agers, not only because the latter consider Christianity no longer viable but also because they compete to convert the same population of spiritual seekers.

Peretti's novel vividly reflects the belief among conservative Christians in a well-organized, secret New Age organization actively seeking to take over the country by infiltrating the government as well as schools and churches.[4] This belief animates *This Present Darkness.* In the fictional town of Ashton that is under attack from these forces of darkness, the female villain is a college professor, the lackey of the New Age organization's corporate leader, and the liberal Christian church has already been compromised, its pastor spouting New Age spirituality in his sermons. Naturally, the forces of good triumph, led by a conservative Christian pastor, well-schooled in intercessory prayer, and the local newspaper editor who becomes his ally.

However, the novel's tale of a town being taken over by the New Age forces of evil is only a thinly disguised metaphor for the conservative Christian sense of their country being taken over by godless humanism that denies students the right to pray in school and allows the abortion of innocent children. As with *Dracula,* the apparent evil in the fiction represents a larger evil that must remain unnamed. It is likely that this association was unintended serendipity for the inexperienced Peretti, who has benefited from the incredible sales of his rather mediocre book. The continued popularity of *This Present Darkness* can be attributed to evangelicals' desire to believe that the righteous ultimately will win the day in America as they do in Ashton. It's a novel that taps into conservative Christians' fear of encroaching secularism and assuages that fear with a story of Christianity triumphant.

While conservative Christians may relish this story of good vanquishing evil, there has been significant concern among evangelicals with Peretti's alleged errors in depicting spiritual warfare.[5] Without detailing the charges, I mention this solely to indicate evangelicals' awareness of the power of fiction to affect belief. Most consumers of popular fiction are unsophisticated readers and easily conflate fact and fiction. Conservative Christian leaders obviously feared that such readers would absorb Peretti's account of spiritual warfare as an orthodox presentation of Biblical truth. From a brief scan of the laudatory reader reviews on Amazon.com, it would seem that their concerns are well founded.

Twenty-one years later, the Left Behind phenomenon began, a series of novels that are the descendents of *This Present Darkness* in the subgenre of Christian spiritual suspense fiction that portrays the warfare between good and evil. The overwhelming sales of the Left Behind books highlight some of the same principles that contributed to the success of Peretti's pioneering work. When writing in this subgenre, tapping into people's fears is far more profitable than producing competent prose.

With a sales estimate of 65 million, the Left Behind series provokes the same question as *The DaVinci Code*—what accounts for this incredible volume of sales? As noted in Chapter 2, best-selling fiction is rarely a result of aesthetic excellence. To appeal to such a large number of readers, the fiction must some-how touch on the *Zeitgeist,* the intellectual and cultural climate of the times, and thereby appeal to a wide range of readers. In considering the enormous popularity of the Left Behind series, however, it is helpful first to establish the nature of the fiction involved in these books.

The Books

Authored by Jerry Jenkins and Tim LaHaye, the Left Behind series is composed of twelve novels that depict the end of the world from a specific perspective that is not shared with mainline Christian churches. Known as "pre-tribulation" escha-tology, it contrasts with the more orthodox version of the end times known as "post-tribulation." The Tribulation is the period of suffering that supposedly precedes the Second Coming of Christ, an event which announces the world's end. In the post-tribulation version of this event, when Jesus descends from heaven, the elect on earth, those Christians who are deemed faithful and worthy, will be gathered to meet Him in the air. This is known as the Rapture. Then the whole gathering, angels and saints, are revealed to the world along with its Savior.

In the pre-tribulation version, the Rapture occurs before the period of Tribula-tion, thus saving the elect from the suffering that will be visited on the earth during the period of Tribulation when the Antichrist tries to dominate the world. Shortly after this Rapture, when the true Christians vanish from their homes and families, the Antichrist begins his work on earth, ushering in a seven-year period of Tribulation. The series authored by LaHaye and Jenkins begins with the Rapture in early pages of the first novel, *Left Behind: A Novel of the Earth's Last Days,* and extends through the final book, *Glorious Appearing: The End of Days,* that describes the coming of Christ to vanquish the Antichrist and begin his millennial reign on earth. Since the authors have already published additional novels as "prequels" to the series, it is doubtful that the end is yet in sight. There may be many more episodes remaining in this marketing marvel. Without debating the theological core narrative of the Left Behind series, it is necessary to clarify its specific "pre-trib" eschatology.

This pre-trib version of the end times is the basis for the narrative core of the Left Behind novels. Historically, this pre-tribulational (also known as pre-millennial) eschatology that locates the Rapture prior to the period of Tribulation has been almost exclusively believed by evangelicals and rejected by most main-stream Christian denominations. They adhere to the post-tribulation version that locates the Rapture at the time of the appearance of Christ, following the Tribula-tion. However, the version of the end times that the majority of Christians embrace may change in the future, given the power of fiction, as more and more readers may come to accept the orthodoxy of the Jenkins/LaHaye version of the demise of our world through reading these books. A cover story in *Time* magazine in 2002 reported that only about half of the readers of the Left Behind series are evangelicals, so the pre-trib version of the apocalypse may be more widely held than ever before.[6] In fact, the plethora of challenges to the Left Behind eschatol-ogy, mainly from Roman Catholics, suggests that mainline denominations are concerned with the effect on belief of their adherents' casual reading of these novels.[7] After all, the average reader cannot understand the arcane Book of Revelation which is the alleged source of these novels, so Left Behind readers can easily accept the LaHaye/Jenkins version of the end times as authoritative, especially since Tim LaHaye promotes his Left Behind books as a virtual transcription of the Book of Revelation.

Christian fiction is often criticized for promoting an agenda, and no fiction is more agenda-driven than the Left Behind series, since it was clearly conceived to popularize the pre-tribulational eschatology for which LaHaye is a major pro-ponent. Almost all sources credit the full development of the pre-tribulation version of the end times to John Nelson Darby, a nineteenth-century, evangelical preacher in England. While Darby mainly synthesized elements from earlier thinkers, one of his contributions was to position the Rapture well before the com-ing of Christ as the first of the various phases that preface the Second Coming. At this moment of Rapture, all true Christians are taken up to heaven and disappear from the earth. Those "left behind" are required to endure the period of Tribula-tion before the final advent of the Savior in His Second Coming. It is interesting to note, in light of the tradition of horror fiction to address readers' primal fears, that one commentator connects Darby's end times theology to that fictional genre, asserting that they derive from a similar impulse:

Darby devised his complicated system at roughly the same time as the horror novel was coming to prominence in England, and both stem from a distrust of reason, science, and the mechanization of society. Both, with their turning to the supernatural or fantastic, were in some part a reaction to the industrial revolution and the Age of Reason.[8]

What cemented Darby's theory in America was a core group of evangelicals who embraced his pre-millennial dispensationalism (the formal term for the pre-trib eschatology). Paramount among them was C.I. Scofield, who edited a Bible in which he footnoted the text to accord with Darby's pre-tribulational views. This *Scofield Reference Bible,* originally published in 1909, became the most popular Bible among evangelicals for the next sixty years, and its readers thus absorbed pre-millennialism as authoritative.[9]

However, in the second half of the twentieth century, the increase in educational opportunities resulted in more scholarly study of Scripture, which called pre-millennialism into question. There was a trend among evangelicals toward the post-tribulation perspective that correlates the Rapture with the appearance of Jesus, considered not only to be more authentically Biblical but also more in accord with the belief of the early church.[10] Concerned by the shift away from what he believed to be the authentic Christian eschatology of pre-tribulationism, Dr. Tim LaHaye published a book on the Rapture in 1992, *No Fear of the Storm.* The following year, he helped found a PTSG (Pre-Trib Study Group) of prophecy scholars and authors, and in 1993, he helped form the PTRC (Pre-Trib Research Center) to encourage "research, teaching, propagation, and defense of the pretribulational rapture and related Bible prophecy doctrines."[11] Within two years, the first novel of the Left Behind series appeared, surely LaHaye's most successful propagation of the pre-trib concept. Thus, the immediate purpose of the Left Behind novels was to reinforce the authority of pre-tribulationism, much as the *Scofield Reference Bible* had done in the preceding era.

In developing the Left Behind series, the authors make no secret of the fact that LaHaye initiated the project and contributed an outline of the events for each novel. Tim LeHaye's web site announces that he "conceived the idea of fictionalizing an account of the Rapture and the Tribulation while sitting on airplanes and watching the pilots. He would think to himself, 'What if the Rapture occurred while flying on an airplane?'"[12] And that provided the opening scene for the first novel, *Left Behind: A Novel of the Earth's Last Days,* which takes place on an airplane, and its pilot becomes the protagonist of the series. Interestingly, in a *Newsweek* story about his successful series, LaHaye's inspiration is described as much closer to the opening scene in his novel:

On an airplane he noticed a pilot, wearing a wedding ring, flirting with a flight attendant. What if this were the moment God had picked to Rapture the faithful, leaving behind only their clothes and a lot of bewildered unbelievers?[13]

One wonders whether the less sexually charged version of inspiration on his official web site is an example of LaHaye accommodating his conservative Christian audience.

Whatever the immediate occasion for conceiving the Left Behind series, LaHaye most certainly would have been aware of the fact that fictionalizing the events of the final days has been a common practice throughout the twentieth century. As Crawford Gribben noted in the evangelical publication *Books and Culture,* end-times fictions have been a feature of evangelicalism throughout the twentieth century with writers rewriting the apocalypse in light of various social and political concerns.[14] And it would be surprising if LaHaye were not familiar with an end-times novel published just two years before the Left Behind series began. *The Third Millennium* by Paul Meier, a psychiatrist publishing his first novel, is a one-volume version of the events chronicled in the entire Left Behind series, from Rapture through Tribulation to the Second Coming of Christ.[15] It is unlikely that LaHaye was unaware of Meier's novel, since both men have been associated with Dallas Theological Seminary and the Biblical prophecy *cognoscenti.*

Ironically, Meier's novel is probably more difficult to slog through than the entire twelve volumes of the Left Behind series, given *The Third Millennium*'s turgid prose and pervasive melodrama. The novel's narrator is an angel, the guardian of the protagonists, a nonobservant Jewish family in California. The serious limitations in technique in Meier's novel would have signaled to LaHaye the importance of a collaborator capable of rendering more polished prose if he wanted to reach a significant audience. But Meier's novel also shows that there is no necessity for a series in depicting the pre-trib end times. The choice of multiple novels, along with the claim of originality, reflects shrewd marketing, helping to establish the brand that is responsible for the enormous sales of the Left Behind books.

With Jerry Jenkins, an experienced writer, as the storyteller, the Left Behind novels follow a core group of characters who are not raptured: the airline pilot Rayford Steele and his college-age daughter Chloe; Rayford's flight attendant, Hattie Durham; and a celebrated journalist, Cameron (Buck) Williams. The Steele father and daughter and Williams soon become ardent Christians and eventually form the core of the Tribulation Force, also the title of the second novel in the series. Through the coincidence of a heavily manipulated plot, Steele, Williams, and Durham all become closely associated with the Antichrist, but only the good guys, Steele and Williams, know his true identity for most of the narrative. Steele and Williams engage in cliff-hanging escapades, and the books are replete with gore and violence normally unacceptable in Christian fiction but here apparently rationalized as consistent with the Biblical imagery in the Book of Revelation.

The Appeal of Left Behind

Following the genre of the political thriller, the Left Behind novels are, like *The Da Vinci Code,* easy reading, plot-driven, "page-turners" that engage the reader. This is the first element in their success, the ability to involve readers in the sensational plot. As one commentator noted, since conservative Christians still deny themselves the novels of Stephen King in fear of their suspected occultism, the Left Behind series provides the satisfactions of the horror story in acceptably orthodox fiction.[16] Frank Peretti's *The Present Darkness* had provided that satisfaction for Christian readers in the 1980s, and the popularity of Peretti's fiction demonstrated that there was a strong market for fiction of spiritual warfare among conservative Christians. Thus, a major factor in the initial success of the Left Behind books is that, like Peretti's fiction, they allow conservative Christian readers to experience the thrill of a type of fiction normally unavailable to them.

Under the guise of Christian fiction, Jenkins can indulge in all sorts of violence because he has a Biblical source to justify the gore. Ironically, however, the conservative strictures on sex *are* observed to the extent that readers are expected to believe that the journalist, Buck Williams, a thirty-year-old man and a professional who has been immersed in America's secular culture and has had a high-profile, international career with all the associations that such celebrity entails, is also a virgin. This is apparently necessary to insure that his post-conversion romance is pure. Apparently, by accommodating conservative Christian readers in such details, the authors can indulge in their Scripture-based violence, allowing readers to satisfy their appetite for such fiction, since it is "Biblical" violence.

Timing of publication was a significant factor in the popularity of the Left Behind books, as it was for its end-times predecessor in popularity, Hal Lindsey's nonfiction narrative of the end times, *The Late Great Planet Earth,* the nonfiction best seller of the 1970s. As Nancy Gibbs points out in her *Time* article on the Left Behind series,

Lindsey's explanation of the Bible's warnings came just as a backlash was stirring against '60s liberalism, an echo of the 18th century reaction to the Enlightenment. Lindsey caught the moment that launched a decade of evangelical resurgence, when for the first time in generations believers organized to put their stamp on this world, rather than the next.[17]

Similarly, the timing of publication surely contributed to the success of Left Behind because a sense of impending doom always fosters sales of apocalyptic fiction. Whether pre-tribulation or post-tribulation, all Christian eschatologies focus on the catastrophic events that mark the end time, and it is natural for people to think of the end when confronted with extreme events. For example, *Time* magazine reported that Left Behind sales increased 60% after the tragedy of 9/11, and Book 9 in the series, published in October of that year, was the best-selling novel of 2001.[18] Similarly, when the first novel in the series appeared in 1995, the American public had been primed by events of the preceding five years—the Gulf War and unsettled conditions in that region, the first attack on the World Trade Center, and the Oklahoma City bombing, domestic terrorism on a previously unimagined scale. And 1995 was also the year in which the federal government partially shut down twice in two months because of disputes over the federal budget. The latest closure was still going on at year's end.

The unsettling nature of the times provides an ideal opportunity for the appearance of apocalyptic fiction. This was also evident in sales of Hal Lindsey's book. During the early 1990s because of the Gulf War and people's fears that Saddam Hussein would create additional conflict in that region, publishers reported an 83% increase in sales of *The Late Great Planet Earth*.[19] This was despite Lindsey's prediction of the world's end in the 1980s, a prophecy that detracted from the overall credibility of his work. Thus, in 1995, the doom-focused reading public was primed to turn to a more readable version of the apocalypse in the pulp fiction of Jenkins and LaHaye.

As noted in Chapter 4, novels in a series tend to engage readers who identify with a small group of characters and want to follow them through their adventures, much as television soap opera viewers become engaged with their characters. The decision by Jenkins and LaHaye to tell the story of end times in a series of novels rather than in a single work, as Meier did, would promote reader engagement and subsequent sales. However, Left Behind differs somewhat from the typical series novels that populate Christian fiction. Despite the fact that Jenkins is quoted as claiming that readers are involved with his characters, the engagement of Left Behind readers is less with the remarkably plastic characters than with the unfolding events of cliff-hanging suspense.[20] It is not the nature of the thriller to create nuanced characters, but Steele and Williams are particularly flat. They function solely as the "good guys" who oppose the ultimate "bad guy," the Antichrist. Less interested in these specific characters' adventures, the readers of Left Behind are eager to explore the events that will mark the demise of civilization. Even those who know the basic outline of the pre-tribulation apocalypse would be eager to see how this scenario of the end times occurs in actual events. This is the latest incarnation of the perennial human quest to know the future, and LaHaye and Jenkins profess to be presenting an accurate future.

It seems from the success of the Left Behind books and readers' reviews on Amazon.com that the ultimate series is one that promises to describe for them what will actually occur at the end of this world, and that's what readers believe they are learning from Jenkins and LaHaye. And one can't entirely blame unsophisticated readers for this misunderstanding of the nature of fiction, since LaHaye clearly believes that's what he's doing when he comments in an interview, "We are using fiction to teach biblical *truth*."[21] What keeps readers coming back to purchase the next installment seems to be a desire to know that ultimate ending. In response to the second book, *Tribulation Force,* one Amazon.com reader commented on April 21, 2006, that the novel keeps you "on the edge of your seat" and that he "could not put it down" because of wanting to know "whats [*sic*] going to happen." Another reader, reviewing the eighth book in the series, *The Mark* on October 8, 2005, comments that despite the fact that he only gave the novel two stars, "If you plan to continue the series to its conclusion, as I do, you will need to read it. It introduces new characters and sets up some of the next events." In other words, despite the poor quality of the prose, that readers frequently mention, people keep buying the novels because they are under the impression that they will learn how this world will end.

The frequent confusion of fiction with reality that is always a danger with unsophisticated readers is one of the factors in sales of the Left Behind books. As was noted in *Time* in its 2002 cover story on the Left Behind phenomenon, many people read the books "not as novels but as tomorrow's newspapers."[22] One appeal of the series is surely that the novels are a lot easier to read than the Bible, especially Revelation, the book that Left Behind claims as the source of its eschatology. Describing the average evangelical Christian, the writer Joe Bageant says,

We are talking about a group of Americans 20% of whose children graduate from high school identifying H2O as a cable channel. Children who, like their parents and grandparents, come from that roughly half of all Americans who can approximately read, but are dysfunctionally literate to the extent they cannot grasp any textual abstraction or overall thematic content.[23]

While Bageant, who comes from an evangelical background, may be considered excessively cynical, the Left Behind novels are obviously written for the most unsophisticated reader. There is no need for reader inference in the Left Behind books. In true "techno-thriller" form, the novels are fast-paced, with the exception of the various sermons that pepper the text. However, Jenkins is adept at keeping the reader involved by pacing the action to compensate for the sermonizing. As one Amazon.com reader summarized, writing about the second book in the series in a review dated August 29, 2005, "It is a fun easy read and the subject matter is fascinating in its own right." We know that readers of popular fiction enjoy gaining knowledge or information, and that is a major attraction for readers of this series. Most of the Left Behind readers believe that they are learning the *facts* about the end of the world from these novels.

For evangelical readers, the Left Behind series offers even more special knowledge. While the Bible is the source of ultimate meaning for evangelicals, the Book of Revelation is difficult to interpret, challenging even to scholars, so it's impenetrable to the average reader. The Left Behind books purport to provide the average evangelical with the key to the meaning of this Biblical text. Thus, the knowledge gained from the series far surpasses the typical knowledge prized by readers of popular fiction. For the evangelical reader, the series is Biblical interpretation in a format that is easily accessible. What they are gaining, they believe, is not simply ordinary knowledge, but Biblical truth.

The appeal of this "truth" is that it affirms evangelical Christians in ways otherwise unavailable in this culture, and that accounts to a large extent for the incredible sales of this series. As a group that feels marginalized in contemporary American culture, evangelicals would delight in a version of the end times that begins with the Rapture. This is when they will all presumably leave the earth, enabling them to not only avoid the calamities of the Tribulation but the physical experience of death as well, something fearful to human beings regardless of their confidence in an afterlife. Moreover, the Rapture assures evangelicals that in true Biblical fashion, the current "first" in American culture will be "last." *They* will be the "first" who are immediately transported to Heaven as a reward for their faithfulness. The impulse to convey this message to as many fellow believers as possible surely helped develop word-of-mouth for the initial novel, *Left Behind: A Novel of the Earth's Last Days,* and has contributed to the success of the entire series.

Moreover, the authors have provided evangelicals with the satisfaction of seeing their current antagonists metaphorically converted to belief in conservative Christianity. Each of the protagonists in the novels not only represents secular American culture, there are also some specific types involved. The pilot Rayford Steele represents every spouse who has been unsympathetic to his wife or husband's religious zeal. Steele has ignored his wife's attempts to involve him in her church; he even justifies his flirtation with the flight attendant, Hattie Durham, as resulting from what he initially calls his wife's obsession with religion. In the process of his eventual conversion, he expresses regret at the way he had ignored his wife and almost committed adultery. Christian men or women whose spouses do not share their zeal can experience satisfaction in knowing that their spouse will eventually regret that attitude of disinterest in Christianity, just as Steele repents in the fiction.

After his conversion, Steele experiences frustration with his daughter Chloe who resists his pleas for her to attend church with him. In his concern, Steele reflects the anxieties of religious parents who see their children seduced by secular culture. And Chloe, who eventually responds to her father's entreaties and prayers, is the wish-fulfillment fantasy child of all religious parents as she finally embraces Christianity wholeheartedly. Finally, Buck Williams, the premier journalist, represents the media that evangelicals perceive as biased against religion. As Buck perches on the brink of faith, he thinks, "Was it possible? Could he be on the cusp of becoming a born-again Christian"? And the narrative continues,

Buck had read and even written about "those kinds" of people, but even at his level of worldly wisdom he had never quite understood the phrase. He had always considered the "born-again" label akin to "ultraright-winger" or "fundamentalist."[24]

Buck realizes that if he takes the leap into faith, "he would also take upon himself a task: educating the world on what that confusing little term really meant."[25] Thus, Christians have the satisfaction of knowing that those who are currently antagonistic to the truth of Christianity will be its apologists, as happens in this idealized conversion narrative. As one commentator noted, "Seeing the self-defeating delusions of erstwhile elites exposed may be the greatest pleasure the Left Behind books offer their readers."[26]

Moreover, as a result of Buck's eventual conversion, he loses his powerful position as a prestigious journalist and is exiled from New York, the epicenter of elitism, to the Chicago office to toil for an inept editor who despises him. Buck, as emblematic of the media elite, is necessarily humbled and forced to undergo personal trials, providing satisfaction for conservative Christian readers. As the conservative columnist Cal Thomas has observed of the Left Behind books,

This is intellectual comfort food, the whole Left Behind phenomenon, because it says to people, in a popularized way, it's all going to pan out in the end....It assures them, in the midst of a general cultural breakdown and a time of growing danger, that God is going to redeem the time.[27]

The authors, however, didn't rely on simply publishing these books in order to assure evangelicals that all will be well; they created the ultimate brand, seeming to hold the patent on the end times. With the cooperation of publisher Tyndale, the Left Behind series has become synonymous with the apocalypse. First, of course, was the decision to develop a series rather than fictionalize the pre-trib eschatology in a single novel. In addition, LaHaye's comments are always designed to suggest that he originated the concept of fictionalizing the end times. On the Left Behind web site, both statements about the origins of the series imply that the idea of novels depicting the apocalypse originated with LaHaye. An introduction to the authors states that "it was LaHaye's idea to fictionalize an account of the Rapture and the Tribulation."[28] This could mean that it was LaHaye's contribution to the collaboration with Jenkins, but the phrasing implies that this idea simply came to him without knowledge of any prior fiction on this topic. The classic explanation that LaHaye offers at every interview is stated both on the Left Behind web site and on LaHaye's own personal web site; he was simply sitting on an airplane and "watching the pilots" when the thought occurred to him, "What if the Rapture occurred on an airplane?" This description is prefaced by the statement, "LaHaye originated the idea of a novel about the Second Coming," strongly suggesting that the idea was original.[29] It seems inconceivable that LaHaye, the major proponent of the pre-tribulation apocalypse today, would be unaware of the various novels that have fictionalized this version of the end times throughout the twentieth century.

It not only would be difficult for LaHaye to be unaware of Paul Meier's *The Third Millennium* but there also have been other well-known pre-trib novels that must have come to his attention. The ancestor of pre-trib fiction writers seems to be Sydney Watson, a British author who published three novels of the end times in the early part of the twentieth century. His *In the Twinkling of an Eye* is actually closer to the inspirational novel that Christian fiction tries to achieve, rather than the fear-mongering so characteristic of Left Behind. *In the Twinkling of an Eye* closes with the Rapture, and it introduces several characters whose spiritual development creates the novel's narrative interest, leading to their eventual disappearance at the moment of Rapture.

Watson's major character is a journalist, Tom Hammond, and in a 2003 essay in *Books and Culture,* Crawford Gribben suggests that Left Behind's Buck William is very close to Watson's character in several details.[30] And in a 2004 article in the *National Review,* Carl Olson compares the Left Behind novels to Salem Kirban's novel *666,* published in 1970, showing even more remarkable similarities in the plot and characters of the Jenkins/LaHaye work.[31] The similarities that Olson describes are too close to be coincidences; Jenkins appears to have simply made two characters, Steele and Williams, from Kirban's journalist protagonist. Thus, far from being unaware of their predecessors in apocalyptic fiction, Jenkins and LaHaye appear to be quite familiar with their work.

Since the Left Behind web site creates a monument to pre-trib eschatology, citing a variety of series that have emerged to parallel the Left Behind books, it seems strange that nowhere do LaHaye and Jenkins mention these earlier apocalyptic novels. By intimating that Left Behind is the original fictional treatment of the end times, LaHaye corners the market, as it were, on this subject. And by means of the extensive series of novels, the authors multiply their sales to monumental proportions. Imagine what Dan Brown's sales would have been had he extended *The Da Vinci Code* to a series.

But Left Behind is more than a series of twelve books and even more than the additional "prequels" that the authors are churning out. A check of the Left Behind web site shows an additional ten "graphic novels," those comic book versions that will surely appeal to more challenged readers, a "military series" by another author, Mel Odom, that parallels the action of Left Behind with a focus on how the military deals with the Rapture and subsequent events of the Tribulation. Then there's a "political series" by Neesa Hart that depicts the situation in Washington, D.C., during the pre-tribulation times. These novels by other Christian writers that parallel the Left Behind books suggest a form of franchising by LaHaye and Jenkins, so strong is the Left Behind brand which seems to own the pre-trib story.

And then there are the products hawked on the web site—boxed sets, calendars, greeting cards, music, and the mysterious "iLumina," which is described as follows:

The revolutionary iLumina software makes the novel Left Behind accessible in ways previously unimaginable, through behind-the-scene video clips, Left Behind Audio Theater clips, and secret information about the making of Left Behind. This is your ultimate interactive resource for exploring Left Behind.[32]

The products allow readers to immerse themselves in the world of Left Behind to a fanatical level.

Finally, and rather disturbingly, there's a "Kids" series for children ten to fourteen that depicts the travails of four children, Judd, Vicki, Lionel, and Ryan, who are orphaned by the Rapture and band together to deal with the events of the last days. While the concept of a "kid's version" of a popular series is commonplace in Christian fiction, it seems totally inappropriate in this case. Children are not a suitable audience for end-times fiction and are more likely to be terrified than inspired by the dire events of the Tribulation. At the very least, a story of children orphaned by the Rapture would tap into every child's abandonment fears. One commentator questions the profit motive of both the authors and their publisher for developing this ancillary series for children, citing his own reading of *The Late Great Planet Earth* in his youth as evidence of the danger of focusing on the apocalypse for children who are thereby given "a distorted and frightening picture of what Christianity is all about."[33] It is undeniable that young people will be attracted to the techno-thriller, fast-paced narrative of *Left Behind: The Kids,* but it is equally true that the focus on the earth's destruction and the annihilation of the enemies of Christ can distort children's understanding of Christianity and terrify many of them who will fixate on the impending doom.

However, it is unlikely that those involved with packaging the Left Behind brand would have any cognizance of such problems because the series has developed beyond just a brand; it approaches a religion in itself. Note the language on the official Left Behind web site, language that seems more appropriate to a church than a series of novels:

It is our hope that the new LeftBehind.com will become your online home for spiritual growth, stimulation, support, and close-knit fellowship as you strive to live and share the message of eternity with others while living every day in light of Christ's imminent return.[34]

Similar to the contemporary megachurch, this is a full-service web site that offers a newsletter, a prophecy club, and opportunities for spiritual growth for both new and mature Christians. It is unlikely that anyone would abandon his or her church community for a web site, but for the American individualist who disdains institutional religion, LeftBehind.com offers a spiritual connection without the bother of pulpits and pews. Hubris, traditionally the fatal flaw of the classic hero, appears to have evolved in the modern world to affect this publishing endeavor. Initially created to promote pre-tribulation eschatology, the Left Behind series is now packaged as a spiritual haven for its disciples. This is unsettling because the extension of the novels to children is not the only problematic aspect of this fiction.

Some Issues

The Left Behind focus on God's wrath rather than God's love is the reason that many mainline Protestant scholars object to the underlying theology of the series.[35] The novels are castigated as "pulp fiction, based on a particular reading of the Bible," and "an unbiblical flight of fancy."[36] This is no accident; LaHaye makes no secret of his agenda to counteract the forces of liberal Christianity. In a *Newsweek* article, LaHaye is quoted as saying,

The liberals have crafted a Jesus that's unscriptural and to their liking. They want their God to be a big, benevolent grandfather who lets them into heaven anyway. The worst thing a person can do against God is to deceive people about the Bible. That's satanically inspired.[37]

Far from his expressed purpose of simply fictionalizing the pre-tribulation end times, LaHaye's narratives skewer most of his perceived opponents, presenting readers with an idiosyncratic and intolerant perspective that they may not realize they're absorbing along with the simple narratives.

The most common adjective that Christian fiction embraces is "inspirational." Most authors of evangelical fiction endeavor to support and strengthen the faith of their readers through their narratives. But the Left Behind series can hardly inspire Christians by modeling ideal behavior, since the true Christians vanish in the opening pages of novel number one via the Rapture. The novels in this series mainly satisfy a lust for vengeance as evangelicals can see their current enemies either converted to the truth and repenting of their secular past or annihilated in the apocalypse. If anyone professes to have been converted to Christianity from reading the novels, it would be those who want to be on the winning side in the ultimate war, those who want to make sure that they are among the raptured.

One critic pointed to the negative effect of this focus on the end times. Believing that there is no long-term future, individuals are less likely to save or work diligently to build a business or a career, or be concerned with any long-range planning.[38] Why sacrifice to save for a future when the end times may be near? Just run up that credit-card balance and hope the Rapture comes soon. In a society where young people are failing to save for the future and accumulating significant debt, a fascination with the end times will not promote responsible behavior. It is important to note that the subject matter is not the main problem in the Left Behind series; it is the authorial choices that created fiction which focuses more on settling the score with enemies rather than inspiring the faithful.

In comparison, Sydney Watson's *In the Twinkling of an Eye,* also a novel of pre-tribulation eschatology, is more consistent with the inspirational quality of Christian fiction. The narrative ends with the Rapture, and it focuses on the protagonists' development as Christians in the months prior to that event. The journalist Tom Hammond, for example, is a good man and sincere Christian who comes to a more authentic Christianity via his understanding of the end times. The moment of Rapture reflects the reward for these good people, all of whom have grown and developed in their faith in the course of the novel.

Perhaps more disturbing than the emphasis on God's wrath is the promotion of LaHaye's political agenda that pervades this fiction. One commentator who is particularly concerned with the political implications of the Left Behind series argues that readers may be inclined to ignore the subtle indoctrination of these books under the impression that they're "just novels," when they are actually "a paint-by-numbers, soulless, and morally didactic blueprint of right-wing political and religious ideologies masquerading as fiction."[39] While this critic's language may seem extreme, it is undeniable that the Left Behind eschatology invites application to current world affairs, and the LaHaye/Jenkins narratives present their authors' perspective on contemporary politics. The fact that the return of Christ depends on a Jewish state in Israel that is under assault by the forces of evil translates into pre-trib enthusiasts who are both obsessed with Israeli self-defense and opposed to any peace plan.[40]

Although many Americans may wonder at times how their fellow citizens can support seemingly disastrous public policy, for believers in Left Behind those very policies may be positive acts that deserve support because they are believed to have Biblical significance. While the relationship between popular culture and politics is complex, it remains disturbing that our government has a less than congenial relationship with the United Nations, and the Antichrist in Left Behind becomes the Secretary General of that organization. We invade Iraq, and in the Left Behind books, Baghdad is Satan's headquarters.[41]

The series is propaganda disguised as fiction, and LaHaye has been very successful in inculcating his political ideas through this medium. Perhaps some conservative Christian readers already believe that faith in Jesus is the only path to salvation, that the government is the enemy of the righteous, that ecumenism is a tool of the devil, and that the Pope is in league with the Antichrist, but there are many other readers who are unconsciously absorbing these ideas while devouring the action-packed scenarios of the Left Behind books. A 2006 survey indicated that nearly 69% of Left Behind readers are Protestants, but that figure includes both mainline and evangelicals, so we can assume that evangelicals are likely no more than half of the Left Behind readership. In addition, 8.6% were identified as Catholic, and 22.8% identified themselves in terms of other world religions, such as Judaism, Islam, and Buddhism.[42] This final group may include the "spiritual seekers" that Robert Wuthnow has described who combine a variety of religious traditions in their search for spirituality.

Unfortunately, for most of these readers, the Left Behind political agenda is identified with Christianity. Asked about their motivations for reading the novels, most people indicated that it was to either compare what the books present to what "the Bible says" or because the novels explain the "events described in the Book of Revelation in an understandable way."[43] If LaHaye's original impulse in fictionalizing the events of the pre-trib end times was to counter the drift toward a post-trib view among evangelicals, he has succeeded beyond even his lofty expectations. Thanks to the Left Behind books, the pre-trib eschatology is assumed to be a standard Christian interpretation of the end times, a vivid and accessible account of the Book of Revelation.

Even the notoriously skeptical CBS program *60 Minutes* described the Left Behind series as mainstream Christianity in a 2004 program on the phenomenon:

The books give a graphic version of the New Testament prophesy of the end of the world, happening in our time, in which only the righteous are saved. It's a triumphant tale—unmistakably Christian, undeniably American.[44]

Of course, the television show was not about eschatology or books on that subject. The goal of *60 Minutes* was to focus on the political power of evangelicals in the Bush administration, and the LaHaye/Jenkins interview was simply a vehicle to present evangelicals via a trendy topic that would draw viewers, such is the power of monumental book sales. However, the more normative the Left Behind perspective appears to be, the more it will be accepted by naïve readers, not only as a reliable version of the end times but as orthodox Christian theology as well.

In times of tension and uncertainty, it is natural for people to look for the "silver lining," and this explains the appeal of the Left Behind books beyond evangelical Christians. If natural and man-made catastrophes are actually events that are a necessary prelude to the end times, believing that those events have a positive meaning is reassuring to the human psyche. But the danger is that reassurance comes with a radical political agenda that is cloaked in Biblical prophecy. When the final book in the series was published, *Glorious Appearing,* one of the largest Christian bookstores in Canada refused to stock the book saying that "it promotes a dangerous worldview that exacerbates global tensions."[45] A spokesman for the bookstore explained:

The book is very American-centric. It suggests the United States is successful because it has supported the state of Israel. It portrays the Antichrist as a Romanian who has risen up to take over the United Nations. It also paints the European Union as entirely demonic.[46]

This is ideology masquerading as fiction, and it has to masquerade because it is neither Christian nor American, regardless of what *60 Minutes* broadcasts. The *New York Times* columnist Nicholas Kristof wrote of that novel, "If a Muslim were to write an Islamic version of 'Glorious Appearing' and publish it in Saudi Arabia, jubilantly describing a massacre of millions of non-Muslims by God, we would have a fit." He added, "It's disconcerting to find ethnic cleansing celebrated as the height of piety."[47] Kristof's invocation of Islam highlights the similarities in any form of extremism. As the *Time* cover story noted, "Extremists on each side look to contemporary events as validation of their sacred texts; each uses the others to define its view of the divine scheme."[48] Another commentator, wondering how the authors of Left Behind can "create a blockbuster media empire" out of such intolerant extremism and not be censored in the press, suggested that one reason may be that "while the novels' popularity has received lots of media attention, their actual *content* is utterly off the radar of the kind of people who write about books."[49] In other words, the tendency to assume that Christian fiction has no literary significance has kept the series from being analyzed seriously by mainstream literary critics and thus has insulated it from scrutiny.

Lest one think that the political ideas are inferred by these readers, a visit to the Left Behind web site will confirm the authors' emphasis on connecting current events to Biblical prophecy. There is an invitation to join the "Left Behind Prophecy Club" which is described as follows, including the boldface:

The Left Behind Prophecy Club is a website and newsletter to **help you understand** how current events may actually relate to End Times prophecy. **Each week you will get Interpreting the Signs,** an online newsletter featuring Tim LaHaye, Jerry Jenkins, Mark Hitchcock and other End Times scholars. You also have access to **exclusive online message boards** where you can discuss these important issues with fellow Christians.

It is our hope that by studying Bible prophecy and world affairs, those who believe will be bold in their faith and those who don't will begin to understand the link between **what is happening today and what was foretold in the Bible.**

Such pre-trib thinking has been influential in the development of web sites like "raptureready.com" which includes a "Rapture Index," described as "a Dow Jones Industrial Average of end time activity." There is advice to view this index as a "prophetic speedometer," with the "higher the number, the faster we're moving toward the occurrence of pre-tribulation rapture."[50] Normally, one would assume only eccentrics indulge in such fascination with the world's end, but given the fact that so many conservative Christians feel marginalized by contemporary culture, they are primed to accept a perspective that proclaims that their enemies will be co-opted by the Antichrist and that they will ultimately triumph. The pious may believe they are simply reading of Revelation when they actually are absorbing a radical, political ideology.

Christian Fiction?

Another problematic aspect of the Left Behind phenomenon is that these books are now touted as the triumph of Christian fiction, the genre's greatest achievement, thanks to their astronomical sales figures.[51] But, in fact, the series is the epitome of what detractors object to in Christian fiction, the pursuit of an agenda rather than the creation of a narrative. As Flannery O'Connor explained in her essay "Novelist and Believer," the inept writer "will think that the eyes of the Church or of the Bible or of his particular theology have already done the seeing for him and that his business is to rearrange this essential vision into satisfying patterns."[52] This very accurately describes the development of the Left Behind novels, as explained by the authors themselves.

Totally agenda driven, the fictional elements in these novels are manipulated to promote the pre-tribulation eschatology and, ultimately, the political agenda of Tim LaHaye. This is simply marketing an ideology in the guise of fiction. Were that agenda merely an obscure theory of the end times, the books would not be as problematic as they are. As is evident to many commentators, the Left Behind phenomenon, the books as well as ancillary materials from the web site, is concerned with marketing the perspective of the radical religious right, a political and cultural agenda that is being promoted through seemingly harmless fiction. And this use of fiction is, at the very least, deceptive.

Fiction is not argument; it creates its worldview through images and themes, and the average reader of popular fiction will rarely consciously consider the ideas presented but will, nevertheless, absorb the message conveyed. Moreover, since the fiction is not posed as argument, it is difficult to challenge its premises. LaHaye's insistence that he is simply transmitting the truths of Scripture lends credence to the entire enterprise. But, as one Protestant theologian has commented, the Bible "does not interpret itself, human beings do the interpreting."[53] Literalism in Bible reading is itself an ideology.[54] Nevertheless, LaHaye's claims that he is providing a readable rendition of the Book of Revelation will convince naïve readers, especially those who are seeking consolation in troubled times. What better assurance than to believe that the various conflicts raging throughout the globe are simply evidence of God's plan for the earth?

Readers may assume that LaHaye and Jenkins do not have such authorial control, since the plot elements are obviously dictated by the details of pre-trib eschatology. To see how much of the authors' personal agenda is involved in the Left Behind books, a comparison to Sydney Watson's 1916 novel *In the Twinkling of an Eye* is instructive, as this earlier book is also based on the events prescribed by the pre-trib apocalypse. The first difference is that Watson's novel is less a political thriller than an exploration of human character. His novel recounts the personal and spiritual development of a journalist, Tom Hammond, in the few months leading to the Rapture. This plot, ending at the Rapture, eliminates the need to describe the violence of the Tribulation—although the entire process of the pre-trib apocalypse is explained for the reader in the lectures that Hammond attends. The emphasis in Watson's novel is on defining the nature of the true Christian, that person who will be raptured, and in his definition, Watson is both generous and ecumenical.

Tom Hammond is a basically good man who, as he explains early in the novel, knows Christianity only "from hearsay." He has "heard parsons preach it," but he himself knows "nothing experimentally about these things."[55] However, having saved a desperate woman, Mrs. Joyce, from drowning, Hammond subsequently learns that the woman had been raised a strict Christian but abandoned her faith along with her family for a husband who turned out to be a drunken, abusive lout; hence, her suicide attempt. Both of these individuals are occasions of grace for the other. In thanking Hammond for saving her, Mrs. Joyce writes that his words had given her "a clearer view of God than any sermon" she had ever listened to, resulting in her passage "from death to life" in Christ.[56] She explains,

I gave myself up to God there and then, Mr. Hammond, and am seeking now to live so that, should Christ come, even before I finish this letter, I may be reader to be caught up to meet Him in the air.[57]

Puzzled by this allusion to the Rapture, Hammond then recalls having been sent a poem for review with a similar idea. He searches for the poem which presents more detail about this future event. Still uncertain as to the poem's meaning, Hammond seeks out Mrs. Joyce for further explanation, and thus begins his journey to full acceptance of Christ through the explication of the end times. During this same time period, Hammond is introduced to an American woman, Madge Finisterre, traveling in Europe, and he is briefly attracted to her, as she is to him. Brought up in a Christian home, Madge had received a marriage proposal from her pastor before leaving on her journey, and when she learns that this man is very ill, she takes the next ship back to America. On that journey, she shares a cabin with a very congenial young woman who speaks of the imminent coming of Christ. Intrigued, Madge listens to her cabin mate's explanations, and before retiring for the night, she, too, is born again by her knowledge of the end times. She realizes "that she had passed from death into life."[58]

Through his newspaper writing, Hammond is contacted by Abraham Cohen, a Jewish craftsman, and while visiting him, the journalist is drawn to Cohen's sister-in-law, Zillah Robart. Hammond later learns that Zillah has been attending meetings designed to acquaint Jews with Jesus as the Messiah, and she is close to accepting Christ. Cohen, observing his sister-in-law's attraction to the gentile Hammond, attends some of the same lectures as the young couple, and he is intrigued by the story of Christ as well. These five people are all raptured as the novel ends, and the major point Watson emphasizes in their separate stories is the importance of not remaining a nominal Christian, as are Tom and Madge when the novel begins, and the importance of openness to new ideas, as is evident with characters of Zillah and Abraham.

In Watson's novel, the hollowness of much institutional religion is reflected in those who are "left behind." The closest that Watson comes to attacking theological enemies is the character of Madge's pastor/husband who violently objects to the concept of the Rapture as "lying, senseless nonsense."[59] His mind is closed to the notion that there might be something to discuss with his new wife about this idea that seems to have influenced her spiritual life so significantly. He, of course, is not raptured. And there is also the fact that no one is raptured from any of the theatres or music halls, thus affirming the conservative Christian prohibition of on such entertainments. But these comments are gentle and without the viciousness with which LaHaye indicts his political opponents. Even the character of the Monk, who represents the traditional evangelical antagonism to Catholicism, is simply one of many aberrant preachers who signal the emergence of the Antichrist rather than actually a cohort of Satan, as Catholicism is represented in LaHaye's novels.

In the various ways that Hammond is brought "from death to life," Watson's central message is one of reconciliation and hope, of the importance of openness to God's action in one's life. It is Hammond's receptivity to the message that effects his salvation and that of the other characters whose lives are intertwined with his. In the absence of violence or vengeance, Watson's novel provides inspiration, as it challenges readers to assess their own receptiveness to Christ. In fact, when Hammond writes his newspaper column on the Rapture, the focus is on how this concept should transform the world—"revolutionize all our national, commercial, domestic, and church life," as he anticipates that individuals anticipating the Rapture would conform their lives to the Gospel to live in accord with the teachings of Christ, but he realistically admits that it will probably take the event of the Rapture itself to convince most people to mend their ways.[60] As this brief description of *In the Twinkling of an Eye* indicates, the blatantly antagonistic and intolerant tone of the Left Behind series is not due to its subject matter. Clearly, it is possible to promote the pre-trib agenda in a more inclusive, tolerant, and *Christian* manner.

Unlike LaHaye, Watson not only acknowledges the actual source of his inspiration to fictionalize the Rapture (a pamphlet titled "Long Odds" by a "General Robertson"), but in his Foreword to the novel, he also mentions his hesitation to use the "fictional form to clothe so sacred a subject" as "the near Return of Our Lord."[61] Watson is referring to the notion of fiction as somewhat decadent, like drinking, gambling, and dancing, which made novel reading problematic in the early part of the twentieth century for most evangelicals. Not only does he justify his use of fiction by invoking his source, the pamphlet by General Robertson, but he also refers to the fact that Jesus himself spoke of his return with the use of stories.[62] So prevalent is the phenomenon of Christian fiction today that it's easy to forget that reading fiction was once considered a dangerous pastime.

In addition, for those who ascribe to a literal reading of Scripture, there can be a danger in combining fiction with the Bible. As one contemporary reviewer noted, for those who believe in Biblical inerrancy, the "fictionalizing of Scripture is an egregious offense in and of itself." And the reviewer further noted,

One can argue that the books are only fiction, but will the intermingling of Bible truth and fiction not leave wrong impressions in the minds of people? Will the average reader be able to tell truth from fiction?[63]

One would imagine that LaHaye who certainly ascribes to a literal reading of Scripture would raise such an issue himself, as Watson did in his novel's Foreword. Instead, a *Washington Times* article mentions that LaHaye is "undeterred by critics," quoting the series creator: "'Our position is essentially what the Bible says,' he said. 'The idea we could be wrong has not occupied much of my serious thought.'"[64] The Manichean thinking at the heart of Left Behind is clearly the product of LaHaye's own epistemology. He sees no issues except those of "right" and "wrong"; there are no shades of gray in his world—or in the Left Behind books. And since he's operating in the political realm, the fiction conveys a take-no-prisoners assault on anyone who disagrees with him in any way. The danger is not so much that readers will confuse fact and fiction as that they will absorb the Manichean perspective of the books and be similarly righteous and condemning of alternative views.

What's disturbing is that the acclamations of the Left Behind books as the acme of Christian fiction are due principally to their sales figures.[65] If Christian publishers are going to use sales as the measure of excellence, they appear to have been seduced by the secular culture of materialism. Their ostensible measure of excellence for Christian fiction is implied in the name of the annual award developed by a group of evangelical publishers, the "Christy." And any discussion of the way Christian fiction may intersect with the mainstream should begin with a look at that novel, which will begin the next chapter.

Notes

1. American Christian Fiction Writers, Mission Statement, http://www.acfw.com/missionstatement.shtml (accessed January 19, 2007).

2. Robert L. Dean, Jr., and Thomas Ice, "Frank Peretti and the New Spiritual Warfare," *Biblical Perspectives* 2, no. 5 (September/October 1989), http://www.rapidnet.com/~jbeard/bdm/exposes/peretti/dark.htm (accessed January 12, 2007). Published initially in 1986, the novel was into its eighth printing by 1989.

3. See, for example, Monique El-Faizy, *God and Country: How Evangelicals Have Become America's New Mainstream* (New York: Bloomsbury, 2006), 61. Her casual comment evidences the common knowledge involved in this assertion.

4. Quoted at http://www.religioustolerance.org/newage.htm (accessed January 12, 2007).

5. Dean, Jr., and Ice, "Frank Peretti and the New Spiritual Warfare."

6. Nancy Gibbs, "Apocalypse Now," *Time,* July 1, 2002, http://www.time.com/time/magazine/article/0,9171,1002759,00.html (accessed December 2, 2005).

7. The writer Carl E. Olson, a Roman Catholic convert from fundamentalist Christianity, has authored several articles about the Left Behind series, as well as a book, *Will Catholics Be Left Behind? A Catholic Critique of the Rapture and Today's Prophecy Preachers,* all of which are designed to educate Catholics about their religion's doctrine concerning the end times. Another writer, Joe Bageant, often writes critically of the Left Behind phenomenon using his upbringing in an evangelical church, a religious heritage he has since abandoned but uses to explain the issues involved that are not readily apparent to most nonevangelicals.

8. El-Faizy, *God and Country,* 61.

9. All sources agree on this etiology of "pre-trib." One of the most accessible is in the *Time* magazine cover story that appeared on July 1, 2002; David Van Biema, "The End: How It Got That Way," available at http://www.time.com/time/magazine/article/0,9171,265420-1,00.html (accessed December 2, 2005).

10. Tim Warner, "Introduction and Methodology," http://www.geocities.com/~lasttrumpet/, accessed February 6, 2006. This site belongs to Last Trumpet, a post-tribulation group, and provides a strong defense of that perspective, an argument not germane to this study but accessible for anyone interested in the basis for the "post trib" perspective.

11. From the Tim LaHaye web site, http://www.timlahaye.com/ (accessed September 26, 2006).

12. Ibid.

13. David Gates, "Religion: The Pop Prophets," *Newsweek,* http://msnbc.msn.com/id/4988269/site/newsweek/ (accessed January 13, 2006).

14. Crawford Gribben, "Before Left Behind," *Books and Culture,* July 1, 2003, http://www.ctlibrary.com/bc/2003/julaug/14.9.html.

15. Paul Meier, *The Third Millennium* (Nashville, TN: WestBow Press, 1993).

16. Brian Wilson of Western Michigan University, quoted by David Van Biema, "The End: How It Got That Way."

17. Ibid.

18. Gibbs, "Apocalypse Now."

19. Ibid.

20. Steve Rabey, "Apocalyptic Sales Out of This World," *Christianity Today,* March 1, 1999, http://www.ctlibrary.com/ct/1999/march1/9t319a.html (accessed October 13, 2006). Jerry Jenkins is quoted as saying that readers "have fallen in love with the characters and want to know what happens with them." Reader reviews on Amazon.com stress the "want to know what happens" as the motivating factor in their reading rather than any interest in the characters themselves. That is, they seem to believe that Jenkins and LaHaye are describing what *will* happen at the end of the world, and that is their primary interest.

21. Ibid, italics mine.

22. John Cloud, "How an Evangelist and Conservative Activist Turned Prophecy into a Fiction Juggernaut," *Time,* July 1, 2002, http://www.time.com/time/magazine/article/0,9171,1002762,00.htm (accessed December 2, 2005).

23. Joe Bageant, "What the 'Left Behind' Series Really Means," http://www.joebageant.com (accessed October 14, 2006).

24. Tim LaHaye and Jerry B. Jenkins, *Left Behind: A Novel of the Earth's Last Days* (Wheaton, IL: Tyndale House Publishers, Inc., 1995), 396.

25. Ibid.

26. Michelle Goldberg, "Fundamentally Unsound," http://www.salon.com/books/feature/2002/07/29/left_behind/, published July 29, 2002 (accessed January 13, 2006).

27. Quoted by Gibbs, "Apocalypse Now."

28. At http://leftbehind.com/channelbooks.asp?pageid=130&channelID;=30#lahaye (accessed October 23, 2006).

29. Ibid.

30. Gribben, "L.B.: Recycling Sydney Watson."

31. Carl E. Olson, "The 12th Coming of Less-Than-Glorious Fiction" The Latest 'Left Behind' Book, *The National Review* (April 2004) , http://www.nationalreview.com/comment/olson20040404020904.asp,)accessed October 14, 2006).

32. From http://wwwleftbehind.com/channelproducts.asp?channelID=170 (accessed October 25, 2006).

33. Jimmy Akin, "False Profit: Money, Prejudice, and Bad Theology in Tim LaHaye's *Left Behind* Series," http://www.catholic.com/library;false_profit.asp (accessed December 2, 2005).

34. From LeftBehind.com (accessed October 18, 2006).

35. David Gates, "Religion: The Pop Prophets."

36. Quoted by David Gates.

37. Ibid.

38. Gary North, "Left Behind Culturally," http://www.lewrockwell.com/north/north30.html (accessed December 2, 2005).

39. Michael Standaert, "The novel, Left Behind," http://www.nthposition.com/thenovel.php, (accessed December 2, 2005).

40. Michelle Goldberg, "Fundamentally unsound."

41. Ibid. Goldberg points out these similarities but does not claim causation. Rather, she argues that "the stories people tell themselves about the world necessarily shape

the way they act in it, and right now [July, 2002], this is the story that's captivating America."

42. Terry Mattingly, "About those 'Left Behind' readers," http://tmatt.gospelcom.net/column/2006/07/19/ (accessed October 25, 2006).

43. Ibid.

44. Rise of the Righteous Army," http://www.cbsnews.com/stories/2004/02/05/60minutes/main598218.shtml, (accessed October 24, 2006).

45. Douglas Todd, "Christian Bookstore Won't Stock Latest Left Behind Book," http://www.beliefnet.com/story/144/story_14412_1.html (accessed October 10, 2006).

46. Ibid.

47. Bill Berkowitz, "The Rapture Racket" at http://www.workingforchange.com/article.cfm?ItemID=17713, accessed February, 6, 2006.

48. Gibbs, "Apocalypse Now." Italics hers.

49. Michelle Goldberg, "Fundamentally unsound."

50. From http://raptureready.com/rap2.html (accessed October 25, 2006).

51. Rabey, "Apocalyptic Sales Out of This World." Rabey even quotes a representative of the publisher who attributes the monumental sales directly to God rather than to marketing.

52. Quoted by Carl E. Olson, "The 12th Coming of Less-Than-Glorious Fiction."

53. Quoted by Gershom Gorenberg, "Intolerance: The Bestseller," http://www.prospect.org/cs/articles?article=book_review (issue date, September 23, 2002; accessed October 24, 2006).

54. Ibid.

55. Sydney Watson, *In the Twinkling of an Eye* (1916; repr., Ohio: Barbour Publishing, 2005), 32.

56. Ibid., 53.

57. Ibid., 54.

58. Ibid., 124.

59. Ibid., 167.

60. Ibid., 172–3.

61. Ibid., 8.

62. Ibid.

63. The *Left Behind* Series at http://www.rapidnet.com/~jbeard/bdm/BookReviews/left.htm (accessed December 1, 2005).

64. Julia Duin, "'Left Behind' finale is The End, literally" *The Washington Times,* http://www.washingtontimes.com/national/20040330-120047-7043r.htm (accessed January 13, 2006).

65. Rabey, "Apocalyptic Sales Out of This World."

— 6 —

Beyond "Christian Fiction"

Writers whose work is nourished by religious concerns are on a pilgrimage to find the source of their faith as individuals and of their strength as artists.

—William Zinsser

Awards are often designed to set a standard, to highlight the nature of achievement in the field. This is true of the "Christy," the award for excellence in Christian fiction, named in honor of Catherine Marshall's 1967 novel and chosen to honor Marshall and her work. In using the novel's title for this award, there is an implication that *Christy* denotes true excellence in the genre of Christian fiction. However, Marshall's novel actually appeared prior to the burgeoning evangelical Christian fiction market, which all sources date as beginning more than a decade later. Indeed, one wonders whether Marshall's work would be accepted by contemporary evangelical publishers, since the book's minister is a confused young man, ineffectual in his dealings with people, and the novel's authentic spiritual leader is a woman—and a Quaker.[1]

The naming of this award, created by a group of evangelical publishers, may be due to more pragmatic concerns. Inaugurated in 1999, the Christy awards seem to be part of a subtle movement in Christian publishing to compensate for the mainstream literary establishment's disdain of their fiction. By associating their award with "one of America's most notable and bestselling Christian writers," as proclaimed on the web site for the Christy awards, evangelical publishers suggest that Christian fiction is deserving of the mainstream status enjoyed by Marshall's novel.[2] In addition to the association with *Christy,* the award's web site features a quotation by Ron Hansen, "Writing, then, can be viewed as a sacrament insofar as it provides graced occasions of encounter between humanity and God." This quotation from Hansen's essay "Writing as Sacrament" appears disingenuous and yet another attempt to conflate mainstream fiction with this distinct genre of

"Christian fiction." Like many other mainstream writers whose fiction is fueled by faith, Ron Hansen has specifically rejected this identification of his writing with the unique "Christian fiction" discussed in Chapter 4.[3]

In his essay, "Faith and Fiction," Hansen writes of the question that writers face in how to "avoid homiletics, the shoehorning in of religious belief, the sabotage of the fictional dream by forcing one's characters to perform the role of mouthpieces."[4] He continues,

So-called Christian fiction is often in fact pallid allegory, or a form of sermonizing, or is a reduction into formula, providing first-century, Pauline solutions to oversimplified problems, sometimes yielding to a Manichean dualism wherein good and evil are plainly at war, or offering as Christianity conservative politics.[5]

Referencing a writer like Hansen who clearly would not want to be associated with evangelical publishing on the Christy Award web site betrays the unspoken attempt to associate conservative Christian fiction with mainstream literature. But this is a case in which the twain should not meet because they are very different species, as I hope will be clear in an analysis of *Christy,* a novel that I believe is very different from the contemporary conservative Christian fiction that has appropriated its reputation.

A Comparison

Catherine Marshall's *Christy* is deceptively simple, an apparent romance novel with a Christian emphasis. In fact, the narrative deals with the spiritual development of its title character much less reductively than is common in contemporary Christian fiction and more consistent with James Fowler's study of faith development. The psychological realism of *Christy* separates it from contemporary Christian fiction which almost universally treats the faith experience reductively. In *Christy,* the crux of the narrative is a young woman's development from immature faith, the Stage 3 of conventional faith, to the more mature, personally appropriated faith experience of Stage 4. Typical contemporary Christian fiction heroines are confirmed in Stage 3, and the tension in the narrative is fending off the secular world rather than any personal development of the protagonist. This is consistent with Fowler's comment that the Stage 3 church is invested in having its members remain in Stage 3 faith, so it is not surprising that conservative Christian fiction would promote that stasis, much as Fowler cites televangelists as simply "offering a tacit version of Christian theology that centers in vicarious interpersonal warmth and meaning."[6] Unlike the spiritual stasis common to contemporary Christian fiction, *Christy* is a novel of growth and development.

When we meet Christy Huddleston, it is the winter of 1912, and she appears to be an idealistic, young, Christian woman, as she is embarking on a missionary endeavor to teach school at a Christian mission in an isolated mountain cove,

Cutter Gap. But very soon, the reader is introduced to the conventionality of her previous religious experience, as Christy explains,

Now I guessed that somewhere—out there—there was something exciting about religion which had not come through to me in my church back home. And I sense that I could have sat in the Huddleston family pew every Sunday until I was an old lady, and it would not have been any different.[7]

Thus, Christy is not simply embarking on a social mission; in recognizing the empty formalism of her worship experiences, she has broken with the authority of her home church, however unconsciously. This break, according to Fowler, is critical in the movement beyond the conventional faith experience of Stage 3.[8] The journey to Stage 4, adult faith, is not an easy one, and the reader is continually reminded of this as some of Christy's seemingly altruistic efforts on behalf of her pupils are identified by the mission's Quaker leader, Miss Alice, as more rooted in self than sacrifice.

Throughout the novel, Christy is both admonished and supported by Miss Alice, who reminds Christy of the fact that spiritual development is a journey, "What you've undertaken here in Cutter Gap in your schoolroom isn't a state of perfection to be arrived at all of a sudden. It's a walk, and a walk isn't static but ever changing."[9] Challenged to explain her Christian beliefs by the unbelieving Dr. MacNeill, Cutter Gap's only physician, Christy is frustrated by her inability to do so. She's comforted by Miss Alice who explains that her awareness of the need to be able to articulate her beliefs is good in itself. The older woman's consoling words echo Fowler's description of the unreflective nature of Stage 3 faith that must be transcended for faith to develop, as Miss Alice explains,

So many people never pause long enough to make up their minds about basic issues of life and death. It's quite possible to go through your whole life, making the mechanical motions of living, adopting as your own sets of ideas you've picked up some place or other, and die—never having come to any conclusion for yourself as to what life is all about.[10]

And when Christy finally comes to a personal awareness of God's love for her, it is not with certitude about the world but simply an awareness of her personal relationship with Transcendence:

The world around me was still full of riddles for which my little mind had not been given answers. . . . Nor could I know what the future held. But the fundamental doubt was for me silenced. I knew now: God *is*. I had found my center, my point of reference. Everything else I needed to know would follow.[11]

Unlike Christy, the heroines of contemporary Christian fiction rarely experience a journey to faith. For them, the faith experience *is* static, despite the appearance of movement. The protagonist of Karen Kingsbury's Firstborn series, Katy Hart, is confident in her Christian identity, explaining that "God and I are sort of best friends, I guess."[12] And in that relationship, Katy, unlike Christy, has answers to all situations because she relies on the repetition of traditional language she has inherited. Faced with a choice, she will "pray about it" and "ask God what to do." For example, the question of whether or not to go to Hollywood for a screen test is reduced to simply awaiting a "sign" from God that will provide the correct answer. And God's voice is easily heard, providing direction as needed. There is never any suggestion that discerning God's will can be difficult or that an individual can confuse his or her own desires with the promptings of God. In this fiction, the Christian communicates with the Creator with ease and clarity.

When the heroine is initially a nonbeliever, like Marty in Janette Oke's *Love Comes Softly,* the journey to faith is similarly uneventful. Forced by circumstances into a marriage of convenience with a stranger, Marty's major vice seems to be an inability to cook. She is a kindhearted, generous woman who, inexplicably, has not had even a conventional Christian background. At her first meal with her new husband, she is astonished when he prays a blessing:

Marty sat wide-eyed looking at this man before her, who spoke, eyes closed, to a God she did not see or know—and him not even a preacher. Of course she had heard of people like that, various ones who had a God outside of church, who had a religion apart from marryin' an' buryin', but she had never rubbed elbows, so to speak, with one before.[13]

The major journey in this novel involves Marty's gradually developing love for this man, which gives the novel its title. Her "conversion" comes, fittingly, at an Easter sunrise service and consists of an instantaneous infusion of awareness of God and His love, resulting in her immediate acceptance. As is typical of the conversion of the nonbeliever in the romance of Christian fiction, this epiphanic moment is static, requiring none of the soul searching and reflection that engage Christy for much of her narrative.

Contemporary Christian fiction is religious romance, applying the conventions of the romance genre to spiritual experience. In this romance, the Christian has a private line to God, while characters who become Christian have an instantaneous experience at the right moment in the plot. The major spiritual challenge for these Christians is avoiding contamination with the sinful world beyond the Christian enclave. It could be argued that these novels are realistic in depicting the unique beliefs of evangelical Christians. As one writer comments, "For those of us who are not believers it is almost impossible to grasp how essential an evangelical's spiritual experience is in his or her life. God is a living, tangible, and daily presence."[14] However, even someone as partisan as an editor for *Books and Culture,* an offshoot of the evangelical *Christianity Today,* refers to Christian fiction as an "alternative universe," populated by "evangelical buffoons," so steeped are these novels in simplistic spirituality.[15]

Undeniably, this fiction serves a purpose. Its reductive presentation of the spiritual life is useful to support its Stage 2 or 3 readers, providing a way for them to participate in an apparently realistic version of their unique Christian culture.

There is no challenge to readers' thinking in this essentially self-reflexive fiction because it is designed to mirror its own culture as an idealized reality. The sales figures indicate that this fiction, however aberrant it may seem from a literary or mainline theological perspective, meets the needs of a significant number of conservative Christians. This "literature of their own" must be understood as the product of a specific cultural moment and as a subgenre that fulfills the needs of a specific group of readers.

The spiritual journey experienced by the heroine in *Christy* is more consonant with mainstream fiction which privileges the growth and development of the protagonist. And the two types of literature should not be conflated, as in the obvious attempt to raise the status of Christian fiction by claiming association with mainstream authors, as in the use of a quotation from a highly praised mainstream writer like Ron Hansen on the Christy Awards web site. Ironically, since Hansen is a Roman Catholic, many evangelicals would not even consider him a Christian, so the use of his name appears to be quite a reach in seeking status for evangelical Christian fiction.

Seeking Credibility

In creating the Christy award, evangelical publishers were clearly not satisfied with booming sales. Their expressed intention was threefold, as explained on the award's web site:

The Christy Award is designed to:

- Nurture and encourage creativity and quality in the writing and publishing of fiction written from a Christian worldview.
- Bring a new awareness of the breadth and depth of fiction choices available, helping to broaden the readership.
- Provide opportunity to recognize novelists whose work may not have reached bestseller status.[16]

Implicit in these goals is the desire to give status to their novels that are not recognized by the mainstream literary establishment and not given consideration for their awards. Since conservative Christians already see themselves marginalized by the dominant culture, the fact that their fiction appears to be similarly marginalized by the literary establishment is surely frustrating and reinforces their outsider status.

The desire to "cross over," to appeal to mainstream readers and, consequently, to the mainstream literary establishment is evident in comments made about the latest sub-genre in Christian fiction, "chick lit." In an article in *Christianity Today,* there's a hope expressed that, "The sense of fun that pervades Christian chick lit almost as much as its core of faith may allow this genre to do something few other books written for the Christian marketplace have done: cross over to the secular market."[17] While such a cross over would increase sales, that seems to be less a goal than the desire to be a part of mainstream literature. This expressed hope of appealing to readers in secular American culture may appear innocuous, even consistent with the evangelical emphasis on spreading the good news. However, a more recent attempt to broaden the concept of Christian fiction is much more problematic.

In a 2006 essay, Charles Colson attempts to elevate the status of conservative Christian fiction by claiming some highly regarded mainstream novels belong to that subgenre and deploring the fact that "for years, most Christian authors wrote only to an audience that was familiar with a certain brand of Christian terminology."[18] In praising Elizabeth Strout's *Abide with Me* as a more "successful" product of Christian fiction, Colson conveniently ignores the fact that the novel is from a mainstream publisher, and, as he himself explains, its author is "more of a 'church-hopper' than a committed churchgoer," and the book has "rough language and a couple of graphic descriptions,"[19] all elements that would disqualify the novel for evangelical publishers—and readers.

What's going on here? Clearly, Colson wants to extend the Christian fiction brand to mainstream fiction, to authors who may not themselves want to be identified as "Christian writers." In doing so, Colson either has missed the point of evangelical Christian fiction or chooses to ignore it. He claims that Christian fiction was designed by authors to "try to spread the message of Christ in their work" but wound up "turning off unbelievers."[20] This is a distortion. While it is true that the Christian writers discussed in Chapter 4 are all engaged in an effort to convey the message of Christ, it's also fairly evident that their use of "a certain brand of Christian terminology" is due to the fact that they envision their audience as fellow Christians, not unbelievers. They *are* preaching to the choir, and that's the reason for their "certain brand of Christian terminology."

However, Colson's concern is very real because evangelicals should always be trying to evangelize in their work, the novelist no less than the preacher. But his concerns may be based on reading some of the less-polished authors. Evangelical publishers have long been working to upgrade the quality of Christian fiction; their creation of the Christy Awards was a part of that effort. Authors like Oke, Karon, Rivers, and Kingsbury certainly produce fiction that can be enjoyed by nonbelievers, especially by contemporary spiritual seekers, those individualists who embrace spirituality while often disdaining institutional religion. The best-selling Christian writers may have a large audience of nonevangelical readers. For example, studies indicate that evangelicals comprise less than half of the readers of the Left Behind books.[21]

The vast majority of Christian fiction is designed to provide conservative Christians with an alternative to the "rough language and graphic descriptions" of mainstream fiction. It is not coincidental that the advent of Christian fiction correlates with mainstream publishers' orientation to more graphic and sexually explicit popular fiction in the mid-1970s, an orientation that alienated conservative readers and created a market for explicitly Christian popular fiction that self-reflexively mirrors the conservative Christian culture. However, there are also many Americans who are not evangelical but similarly alienated from the sordidness of contemporary popular fiction. The relatively muted didacticism in the novels of a Kingsbury or a Henderson will also attract this reader, especially since the most popular authors have managed to claim space on the shelves of the major secular book sellers like Barnes and Noble and Borders.[22] Reaching beyond the conservative Christian community does not seem to be what's motivating Colson in this essay.

Colson begins his essay by expanding the idea of Christian fiction, citing Dostoevsky, Tolstoy, Jane Austen, and Flannery O'Connor as models who "understood that moral literature is one of the most important ways of transmitting Christian truth."[23] Evidently, Colson wants to include most of Western literature under the brand "Christian," and actually he is not incorrect. Literature reflects the values of the society that produces it, so it is hardly surprising to note that much of Western literature reflects "Christian truth." But the manner in which that "truth" is conveyed is radically different in mainstream literature than it is in the contemporary Christian fiction that is currently a publishing phenomenon, as discussed in Chapters 4 and 5. Writers have described this difference in a variety of ways, but the essence is in the nature of the conflict experienced by protagonists.

In evangelical Christian fiction, religious faith is an idealized experience. Like Katy Hart, most Christian protagonists have merely to tune into the voice of God in order to know what to do in any situation. If the protagonists are nonbelievers, as in Dee Henderson's O'Malley series, they are absorbed into the Christian community by the Christians in their lives, and their conversion is similar to the dramatic moment experienced by Marty in *Love Comes Softly,* a sudden manifestation of God to them, as though the Holy Spirit has decided that it's time to swoop them up into the fold. This is the *deus ex machina* of Christian fiction, a plot formula that liberates the author from having to develop any depth in characters. The tension in this fiction is mainly in how long it will take for the "happily ever after." Since the reader has been conditioned by the formulaic nature of the novels to anticipate the inevitable resolution, there is a sense of satisfaction in reading the various stories that ultimately vindicate the Christian worldview, a complacent satisfaction that supports conservative Christians' certitude in the righteousness of their beliefs.

However, the story of authentic religious experience that has been long documented in Judeo-Christian culture and reflected in our best literature is more complex and uncertain, as described in this study of imagination and faith, a description that mirrors James Fowler's chronicle of the path to adult Stage 4 faith:

For all seekers after truth, it is only in leaving the security and certainties of home and going into exile, as it were, into the desert, to a world of uncertainty, that real security will be found. This was behind those changing of names, for example, from Aram to Abraham, and Simon to Peter. It is behind those old customs of those entering religious life changing their names and taking new ones. They are being invited to uncertainty. They are being asked not to lose their identities, but to find out who they truly are.[24]

It is this shift from certitude to uncertainty, from security to insecurity, that is a central difference between contemporary "Christian fiction" and mainstream fiction that may be "nourished by religious concerns." The latter is simply one aspect of the universal story of the novel. In his speech accepting the Nobel Prize for literature, William Faulkner referred to the basic subject for the novelist, "the problems of the human heart in conflict with itself which alone can make good writing because only that is worth writing about."[25] And the "human heart in conflict with itself" characterizes the struggle with faith for adherents of all religions. Thus, although the novels of Graham Greene, for example, are widely recognized as "nourished by religious concerns," anyone familiar with his fiction would agree that there is no better description of his craft than that he is depicting that "human heart in conflict with itself"—in various protagonists and in different situations.

In his essay, Colson has conflated excellent mainstream novels that reflect religious concerns and/or values with the typical products of evangelical publishers, wanting to include them all as "Christian fiction." Since evangelicals view mainstream culture as inherently secularized, Colson may have assumed that this contemporary religious fiction is indeed a sign of some "renaissance" in Christian fiction. Actually, it reflects the fact that the polarized rhetoric of the culture wars masks the complex and varied views of mainstream Americans. Everyone who is concerned with religion in America today is not automatically an evangelical Christian.

It is notable that two of the novels Colson cites in his essay, Elizabeth Strout's *Abide with Me* and Marilynne Robinson's *Gilead,* are both set in the America of the 1950s, perhaps the authors' way of avoiding the current cultural chasm, since the "restructuring of American religion" that Robert Wuthnow documents in his landmark study began in those years following the World War II.[26] By setting their novels in a less fractious era, both authors can avoid the current association of religion with politics. These two novels are not only vastly different from the conservative Christian fiction that is a current publishing phenomenon but also not unique, as Colson suggests. Rather, they represent a strong current in American fiction from the time of Hawthorne, fiction that is "nourished by religious concerns." The contemporary manifestations of this fiction reflect the nonevangelical Christian perspective, and it is a perspective to consider in the interest of an accurate view of the landscape of Christian fiction in America today.

Faith and Frailty

In Gilead, Iowa, the Rev. John Ames, a Congregationalist minister, is facing imminent death from heart disease, and in his seventy-sixth year begins a letter to his only son. That son is only six years old, the issue of Ames' late marriage, and the father who delights in the child now realizes that he must rely on this written missive to communicate the essence of himself to his son, since he will not live to nurture the boy as he grows up. The novel *Gilead* is that letter, a tour de force for author Robinson who must shape the memoir to sustain expectations of novel readers for plot and action. The son and grandson of ministers, Ames knows the conflicts that can exist between fathers and sons. His grandfather was an abolitionist, while his son, Ames's father, was a pacifist. Unspoken in the novel is the fact that this 1956 letter is being written when the conflicts of the Civil Rights Movement have just begun, and Ames can anticipate a different world for his son, although it will be a world that he cannot predict. In his own life, he has seen how things can change, and that all change is not necessarily progress:

I blame the radio for sowing a good deal of confusion where theology is concerned. And television is worse. You can spend forty years teaching people to be awake to the fact of mystery and then some fellow with no more theological sense than a jackrabbit gets himself a radio ministry and all your work is forgotten. I do wonder where it will end.[27]

It's interesting that Robinson inserts a reference to television, no anachronism since by 1955 Oral Roberts had a weekly broadcast on ninety-five stations, but also prophetic since we (and author Robinson) are aware of the deluge of televangelists that will follow in the ensuing years and help change the face of American religion.[28] Ames has a natural concern for the future insofar as it is the world that his son will experience. And although at one level, this is a novel about a father's struggle to transfer his life experience to his son, especially his personal faith, it is also about the nature of institutional religion in American culture. As a clergyman, Ames also longs to be able to transfer his own religious affiliation to his son, and occasionally Ames's voice seems to be speaking with twenty-first century awareness, as in this comment,

The history of the church is very complex, very mingled. I want you to know how aware I am of that fact. These days there are so many people who think loyalty to religion is benighted, if it is not worse than benighted. I am aware of that, and I know the charges that can be brought against the churches are powerful.[29]

Despite Robinson's facility with language, Ames expresses the frustration of being unable to articulate the ineffable in human language:

So you must not judge what I know by what I find words for. If I could only give you what my father gave me. No, what the Lord has given me and must also give you. But I hope you will put yourself in the way of the gift. I am not speaking here of the ministry as such, as I have said.[30]

In the phrasing of "what the Lord has given me and must also give you," Robinson so clearly evokes Paul's introduction to the institution narrative in 1 Corinthians (11:23), "For I received from the Lord what I also delivered to you," that it is very clear that what Ames yearns to be able to do is pass on his faith, what he values most. Yet he knows that it is one gift he cannot confer, since it is a gift that only God can bestow. And thus he urges his son to put himself "in the way of the gift," to be open and receptive. As Ames ultimately acknowledges at the end of the novel, God deals with each person individually, "as an only child."[31]

From a literary perspective, one triumph of *Gilead* is its prose; one reviewer described the novel as "so serenely beautiful, and written in a prose so gravely measured and thoughtful, that one feels touched with grace just to read it."[32] The other major accomplishment is the author's use of history to suggest the moral imperative of social justice for people of faith, not through argument or any other techniques of nonfiction, but simply through the situations in Ames' life. Yet despite general praise, some reviewers reflect the traditional bias of the literary establishment when religion is the subject. Typical is this *New York Times* reviewer who offers somewhat backhand praise: "Robinson's pastor is that most difficult narrator from a novelist's point of view, a truly good and virtuous man, and occasionally you may wish he possessed a bit more malice, avarice or lust—or just an intriguing unreliability."[33]

The reviewer never explains why we would want a more flawed narrator, and later in his review, seems to contradict himself in the comment that "while John Ames may be a good man, he is not an uninteresting one, and he has a real tale to tell." One would think he would praise Robinson for creating a "not uninteresting" good man, since he views such a character as a challenge for the novelist. In an interview, when Robinson was asked about this supposed difficulty of creating a "good" narrator, she denied that such a character is generically uninteresting and suggested that such a view reflects some bias about goodness.

> I know good characters are supposed to be uninteresting.
> That must be a very recent discovery. There are plenty of good people in literature. For one thing, they make reliable and scrupulous narrators. For another, they convey ethical and emotional nuance. Goodness, after all, requires a disciplined attention to other people.[34]

Robinson added a comment suggesting that this belief in the "good" character as negative may be due to the negative imaging of religion in the contemporary culture wars when she comments, "If the word 'good' implies narrowness, judgmentalism or hypocrisy, then 'good' has become a synonym for 'bad,' nothing a writer would wish to explore sympathetically."[35]

If the *Times* reviewer's comments were colored by a negative bias against such an overtly religious novel, a review in *New York Magazine* was much more explicitly biased. In his opening paragraph, the reviewer asserts that "unless you are a believing Christian with strong fundamentalist leanings, you cannot truly understand *Gilead*. Lacking such faith, you're probably not going to like it much, either."[36] The inclusion of the adjective "fundamentalist" is so far wide of the mark that the reviewer's association of Robinson with the religious right seems to be a clear bias against any work with religious content of any kind. Cleverly, the reviewer claims that the acclaim accorded *Gilead* is not for its literary merits but derives from liberal guilt, thus not only maligning Robinson's novel but simultaneously accounting for the enormous praise it received from the literary establishment, a negative rather than positive feature. He writes,

Robinson currently represents everything that liberal, urbane, ironic culturati are now derided for smugly disdaining. And so image-sensitive liberal, urbane, ironic culturati are going to want to prove their complex open-heartedness by indifferently swooning over her book.[37]

Since *Gilead* won the Pulitzer Prize for fiction in 2005, it seems unlikely that it was honored simply as overcompensation by the "culturati," as this reviewer would claim. The reductive dismissal of a novel of this caliber simply because it is informed by a Christian consciousness reflects the generally liberal bias of the media as noted earlier, and the difficulty facing any writer whose work is "nourished by religious concerns."

Despite Colson's attempt to suggest that *Gilead* represents some "renaissance" in evangelical religious fiction, Frederick Buechner's *Godric,* published in 1980, shows that superb fiction "nourished by religious concerns" is no new phenomenon but has existed, along with evangelical fiction, for some time. Buechner shares with Robinson the creation of a narrative voice for a unique protagonist. Godric of Finchale is an actual twelfth-century hermit and saint, and using the scant resources available about his life, Buechner allows the saint to tell his own story. As one commentator notes, Buechner gives Godric "a marvelous narrative voice reminiscent of the cadence and vocabulary of a medieval epic character, but entirely plausible, even likely."[38]

Interestingly, throughout the novel, Godric is parrying with his actual biographer and contemporary, Reginald of Durham, who, in the habit of the times, is determined to create an idealized portrait of the hermit. The hermit, however, is determined to present a more realistic picture of himself as a redeemed sinner. As he advises Reginald,

Know Godric's no true hermit but a gadabout within his mind, a lecher in his dreams. Self-seeking he is and peacock proud. A hypocrite. A ravener of alms and dainty too. A slothful, greedy bear. Not worthy to be called a servant of the Lord when he treats such servants as he has himself like dung, like Reginald. All this and worse than this go say of Godric in your book.[39]

In this novel, holiness is a result of the continual struggle to tame the beast within.[40] The narrator's emphasis on the unsavory aspects of his life is presented as important to counter the tendency to hagiography, a practice that Godric is determined to subvert. Buechner's artistry is in the psychological verisimilitude with which he crafts Godric's narrative, presenting the saint as a human person who is gifted by grace. It is notable that Godric's visions—the appearances to him of St. Cuthbert, the source of his vocation as a hermit, and the Virgin Mary—do not transform him into a saint by some instantaneous canonization.

Buechner presents Christian spirituality as a determined effort to cooperate with the grace given. For the reader, Godric is both a historical figure and a contemporary Christian, since his story is the universal one of the human attempt to be worthy of grace bestowed by God. And Buechner also presents the institutional church and some of its members with comments that suggest that the situation today is much like that of the twelfth century.

Even in his church, the Lord is mocked by lustful, greedy monks and priests that steal. Men travel leagues to see the arm of some dead martyr in a silver sleeve that wouldn't lift a hand to save a living child that's fallen in a well.[41]

Twelve years later, Buechner gave voice to another historical figure, the patriarch Jacob, in his 1993 novel *The Son of Laughter*. Allowing Jacob to narrate his life enables Buechner to bring the modern novel's focus on realism to the Biblical story to revivify that story for contemporary readers. Note the detail with which he describes the simple tower of stones that Jacob and his father-in-law Laban built as a sign of the peace between them:

There were round ones and flat ones, some dusty and dry. Some of them were damp from where we had pried them out of the ground with bits of earth still clinging to them and here and there a worm. We found a stone as thick and long as a man's thigh to fox for a pillar on the top. It had moss on one side, the other side all cracked and scarred. [42]

In his famous description of the art of the novel, Joseph Conrad wrote,

My task which I am trying to achieve is, by the power of the written word, to make you hear, to make you feel — it is, before all, to make you see. That — and no more, and it is everything. If I succeed, you shall find there according to your deserts: encouragement, consolation, fear, charm — all you demand; and, perhaps, also that glimpse of truth for which you have forgotten to ask.[43]

This is an apt description of what Buechner achieves in *The Son of Laughter*. Through the use of realistic detail and psychological realism as well, he brings Jacob to life for the reader. And in Jacob's story, Buechner tells the universal story of faith. In the novel, God is referred to as "the Fear," to correlate with the Biblical injunction that He can have no name. And Jacob reflects on his family's relationship with the Fear:

The Fear gives to the empty-handed, the empty-hearted, as to me from the stone stair he gave promise and blessing, and gave them also to Isaac before me, to Abraham before Isaac, all of us wanderers only, herdsmen and planters moving with the seasons as gales of dry sand move with the wind. In return it is only the heart's trust that the Fear asks.[44]

As the novel ends, Jacob quotes his son Joseph reflecting on his personal experience of God with an apt description of faith, "He speaks to us sometimes in dreams that are like torches to light our way through the dark."[45] And, tellingly, Buechner ends the novel with four questions as Jacob reflects on the Fear's promises to him and asks,

Who knows the full meaning of his words? Who knows from how far he will bring me and to what place even farther still?
 Is his promise only a dream?
 Is it in our dreaming that we glimpse the fullness of his promise?[46]

In eschewing the declarative statement in favor of the question, Buechner reflects in his prose the human experience of faith, the uncertainty and insecurity of relationship with the Divine. Thus, although Buechner is faithful to the events of the Genesis narrative, he goes beyond events to the essence of the reality they signify. Buechner never loses sight of the fact that the story of Abraham, Isaac, and Jacob is a story of the journey of faith.

While *Godric* was nominated for the Pulitzer Prize, *The Son of Laughter* is a less accomplished novel. Ironically, Buechner's strength in this novel is also the source of its weakness. In his absolute fidelity to the events depicted in Genesis, Buechner creates an unusually faithful portrait of the patriarch. As the reviewer for *Theology Today* commented,

Our habit is to read back into the Jacob story the intricately articulated spirituality that has accumulated through our readings of Moses and David and Isaiah. But Abraham, Isaac, and Jacob lived without benefit of most of the preaching and prayers and wisdom that we take for granted.[47]

However, in his allegiance to the Biblical narrative, Buechner created a rather plodding story because he does not allow himself any of the techniques that authors can use to vary the pace of the action and more easily engage readers. And because the events are familiar, there is not even the universal readers' anticipation of "what happens next" to propel the story. Nevertheless, Buechner's readership, although limited, appreciates his work. Although there are only nine reader responses to *The Son of Laughter* on Amazon.com, most of these readers rate the novel very highly and recognize its virtues. Buechner may have a limited number of readers, but they are sophisticated readers who appreciate the literary novel. As one reader commented in a review dated April 2, 2002, *The Son of Laughter* "brings to life like no other author I've read the struggle toward God, the intra-family strife, and the sheer battle to stay alive in harsh times and an unforgiving landscape."

The issue of accessibility in these novels is relevant, not only to their sales figures but to the dominance of the conservative Christian fiction described in Chapters 4 and 5. Both Robinson and Buechner have authored literary novels that are not readily accessible and appeal mainly to educated readers who read for pleasure rather than escape and expect their fiction to be intellectually challenging. That market is not vast, which is why this fiction does not generate the mammoth sales of evangelical Christian fiction. In fact, it is clear from reader responses on Amazon.com that some conservative Christians who read these novels, perhaps having heard that they are "religious," are often disappointed because the fiction fails to conform to their expectations for religious literature.

Gilead, as a Pulitzer Prize winning novel, was naturally selected by many book groups, and the reader responses at Amazon.com are almost perfectly bifurcated. Those familiar with Robinson's earlier novel are almost universally enthralled with *Gilead,* while others admit to not even finishing it. Typical negative comments refer to the book as boring and lacking a plot, with one reader mentioning that it was chosen by her book club and that was the only reason she finished it. Several readers admitted that they expected a "better" novel because of the critical praise and awards, suggesting that it came to their attention because of its reputation. The reader's comment that most aptly reflected the reason for this dissatisfaction described the novel as "something I would expect to encounter in a college class, not something to read for fun."[48] That is, the reader expected the typical escapist novel common to popular fiction rather than a book that would make intellectual demands.

The question of audience for the religious novelist was addressed by Buechner in a 1985 interview. He expressed the belief that his reputation as an ordained minister may alienate the very readers he hoped to influence, the spiritual seekers who are so prominent in our individualistic contemporary culture. Buechner suggested that while such people may be searching for spirituality, they may identify him with more conservative, proselytizing ministers and thus reject his books. He identifies his usual readers as a relatively small group, principally liberal, church-going Christians.[49] The reader reviews of his novels on Amazon.com appear to affirm the accuracy of his estimate. Despite the fact that *Godric* was critically praised and nominated for the Pulitzer, there are only seventeen reviews listed. However, all are highly praiseworthy, detailed reviews that indicate these are informed readers who appreciate the novelist's achievement from both a literary and a religious perspective.

Interestingly, the less well-known *The Son of Laughter* seems to have come to the attention of some untypical Buechner readers, perhaps because conservative Christians are always attracted to fiction with a basis in Scripture. However, although some expressed satisfaction with the novel, they considered it inappropriately risqué. One reader mentioned that although he would love to recommend the novel to those at his church, he would not dare to do so because of its "seamy" details. Sales figures indicate that conservative Christians are the largest group of readers for religious novels, but fiction that does not conform to their norms will not sell among them. And evangelicals' commitment to Biblical inerrancy would make any fiction suspect if it presumes to re-create the actual Biblical narrative, as opposed to a novel that simply alludes to a Biblical source, such as *Redeeming Love.*

Parents and Children

The novel that inspired Chuck Colson's encomium to a renaissance in Christian fiction is Elizabeth Strout's 2006 *Abide with Me*—or more accurately, it was a review of that novel in the *Washington Post* that claimed Colson's attention. But just because a novel involves the Christian religion does not mean it belongs to the body of fiction published by evangelical houses and increasingly devoured by conservative Christians, as described in the preceding chapters. Strout's novel is the story of Tyler Caskey, a young Congregationalist minister in his first pastorate. The northern New England town that is the setting for the novel reflects the tone of the narrative as well, spare and bleak. Rev. Caskey has recently lost his young wife Lauren to cancer, and his congregation is amazed at his strength during her terminal illness. But the reader soon becomes aware that it is not strength so much as denial that is the basis for Caskey's behavior. Strout records that "Tyler didn't think Lauren would die." However, "He should have. His mother knew, her parents knew, the doctor knew. Lauren knew."[50]

Since Lauren dies while Tyler is still in denial, he psychologically retreats from her death by closing himself off to feeling while continuing his ministerial duties with an appearance of still being attentive to others. So emotionally isolated is Tyler that he cannot even relate to the problems that his five-year-old daughter Katherine is experiencing at the loss of her mother, and the child's torment is heart-wrenching. Tyler is totally inwardly focused because he has lost what he calls "The Feeling," that moment when everything in nature surrounding him "would fill the minister with profound and irreducible knowledge that God was right there."[51] Although Strout has wisely written the novel in third person to provide the reader with a little distance from the protagonists' emotional pain, Tyler's internal turmoil is almost palpable, as Strout explains,

There was a fear the man lived with, a dark cave inside him: that he might not feel The Feeling again. That the exhilarating moments of transcendence had merely been the product of a youthful—and perhaps not even manly—form of hysteria.[52]

Strout charts the dissolution of Tyler's congregation as a consequence of his inattentiveness. Their tendency toward petty gossip becomes malicious and spiteful, spiraling out of control when the innocent Tyler is suspected of inappropriate behavior with his housekeeper. Ultimately, the crisis is resolved for all—Tyler, his daughter, and the members of his congregation. And the minister once again experiences The Feeling, but this time in an unexpected way. The novel's ending is an enactment in this New England town of Romans 8:28, "We know that in everything God works for good with those who love him."

Throughout the novel, Strout's prose style is impeccable, as she maintains the narrative in what the *Washington Post* reviewer called "an extraordinarily delicate position." As he explains, "One careless move and the whole novel crystallizes into something shiny and doctrinaire — or, just as bad, dissolves into the pool of sophisticated cynicism about traditional Christian faith."[53] It is Strout's ability to keep her novel from becoming "something shiny and doctrinaire" that most clearly separates this book from typical evangelical Christian fiction.

Ironically, despite excellent critical reviews of *Abide with Me,* many of the reader reviews on Amazon.com express dislike for the novel. The common theme among these reviews is that the readers could not care about any of the characters. One reader reported in a review dated April 23, 2006, that the novel was "dark and depressing," and concluded, "Its [*sic*] an easy book to read, but I ended up not caring about any of the characters, not liking the town, and overall tired of the book. I was glad when it was over." Often relatively unsophisticated but voracious readers who subsist mainly on popular fiction will come across a literary novel like *Abide with Me,* especially those who are attracted to what they perceive to be a "Christian" book. Their difficulty is often due to the fact that inexperienced readers are strongly affected by the climate of the book, unable to separate themselves from the world the author is creating as a more sophisticated reader can. In a novel like this, the reader who unconsciously absorbs Tyler's psychological pain and his daughter's distress will find the book extremely discomforting. In the effort to distance themselves from these emotions, these readers will distance themselves from the novel as well. I believe that's why the inability to "care" about the characters was the common theme in these reviews.

This is significant because a large part of the success of conservative Christian fiction is that it is designed for its readership. And that is not the same reader who can enjoy more literary novels, such as *Gilead* and *Abide with Me.* Note that the reader quoted above begins with a positive comment about Strout's novel, but it's the fact that *Abide with Me* is "an easy book to read." Ironically, this may account for the dislike by many readers. Strout's fluent narrative may be deceptive in suggesting to naïve readers that this is popular fiction. And the unsophisticated reader who is comfortable with such novels may feel betrayed by this literary novel with its bleak landscape, depressing both physically and psychologically. *Abide with Me* is "an easy book to read," but it is deceptively easy; accessible initially, it draws the reader into a literary terrain that may be disconcerting for the reader of popular fiction who is unprepared for the complexity of the novel and the bleakness of its world.

A novelist whose work even more closely approaches popular fiction is Gail Godwin, but as with Strout, the appearance of simplicity can be deceiving. In 1999, Godwin published a novel of a young minister's crisis in *Evensong.* That minister, Margaret Bonner, neé Gower, was introduced to readers earlier in Godwin's 1991 best seller, *Father Melancholy's Daughter,* another novel that reflects the fact that quality fiction "nourished by religious concerns" is no recent phenomenon, as Chuck Colson suggests.

As with Tyler Caskey, the signal event in the life of Rev. Walter Gower, an Episcopalian priest in the fictional small town of Romulus, Virginia, was the loss of his wife. Unlike Lauren Caskey, however, shortly before Walter's wife

Ruth died, she had abandoned him, running off with a former teacher, Madelyn Farley, ostensibly to experience life more fully. When Ruth is killed in an automobile accident, the question of whether she would have eventually returned becomes moot for both Walter and his six-year-old daughter, Margaret. A man temperamentally prone to depression, Walter is devastated by Ruth's departure, and Margaret's youth, chronicled in the novel, is dedicated to parenting her parent.

In one sense, a traditional coming-of-age novel, *Father Melancholy's Daughter* could easily have emphasized the psychological component of Margaret's development, dealing with the sense of abandonment by her mother and coping with the burden of a dependent father. And the psychological is certainly apparent in the novel. However, Godwin's multifaceted narrative is also a story of religious faith, and the journey involved in dealing with that relationship to God. Like Tyler Caskey, Margaret experiences The Feeling, an awareness of the presence of God.

At times like this, when I was simply going about my business, doing whatever it was that presented itself to be done next. . ., a strange sensation sometimes came over me. It was as if another presence were allowing me to become aware of its unwavering attention on my behalf; for it was always there, this larger, luminous, and highly focused consciousness.[54]

And because of Margaret's immersion in the world of religion as the daughter of an Episcopal rector, she struggles to identify her spiritual sensibilities as authentically her own, apart from the cloying piety she often observes among her father's parishioners. Thinking about her habit of reflection, she muses,

If I wanted to express it in religious language, I would have said I was "offering up" the past week, the whole mixed-bag of failures, accomplishments, and incompletes, and inviting the Holy Spirit to contribute its shaping powers to the one ahead. But such language made me squirm. Too many good words and images had been ruined by facile usage and unctuous people.[55]

As the religiously sophisticated daughter of a priest, Margaret is also sensitive to the human tendency to fashion a God to meet one's needs, rather than responding to the actual presence of the Divine. Aware of the gift of God's presence to her in her consciousness, Margaret nevertheless fails to be comforted because it is a challenging presence that asks her "to get on with its work. But I would have liked more of a Parent-God, into whose all-loving embrace I could curl up, into whose perfectly wise care I could give myself over and trust to make the most of me."[56] Having had to parent her own father for so long, this yearning for a Parent-God is understandable, but the image Margaret intellectually knows she must eschew is often the God of conservative Christian fiction, the caretaker who makes human effort unnecessary.

Margaret's story is the search for an authentic faith, the Stage 4 adult faith that Fowler describes. At one point in the novel, she meets a colleague of her father, a priest-psychologist, Adrian Bonner. When asked rather glibly for his definition of sin, he responds, "A falling short of your totality....Choosing to live in ways you know interfere with the harmony of that totality."[57] Margaret questions how one knows his or her "totality," and Bonner responds, "You learn. You unlearn. You pay attention. You feel where things balance for you and where they don't."[58] When the novel ends, Margaret has graduated from college and conquered some of her demons, but there is no happily-ever-after; this is not a romance novel. Margaret's challenge to know her totality and live in harmony with it is a lifetime project which she has come to understand—as has the reader.

Two Worlds of Fiction

It is too facile to suggest that the difference between evangelical Christian fiction and these more nuanced novels is simply that the former is popular fiction and the latter is serious or literary fiction. In fact, the major difference is that they represent two different conceptions of narrative, as was explained in Chapter 4. While contemporary, conservative Christian fiction is rooted in the classical paradigm, promoting the *mythos* that the community regards as authoritative, the novel as a literary form is a post-Enlightenment genre that presents human experience from the unique perspective of the author, a perspective that is developed within the act of creation. As one writer explains it, "The true work of art is not a known thing before its creation. You do not as an artist decide what the novel is going to say and then construct something to say it."[59]

Very often, this is the difference between a literary novel and a work of popular fiction; for most readers, the latter is a more satisfying experience, similar to viewing a favorite television show. Thus, the lack of critical recognition of evangelical Christian fiction by the mainstream literary establishment is understandable, since the genre violates the common understanding of the nature of the novel, an art form identified with the modern paradigm. For the literary critic, evangelical Christian fiction is a debased form of the novel unworthy of critical recognition. But the world of the literary critic and that of the average reader are separated by a wide and deep chasm.

For the average reader, the accessibility of popular fiction is its major virtue. The reader is not looking for ambiguity or metaphoric allusions so much as escapism, light entertainment for relaxation, whether it be the romance or the suspenseful thriller. Sales figures suggest that Christian fiction is not turning off nonbelievers, as Colson argues. Indeed, mainstream publishers are continually trying to recruit best-selling Christian writers to their imprint, cognizant of their ability to attract mainstream readers. For example, Jan Karon moved from her Christian publisher to the mainstream Viking after her first three novels were so successful, and LeHaye and Jenkins have left Tyndale, their Christian publisher, for Putnam, a mainstream house.[60] Colson seems more concerned with literary acceptance of Christian fiction than its ability to attract nonbelievers, but it is difficult for even the most accomplished literary writers to achieve recognition when their subject is religion.

Frederick Buechner has often mentioned in various interviews that he believes his work suffers from its association with religion, and he once cited a comment by the late eminent critic Alfred Kazin in a review of the *Oxford Companion to American Literature,* "Eyebrows will be raised in certain quarters by the amount of space given to Frederick Buechner."[61] As Buechner interpreted that comment, he explained, "I think what he meant was, I'm not really a writer of literature. I'm a writer of propaganda, somebody with a special ax to grind. A lot of reviews assume this."[62] Buechner's explanation of how he actually works helps to identify that fine relationship between faith and fiction,

I'm like any other novelist. I'm trying to listen to what goes on in the lives of my characters and to the interesting things that happen to people; and, because I am a religious person, I always listen for the religious things that go on.[63]

Although Buechner, an ordained minister, identifies himself as a religious person, the piety of the author is not an essential factor in religious fiction. The "religious concerns" that Zinsser alludes to in the epigraph to this chapter are often exploratory and ambiguous, with the writer asking a question as a premise. For example, the popular novelist Jodi Picoult has published an intriguing novel about the religious experience of a child and admits that it derives from the fact that neither she nor her husband is currently connected to their own religious heritage.[64] And Elizabeth Strout who writes so movingly of the crisis for a young minister identified herself in an interview as a "church hopper," explaining, "because I like to go to different churches and observe what they do. I'm really interested in churches and I go to them a lot."[65] Both novelists reflect the individual with no direct ties to a specific denomination but with interests in spirituality and religion.

Indeed, if there is a common denominator for literary novels of "religious concerns," it is that they are more focused on faith than on religion, more concerned with the interaction of human beings with transcendence than with doctrine or dogma. As Buechner explains, the novel is the ideal genre for dealing with issues of faith:

Faith and fiction both journey forward in time and space and draw their life from the journey, *are* in fact the journey....Fiction can hold opposites together simultaneously like love and hate, laughter and tears, despair and hope, and so of course does faith which by its very nature both sees and does not see and whose most characteristic utterance, perhaps, is "Lord I believe, help thou my unbelief." Faith and fiction both start once upon a time and are continually changing and growing in mood, intensity, direction. When faith stops changing and growing, it dies on its feet. So does fiction.[66]

No, there is no renaissance in Christian fiction, as Charles Colson asserts. Rather, fiction that is "nourished by religious concerns" has been a staple of American literature throughout its history. There are political, social, and even publishing industry reasons for the contemporary focus on evangelical Christian fiction, but the real world of literature reveals that there are also other American writers who take both religion and literature seriously. The next chapter looks at that more varied religious landscape.

Notes

1. To reinforce this fact that *Christy* is not considered part of the contemporary subgenre of "Christian novel," when I tried to purchase a copy of the book, it was not in the inventory of two online Christian booksellers—but readily available at Amazon.com.

2. Christy Award web site, http://www.christyawards.com/about.html (accessed September 18, 2006).

3. Ron Hansen, "Faith and Fiction," *A Stay Against Confusion: Essays on Faith and Fiction* (New York: HarperPerennial, 2002), 25.

4. Ibid.

5. Ibid.

6. James W. Fowler, *Stages of Faith: The Psychology of Human Development and the Quest for Meaning* (San Francisco: Harper & Row Publishers, 1981), 164. Note that this 1981 book was published before the proliferation of Christian fiction, and Fowler's comments here about television evangelists and media clubs would apply as well to this form of media.

7. Catherine Marshall, *Christy* (New York: Avon Books, 1968), 20.

8. Fowler, *Stages of Faith,* 179.

9. Marshall, *Christy,* 224.

10. Ibid., 310.

11. Ibid., 434. Italics in text.

12. Karen Kingsbury, *Fame* (Wheaton, IL: Tyndale House Publishers, Inc., 2005), 209.

13. Janette Oke, *Love Comes Softly* (1979; repr., Minneapolis, MN: Bethany House Publishers, 2003), 30.

14. Monique El-Faizy, *God and Country: How Evangelicals Have Become America's New Mainstream* (New York: Bloomsbury, 2006), 7.

15. John Wilson, "God Fearing," *New York Times Book Review,* November 12, 2006, 63.

16. From http://www.christyawards.com/about.html (accessed September 18, 2006).

17. Ramona Richards, "Redeeming 'Chick Lit,'" *Christianity Today,* 25, no. 5 (September/October 2004), http://www.christianitytoday.com/tcw/2004/005/3.50.html (accessed September 26, 2006).

18. Charles Colson, "Modern-Day Renaissance," April 27, 2006, http://www.break point.org/listingarticle.asp?ID=2178 (accessed November 9, 2006).

19. Ibid.

20. Ibid.

21. Terry Mattingly, "About those 'Left Behind' readers," http://tmatt.gospelcom.net/column/2006/07/19/ (accessed October 25, 2006).

22. El-Faizy, *God and Country,* 121.

23. Ibid.

24. William J. Bausch, *Storytelling: Imagination and Faith* (Mystic, CT: Twenty-Third Publications, 1984), 76.

25. William Faulkner, speech at the Nobel Banquet at the City Hall in Stockholm, December 10, 1950, http://nobelprize.org/nobel_prizes/literature/laureates/1949/faulkner-speech.html (accessed November 6, 2006).

26. Robert Wuthnow, *The Restructuring of American Religion: Society and Faith Since World War II* (New Jersey: Princeton University Press, 1988), 5.

27. Marilynne Robinson, *Gilead* (New York: Picador, 2004), 108.

28. Wuthnow, *The Restructuring of American Religion,* 184.

29. Robinson, *Gilead,* 114.

30. Ibid.

31. Ibid., 245.

32. Michael Dirda, "Giliad," *Washington Post,* November 21, 2004, BW15, http://www.washingtonpost.com/wp-dyn/articles/A61308-2004Nov18.html (accessed December 3, 2006).

33. James Wood, "Acts of Devotion," *New York Times,* November 28, 2004, http://query.nytimes.com/gst/fullpage.html?res=9E00E4DC103FF93BA15752C1A9629C8B63&sec=&pagewanted=all (accessed December 2, 2006).

34. Michelle Hunevan, "Divine Invention," *LA Weekly,* January 20, 2005, http://www.laweekly.com/art+books/books/divine-invention/1041/ (accessed December 2, 2006).

35. Ibid.

36. Lee Siegel, "The Believer," http://nymag.com/nymetro/arts/books/reviews/10525/ (accessed December 2, 2006).

37. Ibid.

38. "The Hermit in Lore: Frederick Buechner's *Godric,*" *Hermitary* at http://www.hermitary.com/lore/buechner.html (accessed December 1, 2006).

39. Frederick Buechner, *Godric* (San Francisco, CA: HarperSanFrancisco, 1980), 21.

40. Ibid., 164.

41. Ibid., 141.

42. Buechner, *The Son of Laughter* (San Francisco, CA: HarperSanFrancisco, 1993), 147.

43. Joseph Conrad, "Preface" to *The Nigger of the Narcissus,* http://www.brocku.ca/english/courses/2F55/narcis.html (accessed November 27, 2006).

44. Buechner, *The Son of Laughter,* 184.

45. Ibid., 273.

46. Ibid., 274.

47. Eugene H. Peterson, http://theologytoday.ptsem.edu/jan1994/v50-4-bookreview4.htm (accessed November 27, 2006).

48. Reader review of *Gilead* on Amazon.com dated August 24, 2005.

49. Buechner, "Doubt and Faith," *Of Fiction and Faith: Twelve American Writers Talk about Their Vision and Work,* ed. W. Dale Brown (Grand Rapids, MI: William B. Eerdmans Publishing Company, 1997), 35.

50. Elizabeth Strout, *Abide with Me* (New York: Random House, 2006), 187.

51. Ibid., 15.

52. Ibid.

53. Ron Charles, "Running on Faith," *Washington Post,* March 19, 2006, BW05, http://www.washingtonpost.com/wp-dyn/content/article/2006/03/16/AR2006031601632.html (accessed December 2, 2006).

54. Gail Godwin, *Father Melancholy's Daughter* (New York: Avon Books, 1991), 104–5.

55. Ibid., 185–6.

56. Ibid., 197.

57. Ibid., 207.

58. Ibid.

59. Robert Olen Butler, "On Madness and Longing," *Of Fiction and Faith,* ed., W. Dan Brown, 65.

60. El-Faizy, *God and Country,* 123.

61. Buechner, "Doubt and Faith," *Of Fiction and Faith,* ed. W. Dan Brown, 33–4.

62. Ibid., 34.

63. Ibid., 32.

64. Jodi Picoult, *Keeping Faith* (New York: Harper Perennial, 2000). In an appendix to the novel, "P.S," 11. This information is also available on the author's web site, "A Conversation with Jodi about *Keeping Faith,*" http://www.jodipicoult.com/ (accessed November 5, 2006).

65. Alden Mudge, "Healing Faith," http://www.bookpage.com/0603bp/elizabeth_strout.html (accessed December 4, 2006).

66. Buechner, *The Clown in the Belfry: Writings on Faith and Fiction* (San Francisco, CA: HarperSanFrancisco, 1992), 13.

7

Varieties of Religious Experience

> In fiction, as in faith, something from outside ourselves is breathed into us if we're lucky
> and if we're open enough to inhale it.
>
> —Frederick Buechner

In Giles Gunn's premise that literature is related to religion in "at least three structurally distinctive ways," he explains his three phases of complementary, oppositional, and alternative literature as progressive, paralleling the historical shifts in Western civilization.[1] Thus, in our postmodern culture, we should expect literature to offer an alternative to traditional religion or to substitute for religion, which should be on the wane in our post-Enlightenment society. And this has been a characteristic approach in contemporary American literature in which the subject of religion in mainstream fiction is often treated with suspicion by the literary establishment, as we've seen in the preceding chapter. Yet despite this marginalization of religion, there is no dearth of contemporary writers whose fiction is concerned with issues of religion and spirituality, fiction that is more characteristic of Gunn's complementary phase in which literature "provided a form for the exploration, articulation, and revivification" of religious ideals.[2] In writing about his perspective on writing, the novelist Ron Hansen provides one explanation for this mainstream fiction of religious experience by contemporary writers.

Hansen refers to the novel that epitomizes the alternative phase in which literature serves as a substitute for religion, James Joyce's *A Portrait of the Artist as a Young Man.* As the novel ends, its hero, Stephen Dedalus, announces his renunciation of Ireland and Catholicism in favor of his dedication to his art in a famous declaration:

I will tell you what I will do and what I will not do. I will not serve that I which I no longer believe whether it call itself my home, my fatherland or my church: and I will try to express myself in some mode of art as freely as I can and as wholly as I can, using for my defence the only arms I allow myself to use—silence, exile, and cunning.[3]

As Hansen notes, these lines are famous because they encapsulate the dominant artistic sentiment of the twentieth century, a rebellion against the fetters of tradition and traditional institutions. And he continues, "And so the situation is now, to some, reversed: that in a society that seems increasingly secular and post-biblical it is now writers and artists of faith who may feel exiled or silenced, who may feel they can say the unsayable only through cunning."[4] Later Hansen explains that it was specifically in rebellion against what he believes is the trivialization of religion in contemporary American culture that he decided to fashion novels that dealt more specifically with his religious heritage and with the mystery of faith.[5] In other words, in Giles' schema, the alternative phase reflected the abandonment of religion for art, as expressed by Joyce in his character of Stephen Dedalus, but in a dominantly secular society, some writers are now impelled to provide a corrective to the dominantly secular culture with literature that expresses religious ideals and values.

An interesting point about this contemporary fiction that is nourished by religious concerns is that its authors are not all allied with institutional religion or drawing on their personal religious heritage. Just as we noted with Elizabeth Strout in the last chapter, some of these authors would fit the description of "spiritual shoppers," as documented by Robert Wuthnow in his book on religious diversity.[6] Frederick Buechner, writing about the work of the novelist, commented, "You fashion your story as you fashion your faith, out of the great hodgepodge of your life. . . ."[7] Thus, the prevalence of fiction that reflects religious concerns testifies to the prominence of those concerns in American culture today. In the preceding chapter, we looked at some of the contemporary religious fiction that is not part of the evangelical publishing phenomenon of Christian fiction, and in this chapter, we will continue to look at the variety of this mainstream fiction.

The Challenges of Faith

Understandably, a major concern for contemporary writers of faith is how that faith can be lived effectively in our modern society. Writers approach this issue from various perspectives. *Mr. Ives' Christmas* by Oscar Hijuelos is a slender novel that resonates throughout with allusions to Charles Dickens and his novels, especially *A Christmas Carol,* and appears to be Hijuelos' contemporary American version of the Dickens classic. Rather than the ghosts of Christmas past, present, and future, Hijuelos presents a narrative of the life of Edward Ives, whose story is told with an emphasis on the major life events that occur during the various Christmas seasons—his adoption from a foundling home, meeting his future wife, and, the signal event of the novel, his son's murder just days before the holiday. Mr. Ives is a traditional Roman Catholic of quiet piety, and his faith in a benevolent God is challenged by this senseless murder of his eighteen-year-old only son who was about to enter the seminary to prepare for the priesthood when he is killed by a young street thug, Danny Gomez.

In the years following this defining moment of his life, Ives struggles with the typical reaction of a person of faith; how can God allow this to happen? In resisting his friends' encouragement to take revenge on Gomez, Ives achieves an uneasy peace, and he is even able to help with the rehabilitation of his son's murderer, maintaining communication with Gomez while he is in prison, urging him to continue his education, and even writing in support of his parole. Eventually, he even manages the face-to-face meeting that Gomez had requested several times but Ives had been unable to bear. Ives's faith is expressed in this novel in the kindness and generosity of his actions as well as his reflection on his duties as a husband, father, and citizen of the city of New York, the environment that both challenges him and supports him in his faith life.

As a child, Ives's response to the fact that his adoptive father's employees were mainly Puerto Rican was to begin to learn Spanish, both to understand their culture and to better communicate with them. As an adult, he chooses to remain in his multiethnic Manhattan neighborhood when he can afford to retreat to the suburbs where so many of his business associates have gone. Ives's faith is not armor against others, nor is it some magical protection against baser human instincts. It is a decision for God that he often has to renew as he faces life's struggles. For example, when Gomez has served his initial prison sentence as a juvenile and been released, Ives's friends urge him to take revenge. Among his neighbors are men who can arrange for the killer to "disappear," and Ives is encouraged to accept their help. But he counters his own urge for vengeance, "In those moments, he would pray for guidance, for wishing death upon another seemed so ugly that each time it occurred he felt a blackening of his soul."[8]

Dickens' Christmas story has given us a generic term for personal greed, warning of the "scrooge" in us all. That story of Christmas urges generosity for others less fortunate. In *Mr. Ives' Christmas,* Hijuelos extends the demand for generosity beyond the material. In the character of Edward Ives, faith is faithfulness, a generosity of spirit that is a habit of mind achieved through repeated action. The religious life in this novel is not isolating oneself from the secular world or living only among the like-minded; it is living Christianity in the world. Mr. Ives's deliberate decision to remain in his teeming, multiethnic neighborhood where he is forced to participate in the lives of his neighbors by their very proximity is emblematic of the transforming power of an individual life lived in faith.

In his study of religious diversity in the contemporary United States, Robert Wuthnow emphasizes the importance of "inclusive" Christians, those who have "somehow managed to retain their commitment to Christianity but apparently do not believe in the more exclusionary interpretations that have characterized Christianity in the past."[9] Edward Ives is such an inclusive Christian, a man whose hallmark is a generosity of spirit toward friend and stranger alike. For him, God is most present in "the goodness and piety of others."[10] Reflecting on

the powerful images of Jewish scholars he regularly sees around the theological
seminary in his neighborhood and the Turkish owner of one of his favorite res-
taurants who he had come upon one day when the man was engaged in prayer,
the narrative concludes,

> Of course, there were the pious priests and nuns, but, among the Christians, no one had
> more impressed Ives, through their own goodness, than some of the black congregational-
> ists walking along Broadway on the way to their churches. The serenity, the blissful sense
> of faith, that he saw on their faces was not the evidence of a wrathful nor vindictive God—
> though many of these people, from what Ives knew of history, would have had good
> reason to believe in one—but a kind and loving deity.[11]

The faith of Edward Ives is not merely tolerant of others; it is generously
accepting, a faith that views others truly as children of the same God. In his
contemporary Christmas story, Hijuelos shows what the Incarnation of
Jesus looks like in our pluralistic culture, and it is a challenging image of
faith.

That emphasis on the power of faith in an individual life is also evident in
Anne Tyler's *Saint Maybe.* Her protagonist, Ian Bedloe, is the son of a Baltimore
neighborhood's "ideal, apple-pie family."[12] The novel's plot is generated
when, at the age of eighteen, Ian tells his older brother that his new wife has
been unfaithful, something Ian only suspects but communicates with the certitude of adolescent conviction. Immediately after this conversation, his brother
is killed in a car crash that appears to be suicide. A few months later, his wife
dies of a drug overdose, either accidental or deliberate, due to despair. Three
young children are orphaned. The subsequent narrative chronicles the aftermath
of these deaths. Ian drops out of college because his aging parents are over-
whelmed with the challenge of dealing with such small children, and he spends
the next twenty years raising them, atoning for his role in the deaths of their
parents.

The religious themes appear obvious—sin, guilt, atonement, and redemption.
Yet the novel is as ambiguous as its title. In the novel, Ian is called "Saint Maybe"
by his niece Daphne as a term of derision, referring to his cautiousness and careful
living. But by the end of the narrative, it's apparent that the title refers to Ian
positively, to his refusal to dictate to others or presume to know what's best
for them. As "Saint Maybe," Ian is welcoming and inclusive of others, not
unlike Edward Ives. His equivocation is not only the opposite of the adolescent
arrogant certitude with which he announced his sister-in-law's presumed infidel-
ity but also the counterpoint to the empty dogmatism that infects organized
religion.

The Bedloes are conventional Christians, but at his sister-in-law's funeral, Ian,
who was usually "indifferent to prayers (or to anything else even vaguely religious)," earnestly participates in the service, hoping to assuage his guilt.[13] And,
as the service ends, it seems that his prayers are answered:

His knees were trembling. He felt that everything had been drained away from him, all the grief and self-blame. He was limp and pure and pliant as an infant. He was, in fact, born again.[14]

His redemption is short lived. At home after the funeral, he picks up his ten-month-old niece, orphaned by his indiscretion he believes, and suddenly he is bereft again, Ian "couldn't explain why the radiance left over from church fell away so suddenly. The air in the room seemed dull and brownish. . . . This child was far too heavy."[15]

Continually burdened with his sense of guilt for the deaths, Ian happens upon a storefront church, Church of the Second Chance, whose founder and pastor, Rev. Emmett, has attempted to purify his church, to cleanse it from all of the pomp and idolatry he sees in mainline religion. Seeking conventional forgiveness from Rev. Emmett, Ian is shocked when he is told that he is definitely *not* forgiven. According to the doctrine developed by the founder of Second Chance, specific reparation must be made for the fault, and, in this case, it means raising the children. Ian protests that he can't do that; he is only a college freshman, to which Emmett responds, "Then maybe you should drop out."[16] Anne Tyler has foreshadowed Ian's future in his reflection about children as an arrogant high school senior in the early pages of the novel. Babysitting for his brother's new family of three children, Ian "wondered how people endured children on a long-term basis—the monotony, irritation, and confinement of them."[17] This is the future that he sees before him in the demand that he must devote his life to raising the children.

Ian accepts the word of this rather eccentric minister, and thus begins years in which he sacrifices his own needs to care for his nieces and nephew and actively participate in Church of the Second Chance, with its proscriptions not only against extramarital sex and alcohol, but caffeine and sugar as well. Throughout the years of patient and diligent care of the children, Ian nevertheless feels unsatisfied spiritually and asks himself, "Why didn't he, after all these years of penance, feel that God had forgiven him"?[18] What the reader begins to see is that Ian has been looking for external approval, some magical forgiveness from God, and his humorless participation in the Church of the Second Chance has been to somehow earn that forgiveness. All conversion involves a turning, a change in perspective, and Ian finally comes to appreciate the children as less a burden than a life-giving force for him. At one point, he finally thinks to himself, "You could never call it a penance, to have to take care of these three. They were all that gave his life color, and energy, and. . .well, life."[19]

Later in the novel, Rev. Emmett suggests that Ian should prepare for ministry to eventually assume leadership of Second Chance. Ian considers this but refuses, explaining that it is not his *ability* to give people answers that he questions but his comfort in doing so. Remembering the arrogant certitude of his youth that resulted in two deaths and three orphaned children, Ian eschews any role that will lead him to similar dogmatic assertions. He now is comfortable with uncertainty, a "Saint Maybe." Characteristically, Ian questions his decision, queries that may echo the reader's own wonder: "When is something philosophical acceptance and when is it dumb passivity? When is something a moral decision and when is it scar tissue"?[20] However, Ian realizes that he doesn't need to decide what his true motives are because, at some level, he understands that he cannot know and that it is not important—or possible—to be certain. He has discerned that this is a decision God has led him to, and it doesn't matter whether it stems from weakness or strength.

In understanding that the life of faith is one of uncertainty, characterized more by the qualifiers "maybe" and "perhaps" than the verbs of being, "is" and "are," Ian not only avoids the certitude that led him to *his* original sin, but, in a way, he counters *the* original sin as well. The serpent tempted Eve with the promise that her knowledge would be like God's—that is, omniscient. In *Saint Maybe,* Tyler suggests that the assumption of that type of certain knowledge may be the root of sin, and the faithful life is in living with the uncertainty that is the human condition. Recognizing that it is human nature to be flawed, both people and the institutions they create, Ian Bedloe can remain faithful to a somewhat wacky church, even when its founder eventually reveals his fallibility to Ian, calling into question many of the precepts he had originally established as doctrine.

As the novel ends with the three children grown, Ian is celebrating the birth of his own son, still involved with the Church of Second Chance but now understanding it as a group of mutual support that provides him an opportunity to share with others and be present to them in their struggles. In the novel, Ian Bedloe has enacted the paradox of Matthew 16:25, in losing his life for the orphaned children, he has actually found his life. The tentativeness that his niece accuses him of as "Saint Maybe" is, in fact, an apt expression of faith. In Ian's reluctance to grasp at certitude, he mirrors the faith described by Frederick Buechner, "Faith is a lump in the throat. Faith is less a position *on* than a movement *toward,* less a sure thing than a hunch. Faith is waiting. Faith is journeying through space and through time."[21]

And the faith of Ian Bedloe is not unlike the faith of Edward Ives. In their respective novels, both men reflect openness to experience and a tolerance of others, flexibility in dealing with life, and, above all, the absence of certitude about the mystery of God's presence in the world. Although both protagonists practice their faith via an organized religion, absent from their faith expression is any sense of exclusivity or triumphalism, so often the hallmark of religious people. Thus, when Ian learns the fallibility of Rev. Emmett, how some of his rules have been based on ignorance rather than insight, his faith is not affected because it does not depend on the holiness of his church. Instead, Church of Second Chance offers Ian an opportunity to be supported in his faith, an occasion for worship and fellowship with like-minded believers. Similarly, although Ives is a devout Catholic, his singular experience of God's transcendence happens in midtown Manhattan among throngs of people, not within a church building during a service. For Ives, religion is an *expression* of his faith rather than its source.

Although *Mr. Ives' Christmas* and *Saint Maybe* are very different novels in structure and substance, the concept of faith in both is similar, and it is well expressed in yet another novel. In Jodi Picoult's *Keeping Faith,* a priest advises a young mother, "I don't care what other clergymen say; I've never believed that spirit comes from religion. It comes from deep inside each of us; it draws people to us."[22] And Picoult's novel emphasizes another aspect of faith, the mystery of God's action in the world.

The Mystery of Faith

In Jodi Picoult's *Keeping Faith,* the Whites are a secular, contemporary, American family with a story so typical that it seems trite—adulterous husband, naïve wife, separation, divorce, and custody battle. But that story is mere background to the compelling events involving the Whites' seven-year-old daughter, Faith. It begins with her involvement with an imaginary friend shortly after her parents' separation. While a young child with an imaginary friend is commonplace, it is less usual for that friend to be God. Initially, the child refers to her friend as her "guard," as she apparently misunderstood the Deity's introduction of herself. Yes, Faith also insists that her God is female. Her mother is at first astonished by Faith's casual recitation of Biblical verses, since the child has received no religious instruction whatever, not even Bible stories. And when Faith is asked by a psychologist whether her "guard" has any other friends, she mentions several names that the Roman Catholic psychologist recognizes with astonishment as very obscure medieval saints. She also realizes that the child could not know these names, and in her efforts to authenticate Faith's experience, she unwittingly provides the means for the media to learn of this child who is apparently visited by God.

Subsequently, Faith is credited with physical cures, including the healing of her grandmother who had been declared dead of a heart attack. Finally, and perhaps most disturbingly, Faith physically manifests the wounds of Christ, known as the stigmata, a manifestation usually associated with great saints of the Middle Ages. What makes the child's experience believable as an authentic manifestation of the Divine is that neither of her parents is a churchgoer, and she has been raised without any awareness of the religious heritage of either of her parents, respectively Jewish and Christian. Thus, she would have no religious knowledge or images available to her to create these phenomena from an overactive imagination, the default explanation that everyone in the novel would prefer.

Eventually the clergy become involved, and their reaction is varied. There's a Catholic priest who encourages Faith's mother, Mariah, to believe that her daughter is in communication with the Deity. He argues for an indwelling God:

I don't know if God is speaking to Faith, Mrs. White. I'd like to believe it, though. I don't care what other clergymen say; I've never believed that spirit comes from religion. It comes from deep inside each of us; it draws people to us.[23]

But there is also a Rabbi who disbelieves in Faith's experiences because he cannot believe that God would fail to meet the Rabbi's expectations of how the Deity should behave:

I don't see God telling her that the Israelites are going to cream the PLO. I don't see God telling her to keep kosher. I don't see God even inspiriting her to come to Friday-night services. And I have a very hard time believing that if God did choose to manifest Himself in human form to a Jew, He would choose one who hadn't followed a code of Jewish living.[24]

Eventually, Faith's physical manifestations of the stigmata are healed, and her communications with God end. There is a suggestion in the novel that Mariah's self-absorption and the distraction of her marital problems had kept her from mothering Faith adequately, and that may have been the impetus for God's intervention in the child's life. Through the crisis with Faith, Mariah recovers her mothering instincts, and thus the disappearance of God from an active involvement with Faith would be understandable; the child was no longer emotionally needy. One way to see the supernatural intervention was that it was designed to effect this union between mother and daughter. The obvious question remains. If, indeed, this is a case of God speaking to this child, why this particular child? There are many lonely children in the world, many children who need a better parent. From this perspective, the story is one of the mystery of God's actions, a reminder that God is not answerable to human reason but a Being with designs of His (or Her) own.

In the novel, the Rabbi represents those who would limit God, who would insist that God meet their expectations, and who cannot credit any expression of spirituality without religious observance. It is as though pious practices are an end in themselves rather than a means for fostering the individual's faith life. This is an error that can easily enter into institutional religion, especially long-established religions in which the practices have become so routine that they are devoid of meaning for many people. All four gospels record Jesus commenting on the fact that the scribes and Pharisees had retained the rules of religious observance and lost the true spirit of those practices.[25] Today, Christianity is similarly distanced from its origins and prey to a similar mindless formalism. In the spirit of the genre of the novel, Picoult raises questions in *Keeping Faith* rather than providing answers, but her questions cut to the heart of the issue of whether we can accept as actions of God things that are a mystery to us.

While manifestations of the stigmata are relatively rare in history, amazingly another contemporary novel also deals with this phenomenon, Ron Hansen's *Mariette in Ecstasy*. This is a novel in which such phenomena would be more expected, since it takes place among the members of a religious order. When the story begins, Mariette is a young woman of seventeen entering a cloistered convent in upstate New York in the early part of the twentieth century. She is young, beautiful, and happens to be the younger sister of the convent's prioress, a sibling twenty years her senior. This is a situation ripe for conflict, as the older nuns may resent both Mariette's beauty and her special association with the mother superior.

When Mariette also seems to be exceptionally humble and spiritual, her demeanor opens a rift between the nuns who admire her, some with obvious erotic interest, and those who are jealous of her gifts. After all, these are women who have devoted themselves to prayer and religious devotion for many years, and suddenly this newcomer appears to have a more developed spiritual life than they do. Soon after the death of Mariette's sister, the prioress, from cancer, Mariette manifests signs of the stigmata, and the situation in the convent intensifies. Those jealous of Mariette are more insidious in their claims that she is fabricating and a fraud, while those who admire her are convinced of her sainthood. It takes a great deal of maturity, self-knowledge, and reflection to deal with the idea that God acts in His own ways, and our role is not to question.

In a telling scene, the prioress who has succeeded Mariette's sister explains her suspicions with a comment similar to that of the Rabbi in *Keeping Faith,* "I have been troubled by God's motives for this....I see no possible reasons for it."[26] Once again there is an inability to admit that God's work in our world is a mystery that we may not comprehend. In the Jewish tradition, speaking or writing the name of God is proscribed because to name is to control, and human beings should not presume to control the Deity. Both the Rabbi and the prioress in these two novels are guilty of the hubris that would control God by insisting that He work only in ways comprehensible to them.

Of course, the prioress has a responsibility for discernment to ascertain the validity of these apparently spiritual manifestations, since Mariette is a postulant, an aspirant seeking to join the religious community. Is this truly a manifestation of God's action in the world, or is this the result of spiritual hysteria that would render Mariette unsuitable for religious life? Clearly, Mariette's religious superiors have a responsibility to the community to attempt to discern the authenticity of her situation. In masterful prose, Hansen provides enough evidence for the reader to take either side; nothing is conclusive.

In an address to the community about Mariette's situation, the prioress concludes

We know that there *are* miracles in the gospels, but we show them disrespect if we dispose ourselves to believe in the simply fabulous. And we must keep in mind that there are a good many more pages in holy scripture that show how little pleasure God takes in astounding us with His power....And let us remember that sainthood has little to do with the preternatural but a great deal to do with the simple day-to-day practice of the Christian virtues.[27]

In his book on faith and fiction, Ron Hansen says that in this speech, the character speaks with the view of the author.[28] But if true spirituality is grounded in simple, virtuous living, why then are these two contemporary novels, published in the same decade, concerned with such a dramatic, supernatural manifestation like the stigmata? Interestingly, Picoult and Hansen have very different perspectives as authors, and yet their use of the stigmata in their novels points to a common concern with contemporary culture.

First, it is important to note how very different these novels are despite their common concern with stigmatics. Jodi Picoult is a writer of popular fiction, and her novels are engaging narratives but relatively weak from an aesthetic perspective. In *Keeping Faith,* the symbolism of the child's name is disconcertingly obvious, and the shifts in narrative perspective from first to third person are jarring, as there is no literary reason for the shifts. They seem to be for the convenience of the author in propelling her narrative. Ron Hansen, on the other hand, is a literary novelist. The prose in *Mariette in Ecstasy* is exquisite, and the novel is expertly crafted. My point is that these authors are addressing different readers, both the general reader of fiction in Picoult's case and the more literary reader who would be attracted to Hansen's prose. And the authors themselves have very different backgrounds.

Jodi Picoult comes from a nonobservant Jewish background, and she married a nonpracticing Protestant. According to her explanation, the story of Faith White began when she was engaged in a conversation with her own son about God, a conversation that reminded her that the situation she creates in *Keeping Faith,* a child whose parents are separated from their own religious heritage and have not given their children any introduction to religion, is not unusual in contemporary society.[29] Thus, her story begins with the child in such a situation who is, or seems to be, visited by God.

Ron Hansen has been explicit about his strong Roman Catholic faith and heritage, explaining that the contemporary "culture of disbelief" that Stephen Carter has described impelled him to make religion more central to his art.[30] In developing the story of Mariette, he drew on the literature of his religious heritage, transmuting his sources to create a plot that initially seems removed from contemporary culture, but in its tension between belief and unbelief is very similar to that in *Keeping Faith.* In fact, despite the vast differences in the two novels and in the backgrounds of the two authors, Hansen describes an authorial impulse that seems as true for Picoult as it is for him:

I have identified in my own experience and that of many other Christian and Jewish writers that there comes a time when we find the need and the confidence to face the great issues of God and faith and right conduct more directly.[31]

In both novels, there is an apparent incursion of God into human life, and in both cases, some characters believe that the apparently miraculous is a sham, some hoax being perpetrated. The question raised by both novels for a contemporary reader is whether we have faith or merely religion. That is, has Christianity become part of our cultural heritage rather than a lived experience so that we no longer credit something beyond our comprehension? Granted, such manifestations in history often have been the result of religious hysteria rather than Divine intervention, but in the fiction, the strongest dissent is voiced by representatives of institutional religion. The Rabbi in *Keeping Faith* wants God to favor believers and promote a Jewish agenda, and Mariette's prioress complains that she doesn't know why God would do such a thing, with an implicit jealousy of the young postulant who appears to be so highly favored. As she says at one point to Mariette, "And if it is within your power to heal me of the hate and envy I have for you now, please do that as well."[32] While there is much more to both novels, at the heart of the unbelief in both is the presumption that if the action doesn't make sense, it can't be true. That's the post-Enlightenment paradigm writ large. Human reason is the only transcendent reality, and if something cannot be encompassed by reason, it cannot be real.

In *Keeping Faith,* the child is directed by her imaginary friend to a "book" that she is told is about her. It turns out to be Hebrews 11, the famous disquisition on faith, and there is a reminder in that text of faith's essence, "By faith we understand that the world was created by the word of God, so that what is seen was made out of things which do not appear."[33] In contemporary society, religious faith requires a belief in things beyond our comprehension, and the reluctance of religious people in both novels to accept the incomprehensible is a reflection of the effects of the post-Enlightenment society in which we live. The Enlightenment dethroned the miraculous in favor of human reason, and thus in expressing skepticism of spiritual phenomena as the Rabbi and the prioress do in these novels because their reason cannot comprehend why He would act as He (or She) apparently has, the characters reflect the challenge to faith in a secular culture.

Perhaps that is why so many recent novels are rooted in Scripture. In retelling a Biblical story, product of the traditional paradigm, through a novel, the genre of the modern paradigm, writers can effect a rapprochement between the two paradigms, infusing ancient tales with contemporary relevance. However, since the modern paradigm, unlike the Bible, credits no ruling *mythos,* there is significant variety in such fiction. Authorial intention is the only standard. And that variety can be instructive, as it reflects a variety of attitudes among writers.

Biblical Roots

In the introduction to his book of interviews with religious writers, William Zinsser refers to the long history of faith and fiction:

Every religious writer is of course the inheritor of a timeless body of writing—the efforts of all the men and women who have wrestled with the angels of faith and the demons of doubt to make some accounting of their trip.[34]

In the Judeo-Christian tradition, the origin of that "accounting" is the Bible itself. And Zinsser's mention of wrestling with angels, a clear allusion to the story of Jacob in Genesis,[35] suggests that initial book of the Bible as the bedrock of religious writing, the foundation of the narratives that follow in Scripture and beyond. While those who ascribe to inerrancy would disagree, most liberals would side with scholars who see the narratives of scripture as the classic expressions of such an accounting, the struggle of human persons to understand their relationship with Transcendence. Thus, it is not surprising that writers whose fiction is informed by religious concerns at times create fiction with specific allusion to the Bible.

In the preceding chapter, we saw one approach in Federick Buecher's *Son of Laughter,* a retelling of the story of Jacob in Genesis to effect an immediacy and sense of psychological realism for contemporary readers. Ideally, such a novel would illuminate the Scripture by revitalizing the narrative for readers, helping them understand the Biblical story in a more relevant fashion. In his novel, *Atticus,* Ron Hansen takes a very different approach with a novel based in Scripture.

In commenting on his fiction, Ron Hansen has written that "*Mariette is Ecstasy* is a parable of a young woman's quest for God; *Atticus* is a parable of God's continuing quest for an intimate relationship with us."[36] To create his parable, Hansen uses the Biblical story of the prodigal son as a source. His is not a simple retelling of the Biblical parable but a dense novel, one that takes on the characteristics of a complex murder mystery. Since Hansen is attempting to convey a divine "redeeming love" similar to Francine Rivers in her novel of that name, a brief comparison of *Atticus* and *Redeeming Love* will once again illustrate the difference between more formulaic Christian fiction and mainstream novels informed by faith.

Rivers is an experienced writer, and *Redeeming Love* undeniably evokes the spiritual core of the Book of Hosea, her source. Like Hansen, she creates an original novel using the basic elements of the Biblical narrative, in this case, God's directive to his prophet to wed a prostitute. Setting her novel in nineteenth-century California during the time of the Gold Rush creates an initial difficulty, since the metaphoric style of the Book of Hosea is not easily transferred to the genre of realistic fiction. It is telling that the most developed character in the novel is the prostitute, Angel, who is simply a cipher in the Biblical narrative. The absence of specifics in Scripture frees Rivers to create the character without any constraints, and she provides a heart-wrenching backstory for Angel, one that contributes most to the reader's emotional experience of the novel. Naming her male protagonist Michael Hosea is disconcerting at first, since "Hosea" is such an odd name, and it seems such an unnecessarily obvious allusion to the Biblical story. One wonders whether that was an attempt by either author or editor to justify the inclusion of the sordid details of Angel's life in an evangelical novel by assuring readers with a direct reference to the Biblical source.

More unsettling, however, is the fact that Michael has a direct line to the Creator, who announces, without ambiguity, that Angel is to be his bride. The first time Michael sees her walking down the street, he hears, "This one, beloved."[37] In another scene, Michael explains his behavior to his brother who has questioned his wisdom in marrying Angel by referring to his closeness to the Deity: "I know what *I* think and what God thinks, and that's all that matters."[38] The certitude that is the basic defect of true faith in mainstream fiction is faith's hallmark in evangelical Christian fiction.

While the Biblical narrative of the Book of Hosea conveys God's wishes to the prophet unambiguously, a realistic novel should portray the more complex nature of the human faith experience. It is undeniable that reading *Redeeming Love* can be an inspiring experience for a relatively unsophisticated reader, but Hansen's transmutation of the parable of the prodigal son in *Atticus* is much more consonant with the genre of the novel and with traditional understanding of the human faith experience. His novel presents a contemporary prodigal son in the character of Scott Cody, the forty-year-old profligate son of an affluent Colorado rancher, the title character, Atticus.

The Biblical parallel is evoked early in the novel when Scott is home for a brief holiday visit and his father cannot resist urging him to reform. The frustrated son replies,

You've got one son who's a huge success that any father'd be proud of, and you've got one son who's a slacker and using up your hard-earned cash on just getting from week to week. Hell, I'm forty years old. You oughta be used to me being a failure by now.[39]

Shortly after Scott returns to Mexico where he's house sitting for some friends, Atticus receives a call that his son has committed suicide. He travels to Mexico to bring home Scott's body, but while there becomes troubled by what he perceives are indications that his son did not commit suicide but has been murdered. As Atticus pursues evidence that Scott has been killed, the novel takes on the coloration of a complex murder mystery. Using the basic elements of the parable of the prodigal son—indulgent and loving father, successful elder son, and profligate younger son who has squandered his inheritance—Hansen creates a contemporary story that conveys the Biblical parable's central idea of God's passion for intimacy with us.

Ironically, although Hansen's *Atticus* is far more polished novel than Rivers' *Redeeming Love* from a literary perspective, the issue of accessibility gives Rivers many more readers, and readers who perceive the authorial purpose of communicating the essence of the Biblical source. As the sales figures for Christian fiction indicate, this is literature that does not require advanced education or literary knowledge to enjoy. Hansen's fiction, on the other hand, is more complex, both in content and in structure, and requires a more sophisticated reader. Thus, despite the fact that Hansen includes a specific rendering of the Biblical parable of the prodigal son in the novel, including its source in Luke 15,[40] and echoes the parable in the novel's final lines, a review of Amazon.com reader reviews indicates that few readers make the connection with the Biblical parable. Because of the intricacy of the mystery of Scott's apparent suicide and the narrative complexity with which Hansen presents Atticus's search for evidence, most reader reviews refer to the novel as simply a murder mystery with a few readers also alluding to the love of the father for his son. If we consider the author's expressed intention of conveying God's love for us through the person of Atticus Cody, then despite the technical and aesthetic excellence of Hansen's novel, *Redeeming Love* is more successful in evoking for the reader the essence of its Biblical source, the powerful love of God for His people.

Although it is not fashionable in contemporary literary circles to speak of authorial intention, in fiction that is written from an author's re-creation of a source such as the Bible for contemporary readers, the degree to which that intention is achieved is relevant. It is even more relevant when the author specifically writes about his intention, as Hansen has done. The basic principle is that the more complex the fiction, the less accessible it is to the average reader. Frederick Buechner, speaking about "what a religious novel at its best can be" describes it as "a novel less *about* the religious experience than a novel the reading of which *is* a religious experience...."[41] Thus, despite *Redeeming Love*'s limitations, both from an aesthetic and theological perspective, it may be quite successful religious fiction if it provides a sincere religious experience for its own target audience of conservative Christians and similarly inclined spiritual seekers.

Biblical Feminist

Anita Diamant, creating her novel *The Red Tent* from the same Biblical book that Buechner used for *The Son of Laughter,* is able to reach far more readers because of the nature of the novel she creates. *The Red Tent* tells the story of Jacob's daughter Dinah from *her* perspective. Although the practice of midrash, the retelling of Biblical stories to elaborate and develop, is common in Diamant's Jewish heritage, that is not what the author is doing in *The Red Tent*. In giving Dinah a voice, Diamant appropriates a character from Genesis and creates a story for her that is a classic historical romance with a feminist slant. As Radway emphasizes in her study of the romance genre, the romance novel is not incompatible with feminism, since female readers value the independent and able heroine of the romance.[42] Dinah, who never speaks in Genesis, narrates *The Red Tent,* and her first words in the Prologue establish the contours of the novel:

We have been lost to each other for so long.
My name means nothing to you. My memory is dust.
This is not your fault, or mine. The chain connecting mother to daughter was broken and the word passed to the keeping of men, who had no way of knowing. That is why I became a footnote, my story a brief detour between the well-known history of my father, Jacob, and the celebrated chronicle of Joseph, my brother.[43]

Buechner brought the ancient world of the patriarch Jacob to life through the realism of fiction. For Diamant, who creates an original novel from Genesis, that ancient world supplies a setting in which men and women truly inhabited separate spheres. This provides the opportunity for her to dramatize the special relationship among women in her fictional red tent. Drawing on the Jewish tradition of separating women from men, especially at the time of their menses, Diamant creates the red tent, the special space in Jacob's camp where the women congregate when they must be physically separated from the men. And in that place apart, Diamant is able to explore the special relationships among the women, an element absent from the patriarchal perspective of Genesis. As Diamant explained in an interview, "I did not set out to explain or rewrite the biblical text...but to use Dinah's silence to try to imagine what life was like for women in this historical period."[44] Interestingly, both Buechner and Diamant ignore the traditional interpretation of Dinah's rape at the hands of Shechem and describe the incident as consensual sex among young lovers. In *The Son of Laughter,* Buechner recounts the incident in this way:

Shechem no more ravished her than she ravished him. A boy is as frail with his big feet and strong hands, his lean long legs, as any girl with her fingers in her hair stringing flowers. A boy is as helpless at least against the heart's fury, which is as terrible as an army with banners.

   Somewhere outside the high walls, Shechem and Dinah met and fell. Beauty felled them together.[45]

And in *The Red Tent,* Diamant presents the first meeting of the young couple with images of marriage:

He saw me color and his smile widened. My awkwardness vanished and I smiled back. And it was as though the bride-price had been paid and the dowry agreed to. It was as though we were alone in our bridal tent. The question had been answered.[46]

   Diamant portrays the subsequent slaughter of the men of Shechem as the product of political maneuvering among members of the patriarchy. Jacob grudgingly agrees to Dinah's marriage, believing he has no choice because she is no longer a virgin, which diminishes her value to any other suitor. He can no longer expect to barter her for a favorable political affiliation. However, Dinah's brothers, Levi and Simon, who plan and implement the murders, oppose the marriage "sensing that their own positions would be diminished by such an alliance."[47] In keeping with the feminist perspective of the novel, Dinah is powerless. Her beloved is murdered because her brothers fear losing power and position. In Diamant's narrative, Dinah's story is a metaphor for the powerlessness of women in any patriarchal culture. The subsequent story of Dinah's long life in *The Red Tent* recounts how she eventually settled in Egypt and became a well-regarded midwife, a female nurturer of life rather than a male destroyer.

   Although *The Red Tent* sold a scant 10,000 copies in hardcover, it has sold more than 200,000 in paperback, sales that Diamant credits mainly to word-of-mouth among readers. She also notes, however, that the fact that the novel did well has "something to do with spiritual seeking, that it's an intensely woman's story and had a base in a very literate community that buys books."[48] Although *The Red Tent,* like *The Son of Laughter,* begins with the Genesis story of Jacob, as novels the two books are very different. Buechner's close adherence to the Biblical sequence of events results in a rather tedious narrative, one that exquisitely captures the psychological realism of Jacob's story but would be accessible to primarily the more educated readers of literary fiction. Alas, so strong is the presence of evangelical Christian fiction in the publishing industry that sophisticated readers tend to avoid novels with religious themes because of the assumption that all religious fiction belongs to the evangelical camp. Buechner has commented on his experience with reviewers and critics who seem to believe that all religious writers are "propagandists."[49] Thus, the relatively weak sales of *The Son of Laughter* are largely due to both its Biblical subject and its less engaging narrative that would appeal only to sophisticated readers.

However, Diamant, although drawing on the same Biblical narrative, created a novel with much wider appeal. In developing a plot of her own to chronicle the voiceless Dinah's life both before and beyond the tragic incident at Shechem, she produced a more engaging novel, a historical romance that would interest her target audience of educated women with feminist inclinations who are interested in their religious heritage. *The Red Tent* has broad appeal as both a novel that adds resonance to the Bible by realistically depicting life at that time and a novel that also has the attraction of a romance novel heroine, independent and resourceful. Yet without extensive marketing to her target audience, *The Red Tent* may have not exceeded *The Son of Laughter* in sales.

In interviews, Anita Diamant has described how effectively she marketed *The Red Tent* among Jewish women:

We initially sent the books to the female rabbis in Reform Judaism – about 500 women. The President of the organization was a friend of mine and wrote a cover letter recommending the book. Another friend who was the president of the Reconstructionist Rabbinic Assembly provided a cover letter and we sent copies to all of the Reconstructionist rabbis – both men and women. People preached from it and recommended it to their congregants.[50]

It is hardly surprising, then, that there are a scant nine reader reviews of *The Son of Laughter* on Amazon.com, while *The Red Tent* records 1,290 reviews, so vastly different are the audiences for these novels. And these reviews are revealing in terms of American religious culture. While Buechner regrets his limited readership, all nine reviews give the novel five stars and write glowingly of the effect of the novel's verisimilitude. A typical review, dated April 2, 2002, lauded Buechner because he "brings to life like no other author I've read the struggle toward God, the intra-family strife, and the sheer battle to stay alive in harsh times and an unforgiving landscape." Buechner may lament the paucity of readers, but though few in number, they are educated readers who appreciate his fiction. This is apparent because there are no complaints about the clay feet of Biblical heroes, a common thread among Diamant's dissatisfied readers.

Reader criticism of *The Red Tent* not only reflects the liberal/conservative dichotomy in American society that has been documented by sociologists and political scientists but also shows that split within a specific denomination—Judaism in this instance. As might be expected, conservative readers complained of the use of the Bible, a sacred text, as the background of a fictional story. One Rabbi who distinguishes between fact and fiction nevertheless excoriates Diamant for daring to present the giants of the faith as fallible:

Only sheer audacity would enable an author to rewrite the history of a nation's seminal figures, tarnishing the name of Judaism's noble ancestors. They were fallible, but they were giants. Even historical fiction must be based on history. And in this, she fails.[51]

Diamant confirmed in an interview that the reaction of orthodox rabbis has typically been negative, quoting them as referring to the novel as "an abomination... because they were looking at it as a Torah commentary, not an historical novel."[52] And conservative Christians have had a similarly negative reaction to Diamant's use of the Bible. This November 12, 2006, reader response on Amazon.com is typical of the relatively few negative responses among the 1,290 reviews of *The Red Tent* on that site:

This is definitely not a retelling of Joseph, Leah, Rachel and Dinah's story that meshes with the Bible. As a Christian, that bothered me to a degree; I feel that Diamant could just as easily have used other names, and this book would have been just as compelling.

In terms of readers, religious liberals would be the audience for both *The Son of Laughter* and *The Red Tent.* The higher sales for the latter novel can be attributed to the fact that historical romance can appeal to literary readers and to less sophisticated readers at the same time, while Buechner's fiction makes more demands on the reader and thus is limited to a much smaller group. In addition to being more accessible than *The Son of Laughter, The Red Tent* was marketed, as Diamant has explained, to its logical audience of liberal Jewish women with an interest in their heritage to overcome the reluctance of more educated readers who tend to disdain fiction with religious overtones.

Seeing Within

Not all fiction with spiritual significance is as obviously related to our Judeo-Christian heritage as these novels that derive from the Bible. In an essay on faith and fiction, Ron Hansen commented that "Christ's story is so primary to our literature that the eyes of faith can find it in a thousand variations."[53] Hansen's reference to the "eyes of faith" highlights an important consideration in any discussion of religious fiction. Literature is dynamic rather than static. In a literary novel, the reader is as much a producer as a consumer of meaning, creating the reality of the fiction in tandem with the writer. In *Gilead,* Rev. Ames's description of a good sermon is applicable to the process of reading as well:

A good sermon is one side of a passionate conversation. It has to be heard in that way. There are three parties to it, of course,...the self that yields the thought, the self that acknowledges and in some way responds to the thought, and the Lord. That is a remarkable thing to consider.[54]

As applied to fiction, Ames's description refers to the author and the reader, both involved in perceiving the reality of the narrative. Since, as Hansen notes, the story of Jesus, indeed the entire Biblical canon, can exist subconsciously within an individual, the reader's perception of religious meaning may even enter the fiction without a conscious intention on the part of the author. Indeed, it is commonplace for writers to describe a process of composition in which they are not themselves fully in control of the product. Frederick Buechner, for example, talks about how his twelfth-century saint, Godric, came alive in fiction:

I am talking about how, by something like grace, you are given every once in a while to be better than you are and to write more than you know. Less because of the research I did than in spite of it, Godric came alive for me—that is what I was given: the way he thought, the way he spoke, the humanness of him, the holiness of him. I don't believe any writer can do that just by taking thought and effort and using the customary tools of the craft. Something else has to happen more mysterious than that.[55]

In an interview, Elizabeth Strout also spoke of this mystery in the process of composition. Complimented on her depiction of the character of Katherine, the child who loses her mother to cancer in *Abide with Me,* she responded that the child's point of view came to her rather naturally and easily, explaining, "Who knows where these things come from? My grandmother died when I was five and maybe without knowing it I was drawing on feelings of bafflement I had about that loss."[56] Note that the process Buechner refers to as grace and described by Strout as emanating from the unconscious is true of the sophisticated reader no less than the writer. Both parties to the novel, author and reader, are involved in meaning making. This is why Hansen refers to the mythic elements of the Christ story being apprehended in fiction by those with "eyes of faith." In literary novels, there are layers of meaning, and within the context of ostensibly realistic fiction, symbolic elements can evoke religious ideas or imagery for some readers and not for others.

Hence, although Anne Tyler's *Saint Maybe* appears to be obviously concerned with religion, given its title as well as Ian Bedloe's need for forgiveness and his allegiance to the rather eccentric Church of Second Chance, one of Tyler's earlier novels, *Dinner at the Homesick Restaurant,* has strong religious symbolism at its heart that is not so readily apparent.

Titles are often illuminating, and although *Dinner at the Homesick Restaurant* is often referred to as the story of a dysfunctional family, the Tulls of Baltimore, it's the novel's title that reflects the story's deepest meaning. In the novel, Pearl Tull, deserted by her husband Beck, struggles to raise her three children, Cody, Ezra, and Jenny. There are no villains in this book; Pearl's inability to provide a warm and loving home for her children is more a product of temperament and circumstances than any willful action on her part. Jenny senses the barrenness of her own home when, as a high school student, she visits Ezra's best friend, Josiah, and, as she leaves, compares her own home with the warmth she's just experienced:

Jenny thought of…was it "Jack and the Beanstalk"?…or perhaps some other fairy tale, where the widow, honest and warmhearted, lives in a cottage with her son. Everything else—the cold dark of the streets, the picture of her own bustling mother—seemed brittle by comparison, lacking the smoothly rounded completeness of Josiah's life.[57]

The Tull family's lack of "smoothly rounded completeness" is symbolized in the novel by their repeated inability to finish a meal together at the Homesick Restaurant. The family's deficiencies are more symbolic than literal, a peculiar clash of personalities and failure to communicate with one other. For example, when Jenny avoids returning home during college vacations, the author explains,

It wasn't that she didn't want to see her mother. She often thought of her wiry energy, the strength she had shown in raising her children singlehanded, and her unfailing interest in their progress. But whenever Jenny returned, she was dampened almost instantly by the atmosphere of the house—by its lack of light, the cramped feeling of its papered rooms, a certain grim spareness.[58]

It is the Homesick Restaurant that her brother Ezra creates that serves as a counterpoint to the "grim spareness" of the family home. Although Cody and Jenny complete college, and Jenny goes on to become a physician, Ezra quietly dreams of owning a restaurant, but one very different than the upscale establishment Scarlatti's where he works as a teenager. Everyone in the family expects Ezra to attend college and find a suitable career, but while he is in the Army, Jenny learns from his friend Josiah that her brother has other plans for his future.

"Ezra's going to have him a place where people come just like to a family dinner," Josiah said. "He'll cook them one thing special each day and dish it out on their plates and everything will be solid and wholesome, really homelike."[59]

This is less an idle dream than the expression of a vocation, for Ezra is a nurturer at heart and has used food to comfort others throughout his life. As Tyler notes, "He was always so quick to catch his family's moods, and to offer food and drink and unspoken support."[60] It is this same quality that he wants to bring to his restaurant. Eventually, the widowed and childless Mrs. Scarlatti becomes ill and makes Ezra her partner with the promise that he'll inherit the restaurant when she dies. While she's still in the hospital, Ezra begins the transformation of Scarlatti's, with an emphasis on nurturing, "By December he had replaced three of the somber-suited waiters with cheery, motherly waitresses...."[61] As Ezra begins changing Scarlatti's into the restaurant of his imagination, he searches for exactly how that ideal will be realized and eventually thinks,

He'd cook what people felt homesick for—tacos like those from vendors' carts in California which the Mexican was always pining after; and that wonderful vinegary North Carolina barbecue that Todd Duckett had to have brought by his mother several times a year in cardboard cups. He would call it the Homesick Restaurant.[62]

In an interview about doubt and faith, Frederick Buechner commented, "I think the basic sickness is homesickness, and I think that is true for everybody."[63] And he added, "We're all so hungry, so hungry for each other and for lots of things, but it does seem to me that the basic hunger really is for the Word of God."[64] Ezra's restaurant is a metaphor for spiritual healing, satisfying that hunger of homesickness. Initially, he planned to restrict his menu to seasonal items; then he decided to abandon the menu and offer only "two or three good dishes." Finally, in an image redolent of ministry, he concludes, "Or I'd offer no choice at all; examine people and say, 'You look a little tired. I'll bring you an oxtail stew.'"[65] At the Homesick Restaurant, Ezra's ultimate goal is the solace of his patrons, both physical and spiritual solace. That the restaurant is a form of ministry is reinforced almost a decade later in Tyler's fiction in *Saint Maybe,* when, near the end of that novel, the dwindling Bedloe family goes out for Christmas dinner, and it is noted that "the owner kept his place open on holidays so that people without families had somewhere to go, and at nearly every table just a single, forlorn person sipped a solitary cocktail."[66] And on the next page, the owner is identified by name—Ezra.

The Tull family's inability to finish a meal at Ezra's restaurant is a leitmotif of the novel and a symbol of their continued hunger yet inability to receive the consolation offered. As the novel ends, the family is returning to finish a dinner together, the dinner following Pearl's funeral. At her death, Beck, the absent father, returns, and the children reconcile with him. Was the influence of Pearl the cause of the family's inability to share a meal at the Homesick Restaurant? One reason to suspect that Pearl is the problem is her reaction to Ezra's earlier acceptance of a partnership in Scarlatti's restaurant, an outburst that disrupts the first family meal Ezra plans. Hearing that Mrs. Scarlatti has sold Ezra a partnership for one dollar, Pearl explodes in fury,

It's a favor; partnerships don't cost a dollar; you'll be beholden all your life. Ezra, we Tulls depend on ourselves, only on each other. We don't look to the rest of the world for any help whatsoever. How can you lend yourself to this?[67]

Pearl's extreme self-reliance that isolated her family within their Baltimore house, separating them even from their neighbors, is often referred to as the source of the hunger that pervades our culture, the modern malady. Abandoned by her husband and faced with raising three children and with no marketable skills, Pearl has been forced to emphasize only a single aspect of her personality, an intense focus on survival through sheer will, which will wound both her and her children on a spiritual level even as they manage to survive physically.

In one of the most famous passages in modern literature, the heroine of E.M. Forster's 1910 novel, *Howards End,* having diagnosed the problem in the male protagonist, exhorts him to "only connect," a phrase that the modernist writers repeatedly cited to denote the path to wholeness in our time. In the novel, it is a plea to reconnect two hemispheres of the soul that have been divided,

She would only point out the salvation that was latent in his own soul and in the soul of everyman. Only connect! That was the whole of her sermon. Only connect the prose and the passion, and both will be exalted, and human love will be seen at its height. Live in fragments no longer. Only connect, and the beast and the monk, robbed of the isolation that is life to either, will die.[68]

In *Dinner at the Homesick Restaurant,* Pearl has divided herself, repressing the passion in her in a determined effort to raise her children. The novel's symbol of connectedness is the shared meal, a feeding of people's needs, as Ezra envisions it. This is a symbol common to both Judaism (the Sabbath meal, the Seder) and Christianity (the Eucharist), a healing and salvific meal in common. It is perhaps also significant that the Biblical sage Ezra was known as a "second Moses" because of his involvement with the restoration of Judaism following the return from Babylonian captivity.[69] Anne Tyler's Ezra is employed in a restoration to assuage the spiritual dislocations of our secular society. Thus, the oddly named Homesick Restaurant provides meals redolent with spiritual associations of healing and wholeness, the vision of a modern Ezra. That Tyler shows the restaurant's continued presence in *Saint Maybe,* a novel published nine years after *Dinner at the Homesick Restaurant,* indicates its value in her personal vision of the fictional neighborhood she has spent her career populating through her novels.

Anne Tyler has remarked that she wants to be known as a "serious" novelist, and she describes a serious novel as one that "has to have layers and layers and layers, like life does."[70] *Dinner at the Homesick Restaurant* is surely a serious novel, and one of its many layers is just as surely a spiritual one that speaks to the value of faith in healing and restoring people, feeding them spiritually. Although Tyler is a serious novelist, she has always been popular with both critics and readers, perhaps in part because the religious layers in her fiction have always been muted. That is, she is not known as a religious or Christian writer, a label that would dissuade liberal readers, perhaps her major audience.

Despite the variety of this fiction of religious experience, very few literary novels achieve any significant level of sales compared with the average product of evangelical Christian publishing. The more complex the narrative presentation of religious values, the more sophisticated the reader must be to appreciate that fiction. Popular writers of more accessible fiction, like Picoult and Diamant, sell far better, but these novels do not rival the sales of evangelical Christian fiction, a subgenre that is written for a specific niche in the market, a group of readers captivated by the serial drama produced by the most popular Christian writers. The escalating sales of evangelical fiction reflect the strong interest of conservative Christians in novels that bolster their religious ideals. Nevertheless, as we saw with *The Da Vinci Code,* when any book touches the *Zeitgeist,* it can become a best seller. One recent highly successful novel with a religious theme confirms the fact that a best-selling author has crafted a work that successfully appeals to the widest range of readers. Reader responses to this novel offer further insight into the landscape of contemporary American religion.

Writers and Readers

In an essay on Christianity and art, the poet W. H. Auden wrote:

There can no more be a "Christian" art than there can be a Christian science or a Christian diet. There can only be a Christian spirit in which an artist, a scientist, works or does not work. A painting of the Crucifixion is not necessarily more Christian in spirit than a still life, and may very well be less.[71]

In Chaim Potok's novel *My Name is Asher Lev* discussed in Chapter 1, the artist alienated his Orthodox Jewish community by employing an image of the crucifixion in his painting, perfectly illustrating the point Auden raises about the difference between an artistic work's substance and its spirit. For Asher Lev, the crucifixion was the ideal image to convey suffering, the subject of his painting, but his community's reductive identification of that image solely with its religious source created a problem for the artist. His fellow Hasidim were offended by an Orthodox Jew's use of a Christian symbol. And that difficulty remains with all serious art; perception is reality. Thus, as the poet and critic T. S. Eliot has pointed out, "what a writer does to people is not necessarily what he intends to do."[72] For example, Salinger's *The Catcher in the Rye* is one of the most frequently banned books in the United States, yet Frederick Buechner has written that *Catcher* had a seminal influence in his life, one of the first books he read that communicated to him what is important for living a good life.[73] How a reader perceives a novel is conditioned by the reader as well as the author's text.

This principle is illuminated in reader reception of the best-selling novel *The Secret Life of Bees* by Sue Monk Kidd. At one level, it is an interesting *Bildungsroman,* the story of a young person's growth, a staple genre in American literature. Kidd's engaging female narrator, the fourteen-year-old Lily Owens, can claim as ancestors Twain's Huck Finn and Salinger's Holden Caulfield. Her journey through South Carolina in search of the truth about her mother is no less metaphoric than Huck's travels on a raft in the Mississippi or Holden's sojourn through the streets of New York City.

Serious novels speak their truth at many levels, and one of the most significant aspects of *The Secret Life of Bees* is the religious spirit of the novel. The reader who is familiar with Kidd's nonfiction book *The Dance of the Dissident Daughter,* which chronicles her personal spiritual journey, will readily see how the writer has transmuted that experience and integrated it into *The Secret Life of Bees,* but a familiarity with *Dissident Daughter* is not necessary for an appreciation of the novel; it stands on its own.

The plot of *The Secret Life of Bees* is a simple one. Set in the summer of 1964, it is the story of Lily Owens, an unhappy teen whose mother died in an accident with a gun when Lily was just a toddler. As an additional burden for the child, she has been told that she was holding the gun when it fired and killed her mother. Her belligerent father, known as T. Ray, is a demanding and angry parent, and Lily fantasizes an idealized version of her mother for comfort. Ultimately, she leaves home in search of information about her mother, using one of the few relics she has to guide her, a picture of a black Madonna inscribed with the name of the South Carolina town Tiburon on the back. In Tiburon, she winds up at the bee farm that produces Black Madonna Honey, run by three African-American sisters, May, June, and August Boatwright. Among the community of women who surround the sisters, Lily discovers not only the truth of her mother's brief life, but solace and support for herself as well. The women are part of a small group of worshippers of the Virgin Mary, having reinterpreted orthodox Catholic theology and cast the Madonna as a Goddess.

The Secret Life of Bees is a tribute to individualistic spirituality, identified by Bellah and his colleagues as a dominant trend in American religion.[74] The novel also exhibits the individualists' skepticism of organized religion, a characteristic of Americans since the time of the Transcendentalists. It is Kidd's choice of narrator that enables her to both critique institutional religion with a light touch and present her rather unorthodox spirituality as intriguing rather than eccentric. Lily speaks with a unique voice, a seemingly innocent wry humor that allows Kidd to avoid the sarcasm that an adult voice would convey, as well as the negative tone inherent in such sarcasm. Note how early in the novel, Lily's ostensibly simple comment about her father expresses skepticism about conventional churchgoers and communicates the important idea that worship should influence behavior: "I had asked God repeatedly to do something about T. Ray. He'd gone to church for forty years and was only getting worse. It seemed like this should tell God something."[75] Using the carefully constructed voice of her young narrator, Sue Monk Kidd deftly suggests a sense of the hypocrisy of many supposedly religious people.

The novel's setting during the intense summer of the Civil Rights Movement enables Kidd to use our contemporary awareness to highlight social issues, much as Twain did in setting his 1885 novel of Huck Finn's adventures more than twenty years earlier when slavery was still rampant and accepted. Similarly,

Kidd uses the historical situation to remind the reader of present-day failings. For example, Lily's apparently innocent comment about her church experience indicts institutional religion for a contemporary reader:

Every time a rumor got going about a group of Negroes coming to worship with us on Sunday morning, the deacons stood locked arms across the church steps to turn them away. We loved them in the Lord, Brother Gerald said, but they had their own places.[76]

Having established Lily's insightful and humorous voice, Kidd also presents her as a reliable narrator, admirable in her personal honesty and ability to learn from experience. Much as Twain did with Huck Finn, Kidd creates a distance between Lily and the reader, with the reader more aware than the narrator herself. For example, Lily speaks of herself as bad, but the reader sees her virtue. She is reliable but a naïve narrator, and that point-of-view in the novel promotes the reader's acceptance of her viewpoint. We're on her side. And as with Huck, the historical time of the novel allows the reader to understand the racial bias with which Lily has been indoctrinated and appreciate her ability to learn from experience. When she finds herself in the unusual situation of being part of a household of black women, Lily uses her insight and intelligence to transcend her cultural conditioning, just as Huck Finn did in his friendship with the slave Jim:

T. Ray did not think colored women were smart. Since I want to tell the whole truth, which means the worst parts, I thought they could be smart, but not as smart as me, me being white. Lying on the cot in the honey house, though, all I could think was *August is so intelligent, so cultured,* and I was surprised by this. That's what let me know I had some prejudice buried inside me.[77]

With Lily telling the story, and having established her as admirable in the eyes of the reader, Kidd can gain acceptance for the unorthodox feminist spirituality that she introduces after Lily arrives in Tiburon. The Boatwright sisters who provide a haven for Lily have created their own religion which includes a group of other black women who call themselves the Daughters of Mary. When Lily hears them pray to the Virgin Mary, she asks August if they are Catholic and is told, "May and June and I take our mother's Catholicism and mix in our own ingredients. I'm not sure what you call it, but it suits us."[78] On Mary's special feast day, as part of the celebration, the women stand in a circle and take turns breaking off a piece of honey cake, baked in honor of the Virgin, placing it on the tongue of the next woman with the words, "This is the body of the Blessed Mother." Each woman, in turn, feeds the next, a truly nonhierarchical process of communion. Kidd then affirms the feminine Eucharist with Lily's response:

Me, I had never seen grown-ups feed each other, and I watched with the feeling I might burst out crying. I don't know what got to me about it, but for some reason that circle of feeding made me feel better about the world.[79]

Ultimately, Lily learns that the worship of these women is an outward manifestation of their conviction of the indwelling of the Divine, and that her urge to search for her mother was, in effect, a need to contact that part of herself that provides strength and consolation. As August explains, "Our Lady is not some magical being out there somewhere, like a fairy godmother. She's not the statue in the parlor. She's something *inside* of you."[80] And, in the climactic scene in the novel, Lily draws on that inner strength to stand up to T. Ray and insure her future among these women.

The *Bildungsroman* is a novel of the formation of a young person. That Lily's development is through religious experiences is not only unusual in our supposedly secular society, but equally unusual is the fact that a novel so steeped in religious ideals can be a best seller. More than 3.5 million copies of *The Secret Life of Bees* were reported sold within four years of publication.[81] It is worth noting that among the reader reviews on Amazon.com, there is little mention of religion, and then only as tangential to the plot. The fact that many readers overlooked the spiritual aspect of the novel testifies to the truth of T.S. Eliot's assertion that "what a writer does to people is not necessarily what he intends to do. It may be only what people are capable of having done to them."[82] One aspect of the success of *The Secret Life of Bees* is that Kidd has produced a novel that can engage readers at a variety of levels, thus broadening its appeal.

The Common Reader

To understand the appeal of *The Secret Life of Bees,* it is helpful to consider *To Kill a Mockingbird,* a novel frequently mentioned in reader response to Kidd's work. Like Harper Lee, Sue Monk Kidd has created an irresistible narrator who captivates the reader with her voice and her story. Common to both novels is a narrative involving race relations in the American South and the triumph of love over hate, themes that engage readers easily when they are sentimentalized, as they are in both novels. Moreover, the female world of the bee farm and Kidd's emphasis on the inner mother and female empowerment would appeal to female readers, and reading popular fiction is very much a female occupation.[83]

In terms of religion, *The Secret Life of Bees* is much like *The Da Vinci Code* in its appeal to both liberal and conservative readers. For the liberal reader, the emphasis on individualism, the critique of institutional religion, and the Boatwright sisters' unique feminist adaptation of Catholicism, suggesting the process of spiritual seeking, would be attractive. What would appeal to conservative readers is the way that the Boatwright sisters and their friends live Christian values in their care for Lily. For naïve readers, Lily's story would be their dominant experience of the novel, and it's possible that conservative readers simply ignored the radical theology of the Boatwrights or were not offended by their reformulation of Catholicism, since that religion remains suspect in evangelical circles. As Lily explains it, "According to Brother Gerald, hell was nothing but a bonfire for Catholics."[84] Moreover, Kidd's previous career writing for conservative

Christian nonfiction publications would give her credibility with those readers. In my sampling of reader reviews, there was only one obviously conservative Christian who complained of the worship of Mary rather than Jesus, the use of a statue in a worship service, and T. Ray's profane language.[85]

The majority of readers did not even mention the fact that religion or spirituality is an important aspect of the novel. Their focus was entirely on Lily's adventures, the literal level of the novel. For example, the bees in the novel's title seem relevant on that literal level; the Boatwrights are bee keepers, and the women are essential to Lily's development in the narrative. But in the story, it is revealed that bees are a symbol of the soul, of death and rebirth, and so the bee farm symbolizes the place where Lily experiences a rebirth to wholeness. The "secret life of bees" is then the secret life of the soul, the universal story of human transcendence. However, for readers who perceive mainly the literal level of the narrative, the novel is effective as simply a coming of age story set on a bee farm.

That many readers focus on the most superficial level of the narrative is hardly surprising. In a 2002 interview, the novelist John Updike commented that he believed that readers who can appreciate serious fiction are diminishing in numbers.

I think that the kind of readers that would make it worthwhile to print a literary writer are dwindling. People seem to read more purely for escape than when I was younger. You look at the books that people are reading on an airplane, and you never see a book that you would want to read. It's always these fat thrillers....[86]

Updike attributed this lack of readers for any but popular fiction to the nature of society today and the opportunities for entertainment that offer more immediate gratification than the printed word, television, the Internet, and other technologies that provide information, concluding "who knows what inroads will be made there into the world of the book."[87]

In 1985, the literary critic Cleanth Brooks made a similar point about the diminishing readership for literary fiction in American society. He referred to serious literature as a "rather specialized pleasure."[88] That phrase reflects the often overlooked fact that appreciating the literary novel requires some degree of education in literature, comparable to any specialization, a fact not often noted in discussions of the limited sales for literary fiction. Brooks also expressed an opinion, similar to Updike's, that "the character of the age itself" diminishes the value of serious literature:

A technological age—especially an extremely brilliant and successful one—has difficulty in finding a proper role for literature. Such a society sees literature as a diversion, as a mere amusement at best, and so it is classed as a luxury, perhaps an added grace to adorn the high culture which the technology has itself built.[89]

The religious writer Walter Wangerin made a similar point in a 1995 interview:

Today in our country, we boast of our high literacy rate. But we have ceased to acknowledge the fact that there is complexity in literature. It is still a small group that has been willing to learn the subtleties.[90]

As a consequence of this, Wangerin asserts, "Literature has lost its place, so we sell to the masses, people who can read words, but who have themselves made narrow choices."[91] Thus, the vast sales of Christian fiction are understandable, since these novels are popular fiction, easily accessible, and making few demands on the reader. This fiction functions entirely on the literal level, much like television drama, and viewers can just as easily be readers as watch television. In fact, the popular fiction reading experience, portable and sans commercials, can be more satisfying than television viewing. On the other hand, although the contemporary literary landscape reveals no dearth of serious writers whose work is nourished by spiritual concerns, there's a dearth of readers for this literature. It is, as Brooks noted, a "specialized" pleasure, and even among the educated in today's society, people have chosen other areas for specialization. Hence, it is unsurprising that a best seller like *The Secret Life of Bees* is appreciated mainly at the literal level by the vast majority of readers.

The problem with the literal level of this novel is that it is set during the summer of 1964 when the issue of civil rights was predominant throughout the south, and in that context, Kidd has included scenes that defy reason. What black woman in that era would pour a jug of spit over the shoes of a group of white men who are harassing her? And when that woman is jailed, we are to believe that a fourteen-year-old white girl is capable of effecting her escape. And while Lily's life with a black family can be explained by the farm's isolation, it defies belief that a young black man would invite her to go with him, young black man and white teenager alone together, into the nearby racist town. When that young man is later jailed, August asks Lily to accompany her to visit him, thus advertising the white girl's presence in the Boatwright household, something to be avoided in this racist culture. Was Kidd so focused on her agenda, the metaphoric journey in search of the mother, that she carelessly ignored the reality of life in the Jim Crow south? Or was she trying for magical realism in her narrative, depicting a world that is not based on objective reality but imbued with the supernatural that she's trying to show as operative in the natural world?

Whatever the reason for these anachronisms, the problem is that most of the readers expressed satisfaction with the historical setting of the novel, asserting that they learned a lot about the pre-civil rights south from the narrative. Granted, a few readers noted some of Kidd's lapses, but the majority, reading at the purely literal level, express satisfaction with learning about an important historical time in American history. Given readers' interest in getting information and knowledge from their casual reading, this response is not surprising, but it is unfortunate because Kidd does not accurately reflect this era. This may be the result of the novelist being focused on the metaphysical reality she is trying to present, the feminist journey to empowerment, not realizing that for most readers, the reality of the novel is in its objective, physical world. Thus, it is not surprising that among the readers who have negative views of *The Secret Life of Bees,* the words "fairy tale" and "fantasy" are frequently employed. Reading at the literal level, readers expect a realistic world, and "fantasy" is their derogatory term for the writer's failure to be authentically realistic.

Given the dominance of literal reading, readers' reactions to the religious element in the novel are interesting, specifically the feminist focus on the Virgin Mary. Most readers ignore that aspect of the novel, focusing on Lily's journey in search of her mother and the historical setting in the civil rights era. However, among the few who comment, most of them see the religious elements from a similarly literal perspective. One reader, in a review dated October 25, 2006, refers to the "rituals" as "childish" and "unbelievable," making the women in the novel seem "silly." In another review, dated July 9, 2006, the reader described the "idolization of the Blessed Mother" as unnecessary and argued that Kidd was "pushing her own spirituality," which the reader had deduced from the author's web site. For people who read at the literal level, the characters in the novel become real people to them, and they tend to identify closely with characters they like. Thus, these readers object to the Boatwrights' unique religious expression because it is foreign to them; they want the sisters to be more compatible with their image of how these women should behave.

Even the reader who objected to Kidd's presentation on theological grounds misreads the text. In a review dated June 27, 2006, the reader accurately states the theological fact that "Catholics and other Christians would NEVER worship Mary—or worse, a statue that represents her. Catholics ask Mary to pray for them to Jesus." However, it is clear from the novel that Kidd is not presenting orthodox Catholicism but has deliberately fashioned the Boatwrights' rituals to be unorthodox. She has August explain that the sisters have added their own "ingredients" to Catholicism.[92] And after Lily experiences the feminist communion service, Kidd has her comment that the Pope "would have keeled over" had he seen it.[93] Readers are influenced by fiction, but, as Eliot has noted, they "exercise an unconscious selection in being influenced."[94] What the author intends is not necessarily what the reader perceives. So common is this principle of "misreading" that the literary critic Stanley Fish proposes the primacy of the reader's experience to the virtual extinction of authorial presence.[95] Although I speak of misreading the text, it's important to understand that there is no error involved. It is simply that the reality of the novel for individual readers is in each reader's own perceptions.

Hence, when we refer to "religious fiction," can *The Secret Life of Bees* be included, since the majority of readers tended to focus solely on the novel as a *Bildungsroman,* the story of Lily Owens' search for her mother? And what about novels like *Dinner at the Homesick Restaurant,* where the religious implications are less evident than implicit? The answer to these questions is less in the character of the book than in the experience of the reader. As Buechner expressed it, the religious novel "at its best" is "less *about* the religious experience than a novel the reading of which itself *is* a religious experience. . . ."[96] Thus, the reader does indeed have primacy when we're discussing religious fiction.

Perhaps most interesting among the responses to *The Secret Life of Bees* is the reader who, in a review dated October 16, 2006, refers to the novel as "a wonderful book for a Catholic like myself." The phrase "like myself" is revealing. This reader "enjoyed the characters' unabashed love for Our Lady" but does not seem to notice the heresy in their love being expressed in worship. I suspect that this is because the reader's emphasis is on the novel as an expression of "sisterhood," which the reader recommends "for women looking for a sense of empowerment and bonding." This is a reader who has read at the metaphoric level to appreciate what Kidd is trying to express in the spirituality of the Daughters of Mary and clearly shares the author's feminist ethos. In the spirit of misreading, the reality of the novel for this reader is in its feminist subtext, and minor details like heresy in worshipping Mary are irrelevant. Although the reader identifies as a Catholic, it is important to note that for many religious individualists, relationship to an institutional church may be casual or transient.[97]

Kidd's success with *The Secret Life of Bees* is a result of the fact that she created a novel that appeals to the spectrum of readers, from the least sophisticated who focus on the literal level of the narrative to more experienced readers who identify with the underlying theme of female empowerment. Although this is a novel from a mainstream publisher, Kidd's prior experience writing conservative Christian nonfiction seems to have provided her with insight into those readers because she created a novel that is readily accessible, indeed engaging, for the reader at the most literal level. It is an easy read, something readers of Christian fiction comment on in identifying "good" fiction. Moreover, in keeping with Kidd's overriding feminist perspective, her characters are easily identified as good or bad; most of the women are the former, while the white men are definitely the latter. Such clear-cut distinctions are much preferred to the ambiguity of authentic character development. And many readers comment on the uplifting nature of the story, another aspect of fiction valued by less sophisticated readers. *The Secret Life of Bees* was a best seller because it did not depend on the more "specialized" readers of literary fiction. Like *The Da Vinci Code,* it is a novel that can be read profitably by both conservatives and liberals, both sophisticated readers and naïve readers at the same time.

Evangelical publishing houses produce popular fiction, easily accessible novels that can be fully enjoyed at the most basic, literal level. Reading this fiction is not so very different from watching the made-for-TV movie versions of these stories. In fact, Christian fiction is very suitable for that other contemporary practice, listening to the book rather than reading it, so few are the demands for the reader's attention in these narratives. Moreover, this fiction can accommodate any range of believer, since the concept of Christianity espoused is mainly in the joy of belonging to a loving community of the like-minded. The details of any shared theological belief are kept conveniently vague. Hence, Christian fiction is not only attractive to evangelicals but conservative Christians of any denomination, including Catholics. This fiction can also attract the large number of religious individualists in American society who are inclined to faith but disinclined to join any specific denomination. Such spiritual "shoppers" or "seekers" would be prone to seek out religious literature, since they don't have a strong community in which to participate. Fiction can provide a vicarious community. It's hardly surprising, then, that conservative Christian fiction sells so well.

However, as T. S. Eliot has observed, "It is the literature we read with the least effort that can have the easiest and most insidious influence upon us."[98] As the world becomes more chaotic and moral questions become more complex, conservative Christian fiction provides a safe haven of order and simplicity. The crises faced by characters are always resolved, with God always eventually creating order from chaos and providing answers to all dilemmas. But that reliance on supernatural authority to alleviate all psychological or physical pain promotes a separatist mentality that is not useful for engaging with the larger society. As Bellah explains,

Direct reliance on the Bible provides a second language with which to resist the temptations of the "world," but the almost exclusive concentration on the Bible, especially the New Testament, with no larger memory of how Christians have coped with the world historically, diminishes the capacity of their second language to deal adequately with current social reality.[99]

Insofar as conservative Christian fiction provides reinforcement for a separatist mentality, it exacerbates the culture wars rather than seeking avenues for reconciliation. Perhaps a look at one more novel will help put this issue in perspective as we conclude this study in the next chapter.

Notes

1. Giles Gunn, *The Culture of Criticism and the Criticism of Culture* (New York: Oxford University Press, 1987), 182.

2. Ibid.

3. James Joyce, *A Portrait of the Artist as a Young Man: Text, Criticism, and Notes,* ed. Chester G. Anderson (1916; repr., New York: The Viking Press, 1968), 246–7.

4. Ron Hansen, *A Stay Against Confusion: Essays on Faith and Fiction* (New York: HarperPerennial, 2002), 2. Italics in original.

5. Ibid., 10.

6. Wuthnow, *America and the Challenges of Religious Diversity* (Princeton and Oxford: Princeton University Press, 2005), See especially Chapter Four, 106–29.

7. Frederick Buechner, *The Clown in the Belfry: Writings on Faith and Fiction* (HarperSanFrancisco, 1992), 14.

8. Oscar Hijuelos, *Mr. Ives' Christmas* (New York: HarperCollins Publishers, 1995), 172.

9. Wuthnow, *America and the Challenges of Religious Diversity,* 132–3.

10. Hijuelos, *Mr. Ives' Christmas,* 93.

11. Ibid.

12. Anne Tyler, *Saint Maybe* (New York: Ivy Books, 1991), 1.

13. Ibid., 109.

14. Ibid., 110.

15. Ibid., 112.

16. Ibid., 134.

17. Ibid., 46.

18. Ibid., 214.

19. Ibid., 229; ellipsis in text.

20. Ibid., 292.

21. Buechner, *The Clown in the Belfry,* 12. Italics his.

22. Jodi Picoult, *Keeping Faith* (New York: Harper Perennial, 2000), 126.

23. Ibid.

24. Ibid., 286.

25. See, for example, Matthew 23; Mark 7:1–13; Luke 11:37–44; John 5:37–47.

26. Ron Hansen, *Mariette in Ecstasy* (New York: HarperPerennial, 1991), 159–60.

27. Ibid., 133–4.

28. Ron Hansen, "Stigmata," in *A Stay Against Confusion,* 177.

29. Jodi Picoult, *Keeping Faith,* appendix to the novel, "P.S.," 11.

30. Ron Hansen, "Writing as Sacrament," in *A Stay Against Confusion,* 10.

31. Ibid., 4.

32. Hansen, *Mariette in Ecstasy,* 160.

33. Hebrews 11:3.

34. William Zinsser, ed., *Spiritual Quests: The Art and Craft of Religious Writing* (Boston: Houghton Mifflin Company, 1988), 20.

35. Genesis 32:24–30.

36. Hansen, "Writing as Sacrament," 10.

37. Francine Rivers, *Redeeming Love* (Sisters, OR: Multnomah Publishers, 1997), 53.

38. Ibid., 178. Italics in text.

39. Ron Hansen, *Atticus* (New York: HarperPerennial, 1997), 7.

40. Ibid., 230–1.

41. Buechner, *The Clown in the Belfry,* 21. Italics his.

42. Janice Radway, *Reading the Romance: Women, Patriarchy, and Popular Literature* (Chapel Hill: University of North Carolina Press, 1991), 54.

43. Anita Diamant, *The Red Tent* (New York: Picador, 1997), 1.

44. Diamant, quoted in *Reform Jewish Magazine* at http://reformjudaismmag.net/599 bf.html (accessed November 5, 2006).

45. Frederick Buechner, *The Son of Laughter* (HarperSanFrancisco, 1993), 171.

46. Diamant, *The Red Tent,* 184.

47. Ibid., 197.

48. Faith L. Justice, "An Interview with Anita Diamant," http://www.copperfield review.com/interviews/diamant.html (accessed November 5, 2006).

49. Buechner, "Doubt and Faith," *Of Fiction and Faith: Twelve American Writers Talk about Their Vision and Work,* ed. W. Dale Brown (Grand Rapids, MI: William B. Eerdmans Publishing Company, 1997), 34.

50. Ibid.

51. Rabbi J. Avram Rothman, http://www.aish.com/societyWork/arts/The_Red_ Tent.asp (accessed November 6, 2006).

52. Vicki Cabot, "Woman's voice: 'Red Tent' tells other side of story," *The Jewish News of Greater Phoenix* (January 14, 2000/7 Shevat 5760, vol. 52, no.19), http://www.jewishaz.com/jewishnews/000114/tent.shtml (accessed November 6, 2006).

53. Ron Hansen, "Faith and Fiction," *A Stay Against Confusion,* 20.

54. Marilynne Robinson, *Gilead* (New York: Picador, 2004), 45.

55. Buechner, *The Clown in the Belfry,* 23.

56. Quoted by Alden Mudge, "Healing Faith," http://www.bookpage.com/0603bp/elizabeth_strout.html (accessed December 4, 2006).

57. Anne Tyler, *Dinner at the Homesick Restaurant* (New York: Berkley Books, 1983), 79. Ellipsis in text.

58. Ibid., 84.

59. Ibid., 75.

60. Ibid., 73.

61. Ibid., 124.

62. Ibid.

63. Buechner, "Doubt and Faith," 53.

64. Ibid., 54.

65. Tyler, *Dinner at the Homesick Restaurant,* 120.

66. Tyler, *Saint Maybe,* 329.

67. Ibid., 95.

68. E.M. Forster, *Howards End,* Chapter 22, http://www.doc.ic.ac.uk/~rac101/concord/texts/howards_end/howards_end3.html#8173 (accessed December 8, 2006).

69. Robert Alter and Frank Kermode, eds., *The Literary Guide to the Bible* (Cambridge, MA: The Belknap Press of Harvard University Press, 1987), 357.

70. Marguerite Michaels, "Anne Tyler, Writer 8:05 to 3:30," *New York Times,* May 8, 1977, http://www.nytimes.com/books/98/04/19/specials/tyler-writer.html (accessed December 1, 2006).

71. W.H. Auden, "Postscript: Christianity and Art," *The Dyer's Hand and Other Essays*(New York: Vintage Books, 1968), 458.

72. T.S. Eliot, "Religion and Literature," *Selected Prose of T.S. Eliot,* ed. Frank Kermode (New York: Harcourt Brace Jovanovich, 1975), 103.

73. Buechner, *The Clown in the Belfry,* 78.

74. Robert N. Bellah and others, *Habits of the Heart: Individualism and Commitment in American Life* (New York: Harper & Row Publishers, 1986), 228.

75. Sue Monk Kidd, *The Secret Life of Bees* (New York: Penguin Books, 2002), 3.

76. Ibid., 30.

77. Ibid., 78. Italics in text.

78. Ibid., 90.

79. Ibid., 226.

80. Ibid., 288. Italics are Kidd's.

81. Sales reported at http://kaf.louisville.edu/kidd/ (accessed December 13, 2006).

82. Eliot, "Religion and Literature," 103.

83. Lakshmi Chaudhry, "Why Hemingway Is Chick-Lit," August 16, 2006, http://www.inthesetimes.com/site/main/article/2780/ (accessed December 16, 20006). According to this article, surveys in the United States, Canada, and Great Britain all show that male readers are only 20% of the fiction market, although they read nonfiction at a rate about 10% higher than women.

84. Kidd, *The Secret Life of Bees,* 58.

85. On December 18, 2006, there were 1,221 reader reviews of *The Secret Life of Bees* on Amazon.com, and my comments are based on a review of the most recent 122 reviews.

86. Quoted by Dwight Garner, "The Salon Interview: John Updike," http://www.salon.com/08/features/updike.html (accessed December 8, 2006).

87. Ibid.

88. Cleanth Brooks, "Literature in a Technological Age," *Community, Religion, and Literature* (Columbia: University of Missouri Press, 1995), 212.

89. Ibid., 263.

90. Walter Wangerin, "Man of Letters," *Of Fiction and Faith,* ed. W. Dale Brown, 257.

91. Ibid.

92. Kidd, *The Secret Life of Bees,* 90.

93. Ibid., 226.

94. Eliot, "Religion and Literature," 103.

95. Brooks, "The Primacy of the Reader," *Community, Religion, and Literature,* 249 ff. Brooks presents Fish's perspective, along with a helpful critique of his extremism.

96. Buechner, "Faith and Fiction," *The Clown in the Belfry,* 21. Italics his.

97. Bellah and others, *Habits of the Heart,* 243.

98. Eliot, "Religion and Literature," 103.

99. Bellah and others, *Habits of the Heart,* 232.

— 8 —

Faith, Fiction, and the Future

The more the conditions of men are equalized and assimilated to each other, the more important it is for religion; whilst it carefully abstains from the daily turmoil of secular affairs, not needlessly to run counter to the ideas which generally prevail, or to the permanent interests which exist in the mass of the people.

—Alexis de Tocqueville, *Democracy in America*

In a 2006 review of John Updike's latest work *Terrorist,* the novelist Robert Stone began with the following assessment:

For some 50 years John Updike has been examining America in his fiction and essays, reflecting upon its art and history, documenting its volatile progressions. In their longings, in their occasional self-discoveries and more usually in their self-deceptions, the characters in his novels and stories have demonstrated the desperation with which people in America have sought to find some equilibrium against the background of headlong change.[1]

That succinct overview of Updike's career indicates why his 2002 novel *In the Beauty of the Lilies* provides an apt closure for this study with its insight into American religion in its chronicle of four generations of the Wilmot family. Updike appears to have made his purpose clear, as reported in this review of *In the Beauty of the Lilies*:

In his memoir *Self-Consciousness,* Updike refers to the phrase from the "Battle Hymn of the Republic" that supplies the title, "In the beauty of the lilies, Christ was born across the sea," as "an odd and uplifting line" that "seems to me to summarize what I had to say about America." He told *Publishers Weekly* that in this novel "he has attempted 'to make God a character,' although in ways that illuminate spiritual emptiness in American life."[2]

The novel begins with the story of Clarence Wilmot, a Presbyterian minister who suddenly suffers a loss of faith. Updike describes this singular event as simultaneous with the fainting of Mary Pickford, young star of the incipient movie industry, whose latest film happened to be in production in Paterson, New Jersey, also the location of Rev. Wilmot.

At the moment when Mary Pickford fainted, the Reverend Clarence Arthur Wilmot, down in the rectory of the Fourth Presbyterian Church at the corner of Straight Street and Broadway, felt the last particles of his faith leave him.[3]

In this brief description, Updike introduces the leitmotif that will convey the novel's thesis that the substitution of popular culture for religion is the hallmark of our century. Institutional religion will continue to be a presence in society, but it will be the presence imaged in the character Thomas Dreaver, Wilmot's ecclesiastical superior and the man who advises him that there is no need to leave the ministry simply because he has lost his faith. Updike concisely presents his view of the modern church with his brief description of Dreaver:

Pale and rounded in feature, with short fair hair brushed away from a central parting, he wore a single-breasted, slate-blue business suit and was businesslike in manner, save for an extra smoothness, a honeyed promissory timbre to his voice that marked him as an executive of Christian business.[4]

Dreaver embodies the progressive or liberal church, and he identifies Wilmot's difficulty as having been educated by conservatives who are too inflexible for the modern era. He advises that "Relativity is the word we must live by now. Everything is relative, and what matters is how *we*, we human creatures, relate to one another."[5] What Dreaver is articulating is the shift in American religion resulting from disestablishment and the resultant privatization of religion, a movement "from casuistry to counseling," as Robert Bellah terms it. "In this respect, religion was a precursor of therapy in a utilitarian managerial society."[6] The result of this movement is described in *Habits of the Heart* in an analysis of a late twentieth-century liberal Presbyterian congregation where "Community and attachment comes not from the demands of a tradition, but from the empathetic sharing of feelings among therapeutically attuned selves."[7] Updike's Rev. Dreaver is the embodiment of this modern, liberal religion.

In accounting for his loss of faith, Wilmot explains it as a result of his intellectual pursuits, "I fear I have read too many atheist thinkers, in an attempt to understand and refute them. Meaning to undermine them, I was undermined instead!"[8] At one level, Clarence's distress is emblematic of the Modernist demythologizing of traditional religion, but at the personal level, his loss of faith is also an example of one of the dangers of the mature faith of Fowler's Stage 4. As is true of many psychological phenomena, the strength of this stage of faith, its capacity for critical reflection, is also a signal of its weakness, "an excessive confidence in the conscious mind and in critical thought," whereby the individual overassimilates the perspectives of others.[9] Clarence Wilmot has simply thought himself out of faith, and he is too honorable to continue in ministry, although Dreaver insists that a loss of faith is no barrier to ministry.

So Wilmot leaves the ministry, subjecting his family to a radical alteration in class, as he discovers that the market for former ministers is not as bright as he had anticipated. Reduced to selling encyclopedias door-to-door, Wimot relieves the tedium of his pathetic daily rounds by escaping for a few hours at the local cinema. Thus, in its initial role in the novel, the movies are pure escapism. If, as Marx claimed, religion was the opiate of the people, now the cinema provides that succor instead.

The shift from dogma to sentimentality has been termed the "feminization" of American religion, so it's apt that in the next generation, Clarence's son Teddy wants no part of religion but encourages the participation of his wife and mother in the local church, a symbolic enactment of this shift.[10] But Teddy also illustrates how religion is contextualized by life experiences. He ceased going to church when Clarence died, and, as he explains much latter to his grandson, it was almost a "grudge" against God. Teddy is a child when his father loses his faith and an adolescent when Clarence finally dies, and it's natural that he would have an immature faith. In the Stage 2 faith associated with childhood, the world is "based on reciprocal fairness and immanent justice based on reciprocity."[11] From Teddy's perspective, since God did not fulfill his obligation to Clarence, He was not deserving of Teddy's allegiance. There is no overt hostility in Teddy's decision to abandon God. He encourages his wife to continue her religious practices; as he explains, "I would never take the comfort away from those it comforts," a comment that reflects the role of the church as a solace for the emotions.[12]

Throughout his section of the novel, Teddy is strangely passive, as though his father's loss of faith had somehow removed all ambition from his youngest child. Living with his mother and his aunt, the young Teddy has no career ambitions and is pushed by his Aunt Esther from a job as a soda jerk to his eventual career as a mailman. Teddy accepts these positions and works diligently but appears to have no thought or ambition beyond his daily work and family. Interestingly, Teddy's lassitude reflects a comment by Cleanth Brooks in an essay, "The Crisis in Culture." Brooks writes of a division within the individual soul, "the fruits of which are listlessness and lack of purpose, or an indifference to principle that comes from the individual's basic confusion as to who he is."[13] Brooks attributes this "psychic disorientation" of the individual to times of change in society.[14] Teddy's odd lethargy suggests this disorientation described by Brooks, an effect of his father's loss of faith and symbolic of the cultural dislocation experienced when religion, formerly a source of moral authority, loses meaning for people.

It is Teddy's daughter Essie who epitomizes the American religion of popular culture. Filled with ambition and determined to exploit her good looks, Essie advances from New York modeling to stardom in Hollywood, renamed Alma DeMott during the heyday of the big studio system of the 1940s and 1950s. Essie has absorbed the conventional faith experiences of her childhood and, if asked, would profess belief. But she is the embodiment of radical individualism, the faith expression in which "God is simply the self magnified."[15] Updike reinforces Alma's religion of the self with imagery. When she travels in a limousine to the sound stage, Alma carries herself "like a sacred statue," preparing "to offer up with a static priestly reverence her image to the cameras."[16] In an interview, Updike explained that he used cinema as the substitute for religion in the novel because in his life, and in the movies of the 1940s and 1950s, movies provided a moral compass for Americans:

It was true of my generation, that the movies were terribly vivid and instructive. There were all kinds of things you learned.... It was ethical instruction of a sort that the church purported to be giving you, but in a much less digestible form. Instead of these remote, crabbed biblical verses, you had contemporary people acting out moral dilemmas.[17]

Later, in the same interview, Updike bemoaned the fact that contemporary film is not as morally uplifting as the movies of the previous generation. Talking about a recent film, he complained that it lacked the moral direction of old,

In the old movies, yes, there always was the happy ending and order was restored. As it is in Shakespeare's plays. It's no disgrace to, in the end, restore order. And punish the wicked and, in some way, reward the righteous.[18]

Astute a critic of film that he is, Updike seems unaware of the fact that popular art forms are a reflection of the society that produces them. The changes in movies that he decries reflect changes in cultural values. In Updike's generation, the culture was more closely allied with the values of traditional Christianity. However, once popular culture becomes the source of meaning, values and ideals will conform to the moment rather than to any invariable principles. This is the result of the paradigm shift effected by the Enlightenment; displace transcendent authority, and moral authority is relativized. As the Rev. Dreaver had advised Essie's grandfather, "Relativity is the word we must live by now. Everything is relative...." In the novel, Essie/Alma represents a generation recently unmoored from traditional religion, a time when the culture as a whole shared common moral values that reflected its Christian roots. In Updike's imaging of the cinema as a replacement for religion, he is actually presenting the effect of radical individualism on traditional religion, a subtle substitution of self for God, as he so insightfully presents in depicting Alma's narcissistic conflation of self and religion.

As James Davison Hunter explains in his study of the contemporary culture wars, for progressives, "moral authority tends to be defined by the spirit of the modern age, a spirit of rationalism and subjectivism."[19] He adds that even those liberals who still identify with a religious tradition tend to "resymbolize historical faiths according to the prevailing assumptions of contemporary life."[20] And

for Alma's son Clark, a child of the next generation, those assumptions c
prove sufficiently satisfying.

Burned out by the excesses of Hollywood, Clark is doing menial work at his
uncle's Colorado ski resort when one of the bunnies he attempts to bed brings
him home to her commune, headed by a radically conservative leader, Jesse
Smith. As Updike points out in the character of Alma's son, regardless of one's
family heritage, it is impossible to grow up in American society without some
idea of God and religion. He reports that as a schoolboy Clark was jealous of his
mother, "she had had a God...and in her Hollywood egotism hadn't bothered to
pass Him on to him."[21] Of course, Clark doesn't realize that her "God" and her
"Hollywood egotism" are virtually identical. The longing Clark experiences, for
something beyond "the prevailing assumptions of contemporary life," are no longer satisfied by organized religion in his society; individualistic egotism reigns.

Although the adolescent Clark's need is apparent, he encounters no adults
who can provide the moral direction he craves. While at boarding school, close
to the home of his grandparents, Clark establishes a close relationship with his
grandfather, Teddy, who regularly corresponds with his grandson, but Teddy,
long distanced from religion, is unable to provide for the boy: "Teddy had no faith
to offer; he had only the facts of daily existence. Weather, family news, local
change."[22]

Clark wonders, "Who was this God everybody talked of but no one ever
met?"[23] He cannot find any answer to that question, even at his boarding school
where the Episcopal chapel services

seemed perfunctory and weightless, the same words every time, like a mumbled foreign
language he had never learned, the homilies by faculty members chatty and down-to-
earth if not, in tone, downright mocking. Where was the hidden miracle?[24]

In *Habits of the Heart,* the radical individualism of Americans in religion is
exacerbated by the lack of intellectual leadership by the churches. The argument
is that for "a generation or more, there has been no intellectual voice from mainline Protestant churches," no Tillich or Niebuhr to provide the center for discussion.[25] And in analyzing this lack of an authoritative, intellectual center, the
authors, writing in the early 1980s, seem prescient, describing a process that
certainly applies to Clark—and to the generation he represents:

Without the leavening of a creative intellectual focus, the quasi-therapeutic blandness that
has afflicted much of mainline Protestant religion at the parish level for over a century cannot effectively withstand the competition of the more vigorous forms of radical religious
individualism, with their claims of dramatic self-realization, or the resurgent religious conservatism that spells out clear, if simple, answers in an increasingly bewildered world.[26]

Thus, Clark is ripe for the confident authority of Jesse Smith and the alternative
lifestyle of the commune. The appeal of this radical group is clearly its distance

from the world he's known and Smith's self assurance in matters of religion. Nevertheless, Clark passively drifts into membership, too enervated to make a deliberate choice. Like his grandfather Teddy, Clark exhibits the "psychic disorientation" of those lacking a stable moral center.

In Clark, Updike presents the failure of the movies to provide an alternative to religion. A child of the cinema, Clark's frame of reference in the commune continues to be the industry, the only language available to him. Noting the commune members' reliance on blasphemy, he comments that it "was everywhere, like sex in the movies before the Production Code was abandoned and scenes became explicit, and boring."[27] Handed a gun, "He guessed, from Arnold Schwarzenegger movies, that this was an Uzi."[28] But immersion in the world of film left him without the guidance that Updike referred to in the previous generation when Alma was a star and the movies provided a moral compass. Clark's forays into alcohol and drugs symbolize his generation, seeking relief from a metaphysical emptiness that they don't fully understand.

Updike's obvious model for the commune, the David Koresh–led Branch Davidians of Waco, Texas, suggests an attempt to insure that the reader cannot dismiss this group as simply a creation of Updike's mind. That is, by going beyond verisimilitude to a group and event well known to readers at the time of the novel's publication, Updike stresses that this is not some aberrant group of fanatics he has conjured from his imagination but an actual group straight from the headlines, the type of snare waiting for the Clarks of our world. For it is not only orthodox religions that tend toward authoritarianism, but, in fact, anytime some self-styled guru offers personal liberation and salvation, he or she can acquire excessive control of adherents.[29] The Jesse Smiths and the David Koreshes attract followers because of the vacuum created by the lack of moral authority in society.

Ironically, Clark's search for God is finally satisfied in the conflagration that ends the novel. When Clark's great grandfather, the Rev. Clarence Wilmot, lost his faith, it was in a single moment and with a distinct physical sensation, "a visceral surrender, a set of dark sparkling bubbles escaping upward."[30] As the novel draws to a close, Clark, realizing that Jesse has not only set the fire that is consuming them but is also shooting the women and children and inviting the other men to assist, experiences a "flock of sparkling dark immaterial bubbles" descending into him. In the similarity of the imagery, Updike suggests that Clark has been infused with grace, "and he knew what to do."[31] Clark shoots Jesse and helps the others escape the fire. And while he himself is fatally wounded, Updike records that Clark "wasn't worried; the living God had laid hold of him, the present-tense God beyond betting on."[32]

In her laudatory review of *In the Beauty of the Lilies,* the *New York Times* reviewer Michiko Kakutani called it "an important and impressive novel," adding "a novel that not only shows how we live today, but also how we got there."[33] However, the novel ends with two simple words, "The children."[34] Clearly Updike would like the reader to consider the future, a future that appears to be populated by many spiritual seekers for whom popular culture is not a sufficient substitute for religion, but whose seeking can lead to violence and destruction. They exist in an increasingly bewildered world in which the simple answers of "resurgent religious conservatism" appear to be the preferred response.

In Contemporary America

Updike's vision in this novel is consistent with the perspective of social scientists. At the end of his study of the restructuring of American religion in the decades following World War II, the sociologist Robert Wuthnow concludes that the manner in which religion evolved was "conditioned by the cultural, social, and political environment in which it functioned and by the internal resources with which it was able to adapt to those challenges."[35] *In the Beauty of the Lilies* suggests this has not been an entirely successful transition, since during this process, mainline Protestantism appears to have ceded its authority to popular culture. Indeed, it has been observed that the growing presence of evangelicals has been fueled, to some extent, by the stagnation in mainline denominations.[36] Absent intellectual leadership, seekers will go to the most attractive sources that suggest spiritual fulfillment, and, as with Updike's unfortunate character Clark, they may passively accept the authority of religious opportunists.

Moreover, the lack of significant intellectual voices in mainstream religion has resulted in a religious fundamentalism among American youth who acknowledge religious conviction but are unwilling to engage in dialogue related to their beliefs. In a *New York Times* opinion essay, Professor Mark C. Taylor of Williams College highlighted a problem in higher education that he termed "religious correctness," in which students openly profess religious belief but resist critical analysis of religious principles with professors who attempt to engage them in academic discourse on the subject.[37] And this attitude is not limited to religious conservatives. Taylor notes that "right and left have become mirror images of each other; religious correctness is simply the latest version of political correctness."[38] When religion becomes a proscribed topic for reflection and discussion, the result is a stunting of faith.

The experience of college is often cited as one of the factors that helps individuals negotiate the transition from a Stage 3 adolescent faith to a more mature Stage 4 experience.[39] As Monique El-Faizy argues in her study of contemporary evangelicals, young people who are "truly solid in their faith only come to be that way if they are allowed to look at opposing viewpoints head on, weigh the positive and the negative, and then draw their own conclusions."[40] She categorizes the education offered at most Christian colleges as "not about exploration but about fortification."[41] The phenomenon she describes as imposed at Christian colleges is often the choice of students at secular schools who, as Mark Taylor describes, insulate themselves from alternative views and refuse to open their beliefs to reflection and exploration. These are young people in the conventional Stage 3 of adolescent faith in which beliefs and values are deeply felt, but the person has not reflected on them either explicitly or systematically.[42] Schooled in righteousness, the individual views only the like-minded as allies; others are enemies.

One reason for this refusal to engage in discussion of religion, especially with interlocutors who are perceived as antagonistic, is the well-documented American "culture war" which is primarily a religious battleground. When dealing with the enemy, the most suitable response is fortification, and so the failure of today's college students to develop reflective habits of mind is both a symptom and a consequence of the current cultural moment. This situation portends even more polarization and future discord. As Taylor explains, the dangers of this type of thinking are both religious and political. Not too long ago, the experts prophesied the irrelevance of religion in the public domain in our post-Enlightenment society, but this has obviously not happened as religion has taken center stage in world conflicts.[43] Of course, the danger of such "religious correctness" is that it precludes any dialogue that can lessen tensions among people. Taylor concludes that the current situation should serve as a warning sign, and unless we can develop genuine dialogue on matters of religion, we risk continued, and even more deadly, conflicts in the future.[44]

However, it is difficult to develop dialogue when religion for most Americans is rooted in feeling rather than intellect. More than a generation ago, it was observed that despite the variety of denominations and doctrines throughout the United States, most churches define themselves as "communities of personal support."[45] Even in Catholicism, perhaps the most hierarchical and doctrinal institutional church, the priority of the therapeutic and interpersonal is paramount in this country. When American Catholics were asked in a survey to identify needs for the future, they asked for "personal and accessible priests" and "warmer, more personal parishes."[46] Americans want an emotionally satisfying encounter from their religious affiliation, and the most successful churches are those that meet those needs.

In the decades since Catholics expressed the desire for "more personal parishes," the Church's general failure to respond has resulted in a lack of participation by its people. It is reported that "Mass attendance dropped from 74 percent of self-identified Catholics in 1958 to 25 percent in 2000."[47] Interestingly, the immigration of overwhelmingly Catholic Hispanics in recent years appears to indicate that the Church is currently experiencing a renewal, but critics argue that the Church should not be deceived by these numbers. They argue that this is simply a temporary phenomenon among unassimilated immigrants, much as the Irish and Italians were faithful through the 1950s. But their faith eroded as they become more fully assimilated into American society.[48] Newer immigrants, more in need of assistance from the Church and more apt to submit to its authoritarian attitudes, have simply created an illusion of renewal in American Catholicism. The Church is currently serving its ideal parishioners, but as they become more fully acclimated into American culture, their participation may diminish, as it did among their predecessors.

The absence of strong intellectual leadership in American Protestantism has opened the way for any version of Christianity that adherents find congenial, and the growth of the contemporary evangelical churches, especially the "mega-churches" are an illustration of this phenomenon. It is the growth of the mega-church that parallels and best explains the growth of conservative Christian fiction. In his 2005 study of the challenges of religious diversity in the United States, sociologist Robert Wuthnow wrote of the perspective of conservative Christians, a perspective nurtured in evangelical churches that Wuthnow terms "exclusive" in their belief that only those who accept Jesus Christ as Savior will go to heaven. From his interviews, he arrived at a sense of their specific concept of religion which, ironically, is rather untraditional in terms of Christianity:

Christians talk about personal fulfillment and happiness...more than they do about life beyond death, defining salvation as the key to a prosperous life more than to a heavenly kingdom. Salvation of the kind that Jonathan Edwards preached about has been replaced by self-realization, while Christian therapy, dieting, and self-expression have apparently become more urgent than redemption from divine retribution.[49]

Wuthnow's accuracy appears to be confirmed by the development of the evangelical "megachurch," defined as those that attract at least 2,000 weekly worshippers, a category that developed from 50 in 1980 to an estimated 880 in 2006.[50] Among the most prominent megachurch pastors is Joel Osteen of *Your Best Life Now* fame.[51] His prosperity gospel draws more than 30,000 weekly members to his Lakewood Church, and about 7 million additional people view the broadcast of his Sunday sermons on both network and cable channels.[52] The appeal is obvious for people accustomed to the values of a materialistic culture who are told that material prosperity is God's plan for their lives and that salvation is the equivalent. No more rich man having difficulty getting into heaven; to be rich is to be saved, according to this interpretation of the Gospel message. Osteen explains his church's success with the comment that "Other churches have not kept up, and they lose people by not changing with the times."[53] That, of course, is the critical issue. As Wuthnow has documented, American religion *did* restructure itself in the aftermath of World War II within the context of challenges from the cultural environment. The prosperity gospel can be seen as a similar restructuring—or an aberration of the Christian message.

For fellow megachurch pastor Rick Warren, it's an aberration. He charges that the prosperity gospel is "baloney" and is "creating a false message."[54] But just as Osteen and other prosperity preachers use business tactics to market their brand, Warren uses similar methods to promote *his* brand; in fact, business *is* his brand—or so many traditional Christians believe. Before he authored the best-selling *The Purpose Driven Life,* Warren marketed *The Purpose Driven Church,* a manual for pastors in how to invigorate stagnant congregations. In the process, many churches have been divided over "purpose driven" innovations that some believe undermine traditions and distort the Bible's essential message.[55]

What both Osteen and Warren have in common is the use of business acumen in an attempt to entice those who have drifted away from other Christian denominations, including Catholicism, those spiritual shoppers who are interested in religion but have been turned off by mainline churches. Indeed, if Robert Wuthnow is correct that "spiritual shopping generally is not a quest for a coherent set of beliefs but for experiences that serve as affirmations of the goodness and meaningfulness of life,"[56] then the evangelical megachurch is uniquely suited to the needs of such seekers, and that may account for their rapid growth. Indeed, such megachurches are known among religious scholars and writers as "seeker-sensitive" churches for their focus on adapting the physical church space to avoid people's unpleasant associations with traditional church buildings.[57]

These "seeker sensitive" churches have deliberately excised the traditional accoutrements of religion—the crosses, pews, and stained glass windows—to attract those suspicious of organized religion, and, in tune with the spirit of the times, they've adopted the approach of the self-help movement, replicating the appeal of Oprah and Dr. Phil.[58] The megachurches, like the mall, provide one-stop shopping, a place where mothers can drop off the kids at a youth program or sports team and join friends at a church-sponsored Weight Watchers meeting, aerobics class, or book discussion group. Perhaps the family meets again to share a meal at the Church's café before an evening service or Bible study. As members associate mainly with each other in all aspects of their lives, the evangelical perspective is reinforced and unchallenged; the unreflective Stage 3 faith of members is affirmed. And we drift closer to major conflict, as religious belief is fortified against anyone who thinks differently.

This phenomenon of the church that draws adherents by adapting to the times and meeting people's emotional needs fuels the market for Christian fiction—and vice versa. In her analysis of evangelicals, Monique El-Faizy points out that the road to growth for evangelicals is intensely individualistic.[59] A person may be as inclined to seek guidance from a favorite author as much as a friend or a pastor. Thus, evangelical Christian fiction is an adjunct to people's faith, a form of spiritual reading. Christian novels provide a form of relaxation and escapism untainted by the secular culture, presenting a world in which conservative Christian values are upheld and affirmed in the daily lives of the protagonists. Contemporary evangelical seeker-sensitive churches and conservative Christian fiction function synergistically to create the illusion of a world of shared values in which the faithful will prosper, perhaps not always materially according to Rick Warren's brand of Christianity, but they can be assured that God will resolve all crises in their favor. They can even be assured of escaping any of the chaos of the apocalypse, thanks to the comforting message of the Left Behind fiction.

However much representatives of mainline Christianity criticize evangelists like Osteen and Warren for failing to follow the gospel message, that fact, if true, is likely to be irrelevant to the members of their congregations. As sociologists agree, for the typical American, religion "is a matter of simple experience rather than theology or dogma."[60] Thus, what is attracting members to these churches—

and readers to evangelical Christian fiction—is that their experience is personally satisfying. The theology that informs these churches may not be orthodox Christianity, but it may become the dominant brand of Christianity if growth continues at its current rate. According to a May 2006 Gallup survey, 44% of American adults identified themselves as born-again or evangelical, a group of about 86 million people.[61] It is important to note that although some Protestant denominations are primarily evangelical, evangelicals exist in all denominations, even Catholicism. Indeed, evangelicalism is marked less by church affiliation than by personal belief and is thus the religious spirit most attuned to American individualism. This union of the spirit of evangelicalism with the American preference for individualism is the single factor that suggests continued growth of evangelicals in American society.

More than a generation ago, Robert Bellah's study of individualism and commitment in American life concluded:

Religious individualism is, in many ways, appropriate to our kind of society. It is no more going to go away than is secular individualism. Ours is a society that requires people to be strong and independent.[62]

Bellah and his colleagues added that although many individualists had abandoned the traditions they were raised in, reacting to the authoritarianism and paternalism of mainline churches, it appears that "a vital and enduring religious individualism can only survive in a renewed relationship with established religious bodies."[63] They predicted, however, that churches would need to change to accommodate more autonomy than they might prefer to attract disenfranchised individualists, and it appears that Osteen, Warren, and company are the ones who have ventured to provide such an accommodation. If the sociologists were correct, then mainstream religions' failure to adapt to the contemporary culture as they did in the past may be problematic, not only for American religion but for our nation as well.

Just as a best-selling novel is one that touches on the *Zeitgeist*, a church that attracts vast numbers of people is similarly connected to the *Zeitgeist* , that intellectual and cultural climate of the times. Thus, whether or not the contemporary megachurch is a good idea, it is a present reality that will not disappear because its opponents wish it to vanish. If it is a disturbing trend, it becomes important to understand what that trend signifies. From the perspective of social science, the proliferation of the megachurch is less the sign of a resurgence in religion than a retreat from modernity. As Robert Wuthnow points out in his study of *America and the Challenges of Religious Diversity,* conservative Christians' view that belief in Jesus is the requirement for salvation strongly influences their social and political perspectives. It is no accident that conservative Christians tend to be resistant to the notion of diversity, since theirs is an exclusivist religion in the belief that only Christians will go to heaven. Wuthnow concludes "believing that Christianity is exclusively true is strongly associated with believing that

Christianity is the source of America's greatness and with feeling that immigrants with different religions are a threat to America's distinctive values and lifestyles."[64] And he explains that the threat of diversity is less that presented by other religious traditions than issues believed to be a more immediate threat to conservative Christian values in America—such as the tolerance for homosexuality, heterosexual cohabitation without marriage, and absence of ethical values in public school education.[65]

The response to these threats is a retreat to the security of one's religious community.[66] The rise of the megachurches, with their full-service campuses that provide both spiritual and social services for members, can be seen as a reflection of this tendency to total involvement in the local congregation as a protection against the threat perceived from the secularizing forces of the culture at large. Christian fiction complements this siege mentality, allowing its readers to vicariously dwell in an idealized Christian world, and it would be especially useful to those whose local church is relatively small and unable to provide the total environment of the megachurch. It is important to note the importance of the concept of spiritual warfare for conservative Christians. Faced with the threat of secularizing influences, Christians believe that the suitable response is to be "surrounded by godly things and godly people" to resist.[67] Certainly, the reading of Christian fiction would provide a form of armor, and this explains much of its popularity among conservative Christians.

Similarly, another response to a more diverse culture among conservative Christians is "to associate the growth in diversity with some frightening, apocalyptic vision of the end times," often "the feeling that society is becoming so complex and belief systems so fragmented that the whole universe might just go ratcheting out of control, never to right itself until Jesus miraculously intervenes."[68] The enormous sales of the Left Behind series are a reflection of this phenomenon, another reaction to the societal changes of recent decades that seem to be obliterating not only conservative Christian values but the greatness of America itself. Envisioning the apocalypse, people are naturally impelled toward end-times fiction.

Thus, the emergence of evangelical Christian fiction as a publishing phenomenon is a symptom of a major shift in American religion. In her excellent study of this shift, Monique El-Faizy asserts that "the evangelical community has become America's new mainstream."[69] This radical assertion is credible when we consider that the evangelical community has been most receptive to the spiritual seekers in American society, as evidenced by the growth of evangelical churches. Such a shift portends disastrous consequences if we become a nation of Christian fundamentalists in conflict with nations of Islamic fundamentalists, as Andrew Sullivan warned in a recent essay.[70] Sullivan argued that although in our contemporary world of conflict and confusion, the religious certainty common to fundamentalist thinking is "a balm more in demand than ever," that attitude has, in our own country, "deepened our cultural divisions. And so our political discourse gets more polarized, and our global discourse gets close to impossible."[71] In his essay, Sullivan provides the thoughtful, insightful comments about the nature of religion and its cultural manifestations that are so rarely encountered in public discourse today. Updike ended his American chronicle with a vision of Armageddon, an image of the catastrophe Sullivan suggests as the natural result of the certitude that underscores the current evangelical tendency toward fundamentalist thinking.

In my second chapter, I cited a comment written by Christian pastor to her congregation in response to their concerns about the novel *The Da Vinci Code*. It seems to me that in light of the contemporary American religious landscape presented in this study, her words, with minor additions I've bracketed, are a useful exhortation for all Americans:

The truth is, there are a lot of ideas out there that we need to begin discussing at church [synagogue, mosque], ideas that are challenging, ideas that stretch the limits of our comfort and security, ideas that would reshape and redefine what it means to be a Christian [Jew, Moslem] in a modern setting.[72]

The underlying premise of this study has been that the books people are buying tell us a lot about ourselves as a people. The next step is to heed that information.

Notes

1. Robert Stone, "Updike's Other America," *New York Times,* June 18, 2006, http://www.nytimes.com/2006/06/18/books/review/18stone.html?ex=1165726800&en=40f823 4614427f7b&ei=5070 (accessed December 8, 2006).

2. James M. Wall, "Among the Lilies," 1997, http://www.religion-online.org/showarticle.asp?title=551 (accessed November 14, 2006).

3. John Updike, *In the Beauty of the Lilies* (New York: Alfred A. Knopf, 1996), 5.

4. Ibid., 72–3.

5. Ibid., 76.

6. Robert N. Bellah and others, *Habits of the Heart: Individualism and Commitment in American Life* (New York: Harper & Row Publishers, 1986), 224.

7. Ibid., 232.

8. Updike, *In the Beauty of the Lilies,* 67.

9. James W. Fowler, *Stages of Faith: The Psychology of Human Development and the Quest for Meaning* (San Francisco: Harper & Row Publishers, 1981), 182–3.

10. This shift is explained by Bellah and others, *Habits of the Heart,* 223, citing the landmark study of Ann Douglas, *The Feminization of American Culture* (New York: Knopf, 1977).

11. Fowler, *Stages of Faith,* 149.

12. Updike, *In the Beauty of the Lilies,* 410.

13. Brooks, *Community, Religion, and Literature* (Columbia: University of Missouri Press, 1995), 47.

14. Ibid., 49.

15. Bellah and others, *Habits of the Heart,* 235.

16. Ibid.

17. Dwight Garner, "The Salon Interview: John Updike," http://www.salon.com/08/features/updike.html (accessed December 8, 2006).

18. Ibid.

19. James Davison Hunter, *Culture Wars: The Struggle to Define America* (New York: Basic Books, 1991), 44.

20. Ibid., 44–5. Italics his.

21. Ibid., 408.

22. Ibid., 412.

23. Ibid., 408.

24. Ibid., 409.

25. Bellah and others, *Habits of the Heart,* 238.

26. Ibid.

27. Ibid., 400.

28. Ibid.

29. Ibid., 237.

30. Updike, *In the Beauty of the Lilies,* 5.

31. Ibid., 484.

32. Ibid., 486.

33. Michiko Kakutani, "Seeking Salvation On the Silver Screen," *The New York Times,* January 12, 1996, http://query.nytimes.com/gst/fullpage.html?res=9C0CE7DD1039F931A25752C0A960958260&sec=&pagewanted=2 (accessed December 8, 2006).

34. Updike, *In the Beauty of the Lilies,* 491.

35. Robert Wuthnow, *The Restructuring of American Religion: Society and Faith Since World War II* (New Jersey: Princeton University Press, 1988), 322.

36. Monique El-Faizy, *God and Country: How Evangelicals Have Become America's New Mainstream* (New York: Bloomsbury, 2006), 6.

37. Mark C. Taylor, "The Devoted Student," *New York Times,* December 21, 2006, A39.

38. Ibid.

39. Fowler, *Stages of Faith,* 173.

40. El-Faizy, *God and Country,* 184.

41. Ibid.

42. Fowler, *Stages of Faith,* 173.

43. Taylor, "The Devoted Student," A39.

44. Ibid.

45. Bellah and others, *Habits of the Heart,* 232.

46. Ibid.

47. David Rieff, "Neuvo Catholics," *The New York Times Magazine,* December 24, 2006, 42.

48. Ibid., 43.

49. Wuthnow, *America and the Challenges of Religious Diversity* (Princeton and Oxford: Princeton University Press, 2005), 174.

50. William Symonds, Brian Grow, and John Cady, "Earthly Empires," *Business Week Online,* May 23, 2005. http://www.businessweek.com/magazine/content/05_21/b3934001_mz001.htm (accessed September 25, 2006).

51. See Chapter 4 for a discussion of Osteen and other megachurch pastors who have authored nonfiction best sellers.

52. William C. Symonds with Brian Grow and John Cady, "Earthly Empires."

53. Ibid.

54. David Van Biema, Jeff Chu, "Does God Want You To Be Rich? *Time,* September 18, 2006, http://www.time.com/time/magazine/article/0,9171,1533448,00.html (accessed September 25, 2006).

55. Suzanne Sataline, "A Popular Strategy for Church Growth Splits Congregants," *The Wall Street Journal Online,* September 5, 2006, http://www.post-gazette.com/pg/06248/719178-84.stm (accessed September 11, 2006).

56. Wuthnow, *America and the Challenges of Religious Diversity,* 120.

57. D.A. Carson, "Faith a La Carte?" *Modern Reformation Magazine,* July/August 2005, http://www.modernreformation.org/dac05emerging.htm (accessed January 8, 2007). Carson's essay is actually about the "emerging church" movement, a topic beyond the scope of this study. As he uses the term, "seeker sensitive," it is apparent that it is a term sometimes used negatively by critics of the megachurch phenomenon.

58. El-Faizy, 27.

59. Ibid., 125.

60. Wuthnow, *The Restructuring of American Religion,* 144.

61. El-Faizy, *God and Country,* 5.

62. Bellah and others, *Habits of the Heart,* 247.

63. Ibid., 248.

64. Wuthnow, *America and the Challenges of Religious Diversity,* 229.

65. Ibid., 184.

66. Ibid., 185.

67. Ibid.

68. Ibid., 184. Interestingly, Wuthnow notes a third response to the threat of diversity and that is to criticize other Christian groups who are not authentic enough and advocate a type of "back to basics" approach, often a return to practices of early Christianity. This is an accurate description of the "emergent church" movement, but an analysis of this most recent phenomenon is beyond the scope of this study.

69. El-Faizy, *God and Country,* 5.

70. Andrew Sullivan, "When Not Seeing Is Believing," October 2, 2006, http://www.time.com/time/magazine/printout/0,8816,1541466,00.html (accessed December 28, 2006).

71. Ibid.

72. Rev. Jennifer Fey of the United Church of Christ, June 2006, http://www.occhurch.net/ppage.html (accessed July 24, 2006).

Bibliography

Primary Sources (Fiction)

Brown, Dan. *Angels and Demons*. New York: Pocket Books, 2000.

———. *The Da Vinci Code*. New York: Doubleday and Company, Inc., 2003.

Buechner, Frederick. *Godric*. San Francisco, CA: HarperSanFrancisco, 1980.

———. *The Son of Laughter*. San Francisco, CA: HarperSanFrancisco, 1993.

Dayton, Anne, and May Vanderbilt. *Consider Lily*. New York: Broadway Books, 2006.

———. *Emily Ever After*. New York: Broadway Books, 2005.

Diamant, Anita. *The Red Tent*. New York: Picador, 1997.

Gash, Joe. *Priestly Murders*. New York: Penguin Books, 1984.

Godwin, Gail. *Father Melancholy's Daughter*. New York: Avon Books, 1991.

Gunn, Robin Jones. *Clouds*. Sisters, OR: Multnomah Publishers, 1997.

Hansen, Ron. *Atticus*. New York: HarperPerennial, 1997.

———. *Mariette in Ecstasy*. New York: HarperPerennial, 1991.

Henderson, Dee. *The Negotiator*. Sisters, OR: Multnomah Publishers, 2001.

Hijuelos, Oscar. *Mr. Ives' Christmas*. New York: HarperCollins Publishers, 1995.

Kidd, Sue Monk. *The Secret Life of Bees*. New York: Penguin Books, 2002.

Kingsbury, Karen. *Fame*. Wheaton, IL: Tyndale House Publishers, Inc., 2005.

———. *Like Dandelion Dust*. New York: Center Street, 2006.

Kingsolver, Barbara. *The Poisonwood Bible*. New York: HarperPerennial Modern Classics, 2005.

LaHaye, Tim, and Jerry B. Jenkins. *Left Behind: A Novel of the Earth's Last Days*. Wheaton, IL: Tyndale House Publishers, Inc., 1995.

———. *Tribulation Force*. Carol Stream, IL: Tyndale House Publishers, Inc., 1996.

Lewis, Beverly. *The Covenant*. Minneapolis, MN: Bethany House Publishers, 2002.

Marshall, Catherine. *Christy*. New York: Avon Books, 1968.

McBain, ed. *Vespers*. New York: William Morrow and Company, Inc., 1990.

Meier, Paul. *The Third Millennium*. Nashville, TN: WestBow Press, 1993.

Oke, Janette. *Love Comes Softly.* 1979. Reprint, Minneapolis, MN: Bethany House Publishers, 2003.

Perdue, Lewis. *Daughter of God.* New York: Forge, 2000.

Peretti, Frank. *This Present Darkness.* Carol Stream, IL: Tyndale House Publishers, Inc., 1986.

Picoult, Jodi. *Keeping Faith.* New York: HarperPerennial, 2000.

Rivers, Francine. *Redeeming Love.* Sisters, OR: Multnomah Publishers, 1997.

Robinson, Marilynne. *Gilead.* New York: Picador, 2004.

Strout, Elizabeth. *Abide with Me.* New York: Random House, 2006.

Tyler, Anne. *Dinner at the Homesick Restaurant.* New York: Berkley Books, 1983.

———. *Saint Maybe.* New York: Ivy Books, 1991.

Updike, John. *In the Beauty of the Lilies.* New York: Alfred A. Knopf, 1996.

Watson, Sydney. *In the Twinkling of an Eye.* 1916. Reprint, Ohio: Barbour Publishing, 2005.

Selected Secondary Sources

Bausch, William J. *Storytelling: Imagination and Faith.* Mystic, CN: Twenty-Third Publications, 1984.

Bellah, Robert N. "Civil Religion in America," *Daedalus, Journal of the American Academy of Arts and Sciences* 96, no. 1 (1967), http://hirr.hartsem.edu/Bellah/articles_5.htm.

———, Richard Madsen, William M. Sullivan, Ann Swidler, and Steven M. Tipton. *Habits of the Heart: Individualism and Commitment in American Life.* New York: Harper & Row Publishers, 1986.

Brooks, Cleanth. *Community, Religion and Literature.* Columbia: University of Missouri Press, 1995.

Brown, W. Dale, ed. *Of Fiction and Faith: Twelve American Writers Talk about Their Vision and Work.* Grand Rapids, MI: William B. Eerdmans Publishing Company, 1997.

Buechner, Frederick. *The Clown in the Belfry: Writings on Faith and Fiction.* San Francisco, CA: HarperSanFrancisco, 1992.

de Tocqueville, Alexis. *Democracy in America.* Edited by Richard D. Heffner. New York: Signet Classics, 1984.

Dolan, Jay. *The American Catholic Experience.* New York: Doubleday and Company, Inc., 1985.

El-Faizy, Monique. *God and Country: How Evangelicals Have Become America's New Mainstream.* New York: Bloomsbury, 2006.

Fowler, James W. *Stages of Faith: The Psychology of Human Development and the Quest for Meaning.* San Francisco: Harper & Row Publishers, 1981.

Gandolfo, Anita. *Testing the Faith: The New Catholic Fiction in America.* New York and Westport, CT: Greenwood Press, 1992.

Gottesman, Ronald, Laurence B. Holland, David Kalstone, Francis Murphy, Hershel Parker, and William H. Pritchard. *The Norton Anthology of American Literature.* Vol. 1. New York: W.W. Norton Company, 1979.

Gunn, Giles. *The Culture of Criticism and the Criticism of Culture.* New York: Oxford University Press, 1987.

Hansen, Ron. *A Stay Against Confusion: Essays on Faith and Fiction.* New York: Harper-Perennial, 2002.

Herberg, Will. *Protestant-Catholic-Jew: An Essay in American Religious Sociology.* New York: Anchor Books, 1960.

Hunter, James Davison. *Culture Wars: The Struggle to Define America.* New York: Basic Books, 1991.

Karolides, Nicholas J., Margaret Bald, and Dawn B. Sova. *100 Banned Books: Censorship Histories of World Literature.* New York: Checkmark Books, 1999.

Kuhn, Thomas. *The Structure of Scientific Revolutions.* Chicago: University of Chicago Press, 1970.

Messbarger, Paul R. *Fiction with a Parochial Purpose: Social Uses of American Catholic Literature, 1884-1900.* Boston: Boston University Press, 1971.

Radway, Janice. *Reading the Romance: Women, Patriarchy, and Popular Literature.* Chapel Hill: University of North Carolina Press, 1991.

Shea, John. *Stories of Faith.* Chicago, IL: Thomas More Press, 1980.

Wuthnow, Robert. *America and the Challenges of Religious Diversity.* Princeton and Oxford: Princeton University Press, 2005.

———. *The Restructuring of American Religion: Society and Faith Since World War II.* New Jersey: Princeton University Press, 1988.

———. *The Struggle for America's Soul.* Grand Rapids, MI: William B. Eerdmans Publishing Company, 1989.

Zinsser, William, ed. *Spiritual Quests: The Art and Craft of Religious Writing.* Boston: Houghton Mifflin Company, 1988.

Index

About the Author

ANITA GANDOLFO is Professor Emeritus at the U.S. Military Academy where she was the founding Director of the Center for Teaching Excellence and a Professor of English. She is also the author of "Testing the Faith: The New Catholic Fiction in America" (Greenwood, 1992), for which she won a Choice Outstanding Book award.